Understanding and Managing Sophisticated and Everyday Racism

Race and Education in the Twenty-First Century

Series Editors: Kenneth J. Fasching-Varner, University of Nevada, Las Vegas; Roland Mitchell, Louisiana State University; and Lori Latrice Martin, Louisiana State University

This series asks authors and editors to consider the role of race and education, addressing questions such as "how do communities and educators alike take on issues of race in meaningful and authentic ways?" and "how can education work to disrupt, resolve, and otherwise transform current racial realities?" The series pays close attention to the intersections of difference, recognizing that isolated conversations about race eclipse the dynamic nature of identity development that play out for race as it intersects with gender, sexuality, socioeconomic class, and ability. It welcomes perspectives from across the entire spectrum of education from Pre-K through advanced graduate studies, and it invites work from a variety of disciplines, including counseling, psychology, higher education, curriculum theory, curriculum and instruction, and special education.

Recent Titles in Series

Understanding and Managing Sophisticated and Everyday Racism: Implications for Education and Work, by Victoira Showunmi and Carol Tomlin

Latinx Experiences in U.S. Schools: Voices of Students, Teachers, Teacher Educators and Education Allies in the Age of Trump, edited by Margarita Jimenez-Silva, Janine Bempechat, and Laura Gomez

Implications of Race and Racism in Student Evaluations of Teaching: The Hate U Give, edited by LaVada Taylor

Technology Segregation: Disrupting Racist Frameworks in Early Childhood Education, by Miriam B. Tager

Surviving Becky(s): Pedagogies for Deconstructing Whiteness and Gender, edited by Cheryl E. Matias

Latinx Curriculum Theorizing, edited by Theodorea Regina Berry

Intersectional Care for Black Boys in an Alternative School: They Really Care About Us, by Julia C. Ransom

Culture, Community, and Educational Success: Reimagining the Invisible Knapsack, edited by Toby S. Jenkins, Stephanie Troutman, and Crystal Polite Glover

Whiteness at the Table: Antiracism, Racism, and Identity in Education, edited by Shannon K. McManimon, Zachary A. Casey, and Christina Berchini

The Classroom as Privileged Space: Psychoanalytic Paradigms for Social Justice in Pedagogy, by Tapo Chimbganda

Understanding and Managing Sophisticated and Everyday Racism

Implications for Education and Work

Victoria Showunmi and Carol Tomlin

LEXINGTON BOOKS
Lanham • Boulder • New York • London

Published by Lexington Books
An imprint of The Rowman & Littlefield Publishing Group, Inc.
4501 Forbes Boulevard, Suite 200, Lanham, Maryland 20706
www.rowman.com

86-90 Paul Street, London EC2A 4NE

Copyright © 2022 by The Rowman & Littlefield Publishing Group, Inc.

All rights reserved. No part of this book may be reproduced in any form or by any electronic or mechanical means, including information storage and retrieval systems, without written permission from the publisher, except by a reviewer who may quote passages in a review.

British Library Cataloguing in Publication Information Available

Library of Congress Cataloging-in-Publication Data

Names: Showunmi, Victoria, author. | Tomlin, Carol, author.
Title: Understanding and managing sophisticated and everyday racism : implications for education and work / Victoria Showunmi and Carol Tomlin.
Description: Lanham : Lexington Books, [2022] | Series: Race and education in the twenty-first century | Includes bibliographical references.
Identifiers: LCCN 2022001905 (print) | LCCN 2022001906 (ebook) | ISBN 9781498567091 (cloth) | ISBN 9781498567114 (pbk.) | ISBN 9781498567107 (ebook)
Subjects: LCSH: Racism—Great Britain. | Women, Black—Great Britain. | Blacks—Great Britain. | Discrimination in employment—Great Britain. | Discrimination in education—Great Britain. | Racism in the workplace—Great Britain. | Racism in education—Great Britain.
Classification: LCC DA125.A1 S56 2022 (print) | LCC DA125.A1 (ebook) | DDC 305.800941—dc23/eng/20220203
LC record available at https://lccn.loc.gov/2022001905
LC ebook record available at https://lccn.loc.gov/2022001906

Frontispiece: The Black Swan

The black swan appears to be gliding forwards gracefully on smooth waters. Yet in and beneath the surface lurk devastating dangers. There are toxins in the environment. There are also predators threatening to harm or devour the black swan and at any moment the calm waters may change into a destructive maelstrom of huge engulfing waves. The black swan's existence is not as calm as it seems.

In the same way, Black women may seem to be progressing, but in reality, sophisticated and everyday racism poses a constant threat to their equanimity.

*For my daughters Chantal, Monique
and Charlotte and Carol's family*

Contents

Acknowledgments		xi
List of Figures		xiii
Preface		xv
Introduction		1
1	Race and Racism(s)	9
2	The Tangled Web of Blackness, *Identity* and Race	17
3	Sophisticated and Everyday Racism: What Does It Look Like?	43
4	The Language Style of Black Women and Its Implications for Education and Work	61
5	Challenges Hindering the Success of Some Black Women: Education, Parenting and the Labour Market	75
6	Suffering in Silence: *Black British Young Women and Their Well-Being*	97
7	Black Women Reflecting on Being Black in the Academy: Uvanney Maylor and Victoria Showunmi	113
8	Flip the Script and Change the Narrative	133
9	Conclusion	143
References		149
Index		173
About the Authors		181

Acknowledgments

VICTORIA SHOWUNMI

Understanding and Managing Sophisticated and Everyday Racism came to fruition during COVID-19. I had long wanted to publish and disseminate the ideas which had emerged during many conversations with my colleague and friend Dr. Carol Tomlin. I would also like to thank Uvanney Maylor for co-authoring chapter 7. It was only in 2020 that the time became available. The book is based on the lived experiences of Black women and suggests ways of managing sophisticated and everyday racism. My thanks go to Carol for accompanying me on this journey. I must include the endless support from Dr. Rosalind Duhs who has worked with me to edit and proofread the different stages of the manuscript. I would also like to thank Dr. Stephen Hancock who became an international sounding board and assisted with the editing of parts of the book. Finally, my thanks to Dee Cunningham, Alice Chivers, Dawn Grant, Teresa Dawkins and Dr. Paul Mocombe who have helped in their many different ways.

CAROL TOMLIN

I would like to express special thanks first to the Lord Jesus Christ for the inspiration of this book. Thank you to my blood family Sylvie (my mum), Beryl and Tony, for their patience and enduring support. Thank you to my extended family Tamika, Sharon and the Restoration Fellowship Ministries. Last but not least, thank you to the many friends who have helped me craft my ideas.

List of Figures

Figure 2.1   The Tangled Web of the Big House   20
Figure 2.2   From the Big House to the Workplace: Patterns Persist   22
Figure 3.1   The Sophisticated Racism Framework   46

Preface

The Black Lives Matter (BLM) movement erupted across the globe in 2020 following the brutal murder of Mr George Floyd, a 46-year-old Black man, by Derek Chauvin, a White police officer, on 25 May in Minneapolis, Minnesota. This horrific incident marked another turning point in race relations. The brutal killing of Breonna Taylor by Louisville police officers on 13 March 2020 reminded many of us that she, like George, could have been one of our relatives. We, the authors of this book, are two Black women. The stark reality is that Breonna could have been either one of us. Anti-Blackness is a global phenomenon. While writing this book, we had no idea of the turn of events but what we can say is that this book has been birthed from years of labour pains. The embryo was formed from numerous discussions of our experiences in everyday encounters, in social and professional settings, and the academy. Sometimes conversations between ourselves and with other Black women on both sides of the Atlantic would last for hours. Like the experience of women giving birth, the journey to this book has been both arduous and exciting.

We wanted to capture our experiences as women of colour from two very different backgrounds. We wanted to explore the morass of racial identity, highlighting some of the complexities by recounting our own experiences and analysing the interplay of our multiple identities.

What are these backgrounds? We were both born in Britain where the interplay of race, class and gender is complex. Victoria is of Nigerian origin but was adopted by a White German Jewish upper-middle-class couple in England. Carol's parents came from rural Jamaica. She grew up in Chapeltown in Leeds, West Yorkshire. In the 1970s Chapeltown had a large Black population and proportionately among the highest in the United Kingdom (Woolmore, 2016).

The personal pain of the experiences of many Black women is relevant to our own process of untangling and exploring our identities as Black in Britain. Typically, academic writing is usually seen as requiring distance and objectivity from the author(s). We have instead chosen to bring the lives of Black women, including ourselves, into parts of the work and follow Lea and Helfand (2007) in using our scholarship to inform our insights into how we have experienced the world. Recounting the various significant events that occur in one's own life is necessary as they provide the opportunity to explore, understand and build and develop our differing identities. Some of the ideas presented in the following accounts result from many critical and reflective conversations with friends, locally, nationally and internationally. The first example recounts Victoria's experiences.

VICTORIA'S STORY

I became friendly with a Black woman I will call Maxi at the school my daughters attended. She had a child of similar age to my daughters. I found this to be both comforting and welcoming. I trusted my new friend and valued our new friendship. The school was different from the school my daughters had previously attended in Broadstairs, which was all White, as the pupils came from more diverse backgrounds. My excitement led me to overlook the monolithic view of Blackness operating within the school. The consequences were painful, as discussed here. Suffice it to say at this point that my upbringing by upper-middle-class White German Jewish parents in an exclusively White area meant that my experiences were different from those of a significant number of Black people from an inner-city working-class background.

What is significant about this event? I had never experienced growing up with Black friends or living in a Black family, so Whiteness surrounded me prior to interacting with Black Londoners. To me, any connection with Blackness was exciting, and I cherished and embraced the moment with each person I met.

Going back to the story concerning the parent I met at the new school, we became very friendly. She volunteered to plait my daughters' hair at an agreed price. While she took on the task of braiding their hair, our friendship blossomed, which I thought was genuine, but at the time, it was just surface level. It would be appropriate to ask: 'So what has this got to do with the notion of blackness?' I need to explain the essence of the story. There was a sense of frustration at the heart of our 'friendship'. I finally understood the root of the problem when my 'friend' commented: 'You don't know what it's like to be Black . . .'

I remember these words, as they were similar to words thrown at me when I was hanging out with some newly found Black women friends. At the time, I felt numb and did not know what to do. I knew I was visibly Black, but I was now being thrown into an unknown identity, which in my mind felt uncomfortable. How can I be questioned about my Blackness? Did I not face the same experiences as other Black people? They clearly thought not. The words still haunt me as I put pen to paper for this preface. At the time, I tried to shrug off the comments and felt it must have been something to do with me needing to change myself. It was the first time that I had been questioned about my Blackness, a very new experience. Where I had grown up, just one 'drop' of Blackness was all you needed to be seen as different. What I came to learn as part of some of the cultural ways of being in London is that there was more to it than this; there was Black and then there was *Black* and this is where the idea of the tangled web and the Big House originates (see chapter 2). As I reflect on that encounter, I realise that my 'friend's' identity is as a Black working-class woman whose life experiences have been within a Black British Caribbean context in London. Her interactions with me shifted the dynamics of her own understanding of Blackness, which had been disrupted as I do not 'fit the Black script'. The notion of Blackness for Maxi was relatively narrow. She saw her origin and resultant identity as the norm.

Regarding my own experience, I grew up with constant name-calling and projected and targeted discrimination from my peers over a long period of time, similar to many young people. Very often, the perpetrators were ignored and excused as innocent children. Rigby (1996, p. 303) defines bullying as the 'repeated oppression, psychological or physical of a less powerful person by a more powerful individual or group of persons'. He also points out that bullying, whether physical or psychological, lives in the mind of the victimised person, not only at the actual time of being bullied but in anticipation of being bullied again. He notes that a central feature is the imbalance of power between the bully or bullies and the victim. This takes me back to when I had my first experience of racism within a school at the age of four and how my adopted mother dealt with the 'difficult' conversation required to ensure that I would survive. We had just moved into a quaint village that had previously submitted a petition in an attempt to stop my adoptive parents from buying a house in the village. The villagers appeared to be afraid of the affluent family that had moved in with Black children. I can recall my first morning at the village school in the southwest of England. The school was surrounded by lush green fields. As we walked up to the school gate, I sensed the parents and children looking at me. I was the only Black child in the playground with so many eyes watching me. I did not know what to expect as I was shielded by Whiteness; even though I knew I was different, I was still very naïve. The worst part of the day was during playtime when children would call out a range of names: Blackie, wog, gollywog; the list was endless. It was the time of day that I hated the most and when felt most vulnerable.

For many minority ethnic children, racist intimidation and bullying are a feature of their lives evidenced in the classroom, the playground and the world at large on a daily basis. These young people are often told to dismiss name-calling as there is no physical harm to the person. However, over time this has been proven to be incorrect. For instance, Sullivan's (2005) work discusses the need for educators to acknowledge that racist bullying exists. He argues that racist bullying is where racism and bullying meet. I am not an isolated case in my experience of racist bullying, as so many Black people I have conversed with have reported that they too have had similar experiences. Sometimes they reacted in ways that caused them to be removed from the school. Like so many others, I internalised the experience and used words such as 'Blackie' as a form of endearment towards my younger brother as we grew up together. We both experienced the rawness of racism, yet at the same time, my brother and I were being indoctrinated into Whiteness. We were unaware that using the word 'Blackie' was derogatory. We both grew up knowing we were Black and that the name-calling was aimed at us. As a young person, Blackie was the name I responded to, along with my surname that people were unable to pronounce.

If I assimilate myself into Whiteness, I will be seen as an outsider by my Black peers. This contributes to the ongoing complexity of Blackness. So when my Black 'friends' declare that I do not understand the Black experience, they subconsciously infer that I am exploiting Whiteness as leverage to accrue benefits to position myself in a better place in society. It could be argued that my class is being unveiled and they have associated me with the negative aspects of White middle-classness associated with snobbery and a pariah culture (Archer, 2011). This prevents them from journeying with me. They have also failed to understand my traumatic experiences of Blackness in White spaces, despite my class position, mirroring their own experiences. A critical difference, however, is that they have experienced sophisticated racism (Showunmi, 2021) as a consequence of living in the cosmopolitan city of London, in contrast to the 'raw' racism that I experienced living in a small town where my brother and I were the only Black people. Adding another layer of complexity to this situation is that I believe many individuals in Britain, in particular, cannot assign me to the 'black box' (concerning ethnicity on application forms), but neither can they put me in the white box. If I were mixed heritage, that is, with a Black and a White parent, how they perceive me would be more defined and my behaviour would be attributed to having one White parent. My visible dark skin tone reflects that I do not have a White parent, contributing to the confusion in how they relate to me. Interestingly, I do not have this experience with my African

American colleagues, irrespective of the class from which they originate. It would appear that for the African Americans, I am Black regardless of my class positioning and they relate to me accordingly. They may associate my behaviour as being typically British, whereas, in the United Kingdom, it appears that the assumption is that I wish to be White. The recoiling among some Black people in Britain is because when they first see a person who is different from their reference point of what it means to be Black, they cannot comprehend the individual. Yet, the irony of the matter is that I have never wanted to be White. I, like all Black people in the West, have been 'othered'.

The effects of Black people being othered in the United Kingdom have a long history rooted in the dehumanising of the 'other'. Saarti (Sarah) Baartman is a classic case in point. She was a member of the Khoisan tribe of South Africa who was abducted to Britain in 1810 and viewed as a biological abnormality because of her pronounced buttocks and genitalia. Her buttocks were objectified in London and Paris as a part of the freak show tradition. She became known as the 'Hottentot Venus', a symbol of racial inferiority and Black female sexuality.

Positioning oneself as the other has become second nature for Black people due to how the British system operates. For instance, in the context of our children's education, we seek to engage with educators and embrace school policies. However, when scrutinised, many of these policies are actually designed as a subterfuge to keep non-Whites in their place (Britton and Goldsmith, 2013). The school environment should be a place where young people can gain the skills and knowledge to enable them to develop into future leaders; instead, many face hostility and what I have termed 'sophisticated racism' (see chapter 3). The inability of many young people to identify their discriminatory experience as sophisticated racism ('sophisticated' because it is practised unconsciously and subconsciously) contributes to the rise in mental health issues and especially overall ill-health among some Black women. One could argue that this covert but insidious form of racism operates to maintain the status quo by reproducing inequalities and masks a fundamental problem within British society.

CAROL'S STORY

I was raised by a Jamaican mother and was very confident about what it meant to be *Black* culturally, at least from a Black British perspective, as I grew up in the predominantly Caribbean neighbourhood, Chapeltown, in Leeds. I was a child of the 1960s and remembered hearing about Dr. Martin Luther King and the Black Power movement, which fascinated me. I also remembered watching the television series *Roots* in the 1970s, based on Alex Haley's story of

Kunta Kinte captured from the Gambia and sold as a slave in North America. I went to an all-Caribbean Pentecostal Church, New Testament Church of God, from the age of five. At the age of 10, I would sit in 'big people' church mesmerised by the highly stylised sermons, a fascination that remained, resulting in my research on Black preaching style when I became an adult. As a child, I was also enthralled by the Jamaican Creole language, and when my Jamaican mother spoke, even when she reprimanded me, her voice sounded like sheer poetry. My family would make the trip to Doncaster every school holiday, which I would write about when I returned to school, much to my mother's annoyance, who would say, 'why you have to tell everyone your business'. It appears that a degree of privacy is highly valued in African and diasporic communities as I have heard the same caution regarding the need to be 'private' among many Black people that I have encountered in various geographical settings. I loved listening to stories of 'back home', which my relatives would enact with passion and vibrancy. I loved 'the noise'.

As I reflect on these encounters in my adult life, I realise that those moments for these Jamaican adults from rural backgrounds were opportunities to be themselves. The teachers throughout all my schooling were White. In my primary school, I recall an elderly teacher whom many of the Black children adored, but whom I detested because she would sometimes say, 'You West Indian children . . .' followed by a negative comment. I remember thinking at the time that I have never been to the West Indies. I was born in England. Although I love traditional Caribbean food such as rice and peas (beans), I also like eating Yorkshire pudding, baking scones and for me Bakewell Tart is the best dessert in the world. I cannot remember any of my secondary teachers exhibiting overt racism and I had many Black friends, especially in my secondary school, where almost half of the pupils were Black. When I went to a teacher training college, my experience changed significantly. All the students were White and you could literally 'spot the Blacks'. However, I became very close with the few Black and Asian female students and attended another Caribbean Pentecostal Church.

Interestingly, it was not until I was in America that I embraced more of my British background as an essential aspect of my identity. Before that time, I had tended to be proud of my Jamaican heritage and collective Black identity and placed my British identity on the backburner. During my interactions with African Americans and Caribbean people, I became more aware of the British part of my identity. For example, during an international day at the predominantly African American church, I was asked to represent Britain and did so with a modicum of pride. After all, I reasoned African Americans, despite the torrid aspects of their history, never denounce their American heritage, although they benefit from the Constitution to support their American identity.

Identities are not fixed but are constructed, reconstructed, negotiated and renegotiated. In predominant White societies, I am primarily defined through a racialised lens. However, I am not merely a Black woman because I also define myself as a Christian, a minister, an academic, a friend and a sister. I embrace all of these identities by weaving in and out as the occasion merits. For instance, whenever I attend a predominantly Black church gathering in America or Caribbean or Africa, my posture changes. I engage in the cultural, religious norms and practices of a Black Pentecostal worshipper. When I am in a Black church space, despite the variation in different geographical locations, which require some social and cultural adaptation, I do not have to make a conscious effort to 'fit in'. There is nothing for me like the vibrancy, potency and atmosphere of a Black Pentecostal Church. Similarly, when I am teaching or presenting at a conference, my language and behaviour change accordingly. I do not have to consider these aspects unduly because they are a natural part of my professional identity. Some of the peers with whom I grew up are not quite sure of how to position me. They tell me that they have observed that I relate to White people effectively and attribute this to my personality as well as professional background, having worked in all-White academic settings. In a West African Pentecostal Church that I attended, they thought that some of my behaviours and attitude reminded them of a White person. Not quite sure what they meant and I think I was too nervous to ask. My sister sometimes remarks that she is fascinated at the duality of my posture, that is, my ability to adapt to both the Black and White world, which I appear to embrace with ease. Adapting to the White world of academia is now second nature but I can honestly say that when I moved from my hometown of Chapeltown as a young student, it was at times rather challenging. I found the ignorance of some of my fellow White peers and lecturers disheartening. I too experienced racist comments, for example, about my hair and that story is for another book.

In America, I had the privilege of teaching in two HBCUs (historically Black colleges and universities) where the workforce was multiracial but the management was predominantly Black. It was an exciting experience in terms of the dynamics of race and gender. I remember being interviewed by a panel of five Black women and one White woman, a converse situation to my experiences in Britain. In fact, in Britain, I have never been interviewed by a Black woman. For the first time in my professional career, I was not the 'only one'; while gazing at the sea of other Black faces, I thought I was the norm, in the majority and not the exception in this environment. I blended in, although as I became known around the respective campuses, there was some degree of curiosity because I did not sound American. Despite my different cultural experiences from my African American peers, I was still seen as an insider among the African American students and staff members because I shared their experience of being Black in a majority White society. The few White students at the universities were intrigued as they had never interacted with a Black person from Britain and I am not sure if they thought I was an anomaly.

Our book highlights the experiences of Black women in encountering sophisticated racism in Britain. We are aware that Black women are multilayered as they come from various backgrounds and countries, making for an exciting mix. Living in the United Kingdom presents hopeful possibilities and unending challenges for Black women marked by harrowing accounts of discrimination that we document. We intend to provide strategies for Black women to manage sophisticated forms of racism, which seems absent within the British context. Susan Cousins's book *Overcoming Everyday Racism* is a practical guide, and Reena Bhavnani, Mirza and Meetoo's book *Tackling the Roots of Racism* focuses on social policy interventions in race equality but does not 'detail the struggles or strategies of the recipients of racism' (p. 2). Unlike the books *Why I'm No Longer Talking to White People about Race* by Reni Eddo-Lodge (2018) and *White Fragility: Why It's So Hard for White People to Talk About Racism* (2018) by Robin Diangelo, both aimed at White audiences, this book addresses Black audiences, primarily females. It should also enable White people to gain insights into the lives of Black women and contribute to shaping policy for those who are in positions of power.

To return to the metaphor of the birthing process, other women may not have experienced our labour pains and inevitably have their own story to recount. We recognise that many women, like myself, have never given birth to a baby, biologically speaking; however, I play a 'mothering' role as a church minister. We believe that this book will be of particular interest to Black women, the primary audience, to support them as they map out their space and place within gendered and racialised societies such as the United Kingdom and elsewhere.

It will engage a wider audience and has also been written for the academy as a text for disciplines such as sociology, sociolinguistics, psychology and education, to name a few. In addition, it is intended for professional practice, such as civil service, military, social work and healthcare. We hope the book will have a broad appeal to all individuals, both novice and expert, concerned with social justice across social, economic, political and ethnic divides. We believe this is a timely book!

Introduction

The aim of this book is to examine the everyday racism experienced by Black girls and women, primarily in Britain. Strategies are provided to enable them to manage the racism they encounter. Institutional and structural or systemic racism are also scrutinised as these impact significantly on every facet of Black women's lives, including their education and their emotional stability. Much of the research on Black women tends to be informed by the American literature so we draw on this where relevant. Writing about the experiences of Black women in other regions is less prolific. As a result, there has been a tendency to ignore the social and cultural circumstances of Black women who are not African American. Their gendered identities are situated within a different historical and geographical context (Hall, 1990). In recent years, however, literature which documents the unique experiences of Black women in Britain has begun to emerge (see, for instance, Bryan et al., 1985; Mirza, 1993, 1997, 2006, 2012; Reynolds, 2001, 2009).

Although this book focuses mainly on Black girls and women in the United Kingdom, it will resonate with Black women across the globe wherever they live as an ethnic minority, from the Americas to Europe and Australia.

BLACK WOMEN IN THE UNITED KINGDOM

First, it is important to identify Black girls and women in Britain, as ethnic identity is a construct. Black women are generally divided into two groups. The first are collectively referred to as Africans; they or their parents come from the continent of Africa. The second group are Caribbean or African Caribbean and originate from the Caribbean with African ancestry. In addition to the aforementioned terms, the literature and policy documents use 'Black' to denote ethnicity as in 'Black African' and 'Black Caribbean'. It is appropriate to use the term 'Black British' for individuals born and raised in the United Kingdom from either an African or an African Caribbean background. Women of mixed heritage, that is with one parent from either Africa or the Caribbean and the other White British parent, are also included if they identify themselves as Black culturally or ethnically. So too are other mixed heritage individuals, where one parent is Black and the other Indian, for example. It is also appropriate to use the term 'people/women of colour' to describe Black women, used as a synonym for non-White women, in line with usage in the literature.

We do not wish to posit an essentialist view of Black women in Britain. We are sensitive to the cultural differences between women who come from Africa with a geographically huge landmass which has evolved over thousands of years with many different societies and cultures (Zeleza, 2006). Similarly, women from a Caribbean background come from different islands or countries and cultures primarily arising from African cultural retentions and corollaries of the transatlantic slave trade or chattel slavery, the institution established from the fifteenth century responsible for the spread of Africans into the Americas and Europe. The cultures of women from different African and Caribbean countries have developed from varied social, historical and political contexts. The characterisation of Black women in Britain does not operate in a historical vacuum. The transatlantic slave trade and British colonisation of several Caribbean islands such as Jamaica, and the colonisation of African countries such as Nigeria, are partly responsible for the recent settlement of Black people in Britain. In fact, Black people have been in Britain for centuries. David Olusoga's (2016) brilliant and evocative research popularised in the BBC television series *Black and British* attests to the long history of people of African descent in the British Isles, dating back to the third-century AD. However, the post-war twentieth-century period marked the beginning of mass migration of people from the Caribbean who came to fill the labour gap (see Phillips and Phillips, 2009) together with people from other former British colonies in South Asia. The settlement of Africans from the 1980s onwards has resulted in a substantial Black population forming a major minority ethnic group. According to the 2011 population census, the total Black population comprised 1,864,890, 3.4 per cent of the total British population of 56.1 million. Fifty-two per cent of the Black population was women.[1]

Policy research on Black people or women is often subsumed in studies of minority ethnic populations as a whole, even when alluding to considerable distinctions between different groups, as can be seen for instance in the Race Disparity Audit (2017). Consequently, British policy and scholarly studies on minority ethnic people currently use the term 'BAME' (Black and minority ethnic) to describe communities such as African, Caribbean, Pakistani, Indian and so on, thereby conflating all minority ethnic groups despite cultural differences between the groups. Calls for the term BAME to be abolished as a category have increasingly become louder (see, for instance, Ifejola, 2019). Pan-Africanists in Britain disavow the label as a generic ethnic marker and identify people of African heritage as Africans including those who are from the diaspora. However, as Ackah et al. (2017) suggest, African and diasporic communities are dynamic and diverse and a number of forces such as enslavement, colonialism and globalisation have shaped the peoples. The after-effects of slavery and colonisation embedded in racial discourses shape the lives of Black women in diasporic communities such as Britain.

White male academics (e.g., Mac and Ghaill, 1988, 1994; Gillborn, 1990, 2008) have written a great deal on 'race', particularly in relation to the education of Black men in British literature. More recently White women have also written on 'race' (see Archer and Francis, 2007; Archer, 2011). These writers have not experienced daily racialised encounters. Despite the insightful work carried out by some White writers, in some ways, they have colonised and capitalised on 'race' or issues around diversity on an industrial scale (Ahmed, 2012). Even discourses and scholarship on gender continue to be dominated by Western frames, and very often, Black women question the term 'feminism' because of the implications of its inextricable connection with White feminism (Syed and Ali, 2011). Some Black women prefer the term 'womanist', coined by Walker (1983). In relation to Black women, it is argued by scholars such as Collins (1999) that one of the unwitting consequences of the increased accessibility of knowledge about the lives of Black women is that they are objectified rather than being subjects of investigation. Hill Collins suggests that a process of 'knowing without knowing' occurs, whereby dominant groups in society who have a particular interest in understanding the lives of Black women can observe them from a distance, and without having to personally interact or critically engage with these women. Such investigators do not have to critically analyse their own lives. In contrast, the racial and gender status of Black women means that they are not afforded the opportunity to view other social groups objectively because any understanding of their own lives is interpersonal and based on their status as the racialised and gendered 'other' (Reynolds, 2002).

WAYS OF KNOWING

This book explores sophisticated and everyday racism. 'Everyday racism' is a term first coined by Essed (1991). The book illuminates the power play of racism both institutionally and structurally in terms of individual conduct and manifestations of micro-aggressive encounters. Our analysis is based on the 'interpretation of Black women's experiences by those who participate in them' (Collins, 1990, p. 15). In essence, the book has been written by Black women scholars, and grounded in principles that emphasise participants' voice and a commitment to understanding the experiences of participants. This line of enquiry is modelled on Shealey (2006, p. 7) who suggests 'new ways of knowing' which call for 'a community of scholars engaged in high-quality research driven by the need to heighten awareness of the issues'. New ways of knowing are critical to unpacking the daily experiences of Black women living in racialised societies such as Britain. Significantly, we aim to examine agentic tools for managing sophisticated racism and, as Black British women scholars, we employ 'community nomination'. The idea of 'community nomination' is a process whereby insiders' perspectives are used in analysis (see Foster, 1991). This allows new ways of knowing to emerge. Black women's ways of knowing the world are important to the creation of theory and knowledge yielded by critical analysis of the lives of these women (Griffins, 1996).

Black women are not a homogenous group, so a multifaceted lens must be adopted when analysing Black women's ways of knowing. According to Reynolds (2002), they are often represented in popular discourse through the lens of dysfunctionality such as abuse or discrimination. There has been much pathologizing of Black women on both sides of the Atlantic, because as Reynolds so aptly states, 'they are unable to be conceived other than in a problem/victim context' (2002, p. 594). She also argues that Black female writers tend to validate a discourse of global connection that is informed by notions of Black women's collective history involving racial struggle, suffering and marginalisation. Also, implicated within this collective definition of Black womanhood is the legacy of 'triple oppression' that is based on race, gender and subordinated class status (Collins, 1990). Reynolds believes that the 'triple oppression' and collective history are an outdated way of appraising Black women's lives, but this view of oppression and collective history based on struggle, pain and marginalisation, though key, remain predominant in how they are represented. Furthermore, she urges caution in relation to the dominant American discourse that limits the theoretical attention of Black women's experiences in other geographical settings, outside the West. Her views are plausible. Following Reynolds (2002) we do not seek to present a one-dimensional approach to the lives of these women in Britain but are sensitive to the 'range', 'scope' and 'complexities' (p. 594) of their experience which we attempt to document. However, we interrogate the sophisticated and everyday racism and that all Black women in Britain experience. Black women have to confront, disentangle and overcome obstacles, particularly in majority White contexts and writers such as Reynolds (2002, 2010) and

Mirza (2006) rightly explore Black women's own agency in challenging systemic and oppressive practices. Importantly, we examine agentic tools for managing sophisticated racism by offering strategies for circumventing and negotiating space and place. These tools are equally appropriate to other women of colour who are in minority settings. In chapter 8, we suggest how Black women can be re-positioned as agents to challenge the dominant discourses of both racism and sexism that marginalise and pathologise their experiences.

STRUCTURE OF THE BOOK

The book comprises nine chapters. Chapters 1, 2, 3, and 4, provide the theoretical and background contexts to the notion of sophisticated and everyday racism. In chapter 1 racial discourses are contextualised by briefly examining concepts of 'race' and racism(s). The chapter provides a summation of institutional and structural racism as well as discusses sophisticated and everyday racism. Anti-Black racism and White supremacy and privilege are also examined. The latest national report on race in Britain, *Commission on Race and Ethnic Disparities: 2021 Report*, is critiqued and sophisticated and everyday racism is further defined and explained.

Chapter 2 considers nomenclature to describe Black women and people of colour. It interrogates diverse terminologies used to describe ethnicity and provides a historical analysis of 'Blackness' in relation to slavery. The chapter utilises the metaphor of the 'Big House' historically within the plantocracy system of slavery and analyses the negotiation of power within the slave system which has contemporary resonance. Critically, the concept of sophisticated racism is theorized. The interrogation of a Black identity within a British frame also forms an integral part of the discussion, drawing attention to its intricate layers.

Chapter 3 focuses on the meaning of sophisticated and everyday racism, its manifestations in the lives of Black people and its multi-layered impact. The reproduction of everyday racism between individuals and groups informs the analysis of real-life case studies taken from within and outside organisations. The chapter offers the opportunity to think through the way sophisticated and everyday racism works and how it can easily be overlooked and mistaken for something less malevolent.

Language is an essential part of identity and the tool for the rules of engagement, and in chapter 4 we focus on language by first identifying the different languages spoken by Black women in Britain. It concentrates on the language style of Black women in the diaspora by highlighting the African world view. Utilising the ethnography of speech, commonalities in the style of communication among Black people in the diaspora are discussed. The chapter considers the stylised forms of speech referred to as Black British talk (BBT) embraced by the younger generation. Significantly, it draws attention to the presentation of self with ideas of loudness and symbolic representation of silence in diasporic female talk as countering White hegemony. The implications of the Black female style of communicating in the educational setting and places of work are robustly interrogated throughout this chapter.

Chapters 5 to 8 outline the challenges in managing sophisticated and everyday racism. The insurmountable obstacles hindering the success of some Black women are discussed in chapter 5. An understanding of success is necessary, and the chapter attempts to provide an evolving understanding of the meaning of success. It examines educational achievement, as education is a contested site understood as a foundation for acquiring social and economic resources. Much of the literature on education has centred on African Caribbean students with reports of young Black Caribbean women and girls achieving more than their male counterparts. Black Caribbean women along with their Black African counterparts have fairly high rates of participation in higher education but sometimes lower retention rates. We analyse the mitigating factors contributing to many African Caribbean women entering higher education as mature students and the effects that this could have on their success. In exploring the pursuit of education for some West African women, who have a long history with several British universities, this chapter identifies that some of these women have been involved in private fostering for their children, which has been traumatising. The education of the children of Black women has also been fraught with difficulties evidenced in the literature, irrespective of class. The participation of Black women in the labour market is an issue of concern, more so as many women from West Africa and Zimbabwe are among the highest achieving groups, yet their professional careers and income levels do not match their academic profile. Employment rates for Black women generally lag behind those for White women and they suffer from a greater gender pay gap.

Chapter 6 presents the body of evidence which demonstrates that Black women are more likely to experience mental health disorders compared to their White counterparts. Even more concerning is that there is a lower engagement with health services for Black women, despite urgent calls for more access to mental health care services. One of the consequences of living in racialised spaces such as Britain is the adverse effect on the well-being of the Black population. The mental and emotional condition of Black women has often been concealed. Significantly, this chapter presents a study conducted by Showunmi on the mental and emotional well-being of young Black women. The data shows that young Black women appear to be suffering in silence, contrary to the popular stereotypical view of the 'strong Black woman'.

Chapter 7 features the narrative process of self-enquiry based on an analysis of the academic experiences of two Black women working in British universities. By disrupting the 'Whiteness' of the academy, it describes how Black women construct their 'Black' identities in a context where Black staff are not only underrepresented in academic positions but rarely occupy senior posts. The impact of institutionalised racism within the academy and its effects on Black women on a personal level are discussed poignantly in this chapter.

Chapter 8 is pivotal. It details how Black women and girls can manage sophisticated and everyday racism in educational and professional contexts. The chapter suggests that Black women can utilise agentic means to manage everyday racism and 'flip the script' to change the narrative. Through accounts of real-life encounters, this chapter identifies specific strategies and negotiating tools which can serve as a template for Black women in White spaces thus engendering their own agency. The agentic tools are designed to furnish Black individuals with opportunities to adopt effective strategies during interactions or encounters where they find themselves the victims of sophisticated and everyday racism.

Chapter 9 brings together the themes of the book. The concepts presented in previous chapters are summarised and conclusions are drawn from earlier discussions. A critical lens is adopted to emphasise the complexity of multiple manifestations of diverse forms of racism.

We foreground the dynamic nature of the recognition of the negative and destructive effects of racism which are beginning to be reported although most encounters are still hidden. This book therefore enriches the body of literature which examines the phenomenon of 'race' and the experiences of Black people in society.

NOTE

1. Source: England and Wales 2011 Census/Ethnicity Facts and Figures GOV. UK https://www.ethnicity-facts-figures.service.gov.uk/uk-population-by-ethnicity/national-and-regional-populations/population-of-england-and-wales/latest

Chapter 1

Race and Racism(s)

While race is often theorised as a social construct without biological validity, it is hard to ignore race's power to affect one's lifestyle, choices and opportunities.
—Syed and Ali, 2011, p. 350

The aim of this chapter is to provide theoretical understandings of 'race' and racism(s). A brief overview of 'race' as a social construct is provided. The word 'racism' is also pluralised to signal how racism is aimed at people of colour in minority geographical settings and reflected historically to people groups not based on colour. The forms of institutional and structural racism are examined as a launching pad for sophisticated racism.

Husband (1982, p. 206) writes, 'Race is a classification based on the belief that the perceived difference is immutable and fixed. . . . Although the concept of "race" has no scientific backing, its salience as a social category is evident throughout British society.' Historically, the upsurge in science had set the stage for pseudo-scientific racial hierarchy between Africans, deemed inferior, and Europeans, deemed superior, coinciding with the growth of the slave trade in the seventeenth and eighteenth centuries. Social Darwinism, the theory of evolution by natural selection, constructed the separation of people groups into designated races by ascribing diverse traits for economic gain and had widespread appeal. The innate and unchanging dimensions of race challenged by Darwin's *On the Origin of the Species*, which argued that races had to be kept apart, especially European Whites, to maintain their racial purity (Husband, 1982), subsequently led to the horrors of the Eugenics movement emerging in the late nineteenth century, aimed at improving the human species through selective breeding.

The idea of racism denotes attitudes, beliefs and systems such as economic and political that promote and maintain the superiority of a particular racial group. Bhavnani et al. (2005) identify different types of 'racisms' aimed at specific groups – for example, asylum seekers, South Asians, Chinese, Jews and the Traveller community. These intersect with other discriminations based on class, age, disability and so on. Often racism or racisms are manifested in racial tropes, which historically have not always been conferred to people of colour, as can be seen in gross caricatures of Irish people who have been depicted as apes with protruding mouths (Wade, 2020), a motif replicated in portrayals of Jews (Stepakoff, 2020). Apelike imagery and outthrust mouths analogous to representations of Africans suggest that these images are tactics of oppression (Wade, 2020). Unlike Blacks, Irish and to a lesser extent Jews (Ashkenazi Jews from Europe) have been able to assimilate into British or American society based on their 'White' skin colour. Ignatiev's classic book *How the Irish became White* (1995/2009) recounts Catholic Irish labourers fleeing to America due to landlordism and a caste system that perceived them as sub-human. Initially experiencing servitude and comrade with free Blacks, 'the assimilation of the Irish into the White race made it possible to maintain slavery' (p. 69), and through their rites of passage to eventually 'becoming White' they were able to participate in a system that subjugates African Americans. In his fascinating research on the Jews, Parfitt (2020) surmises that racism manifests in different geographical spheres, anti-Semitism in places like Germany and Russia, and anti-Blackness in Britain and America. Throughout the nineteenth and early twentieth centuries, Jews in Germany were consigned to the Negroid race. The colour question in the ancestry of Ashkenazi Jews began historically with European encounters of Black Jews in the West African kingdom of Loango, contributing to the merging of racial ideas about Jews and Blacks. As Parfitt (2020) explains, Western thinkers and race theorists' racial construction of both Jews and Blacks were often fused. Brodkin's (1999) notes how European Jews (Ashkenazic) have often been assigned to the White race though at other times an off-White or middle racial designation suggesting the complexity in the ethno-religious categorisation of Jews (Green, 2016). Contemporarily, Ashkenazic Jews can choose to become White, in contrast to other non-White people, including Jews – possibly a reason why they are perceived as part of the White system that oppresses people of colour (Green, 2016). Yet, Jews experience racial bigotry by groups such as the alt-right in America and various neo-Nazi groups in Europe. At the same time, without minimalizing 'racisms' experienced by some groups, Diangelo (2018) reminds us of the uniquely anti-Black sentiment, which we will discuss later.

Moreover, according to Bhavnani et al. (2005), the form of racism changes dependent on social and political conditions. Over the past 35 years, the new racism in dominant discourse has moved from a scientific biological basis to a notion of cultural racism. Anti-colonial struggles of the 1960s and 1970s and civil rights movements, and the United Nations' introduction of various human rights/equality policies catalysed the era of integration and cultural differences. Thus, the new racism is culturalized with minorities seen as culturally different rather than biologically deficient and legitimised with terms such as ethnicity and ethnic minorities. However, inequalities are still attributed to cultural deficit models. Culturalized racism is exhibited in many forms, such as overt, covert and unintentional, while simultaneously operating at three distinct levels psychologically, including conscious, subconscious and unconscious.

Drawing on a discourse analytical approach, Van Dijk (2000) argues that the new racism is reproduced through discursive practices and sourced in symbolic and subtle ways through text as in material artefacts such as newspaper reports and text as talk or communication. As he goes on to explain,

> They are expressed, enacted and confirmed by text and talk, such as everyday conversations, board meetings, job interviews, policies, laws, parliamentary debates, political propaganda, textbooks, scholarly articles, movies, TV programmes and news reports in the press, among hundreds of other genres. (p. 34)

More disturbingly, according to Van Dijk, they are a form of 'ethnic hegemony', contingent on apparently valid belief systems and attitudes and often tacitly accepted by the majority of the dominant group. New racism, or old for that matter, is translated into the practices of everyday racism (Essed, 1991). Racism intersects with other discriminations based on class, age, disability and so on (Bhavnani et al., 2005). The intertwining dynamics of race, class and gender are critical to any discussion on racism (Davis, 1982, 2011; Crenshaw, 1989). Racism is often prevalent institutionally through organisational practices and structurally interwoven in the fabric of society resulting in unfortunate outcomes for Black females in all spheres of life. The experiences of Black women must also be seen in the light of Black people in general.

Therefore, it is relevant to give some attention to the latest national Report on race (at the time of writing), the controversial *Commission on Race and Ethnic Disparities 2021*, the British government's Commission in response to Black Lives Matter (BLM) protests. The Report, hereafter referred to as CRED or Sewell (after Dr. Tony Sewell, the Commission's chairperson), references institutional and structural racism. The definition of institutional racism is stated in the MacPherson Report arising from the Stephen Lawrence Inquiry, the Black teenager who died in a racially motivated murder, and described as:

> The collective failure of an organisation to provide an appropriate and professional service to people because of their colour, culture, or ethnic origin. It can be seen or detected in processes, attitudes and behaviour that amount to discrimination through prejudice, ignorance, thoughtlessness, and racist stereotyping which disadvantage minority ethnic people. (MacPherson, 1999, p. 28)

Though acknowledging the existence of racism in British society and MacPherson's definition, the Sewell Report criticises the application of the term 'institutional racism'. Sewell argues that the term describes practices and behaviours that were commonplace and approved by authorities in the twentieth century, but has been used 'liberally' and too 'casually' to explain ethnic disparities (p. 34), and finds a lack of evidence for continuing with the use of the term; suggesting it is a relic of the past. The Report also contends that structural racism is misapplied and refers to a dismantling of the capitalist system. It would be beneficial here to explain the concept of structural racism often used interchangeably with systemic racism. Caldwell and Bledsoe (2019, p. 6) write that 'structural racism refers to the totality of ways in which societies foster racial discrimination through mutually reinforcing systems of housing, education, employment, earnings, benefits, credit, media, health care, and criminal justice'. There are iniquitous features of the system that need to be demolished and replaced with ones more equitable. Whether that is achievable is for another debate, but challenging terminologies do not obliterate the existence of racism. It appears that on both sides of the Atlantic, the words 'racism' or 'racists' are being sanitised for more acceptable terms such as racial slurs and bias (Pulido, 2015). Both institutional and structural racism remain major causes of concern, evidenced by a total of 375 government recommendations to combat racism in recent official reports and reviews such as the following: The Adebowale Report (2013); The Young Review (2014); The Parker Review (2017); The McGregor-Smith Review (2017); The Angiolini Review (2017) and The Lammy Review (2017) (see Chakelian, 2020).

The Race Disparity Audit (2017) paints an accurate but complex and vivid picture of how minority ethnic groups, including Black women, are treated across society compared to their White counterparts. The Audit demonstrates that substantial inequalities remain a crucial feature of life for Black Caribbean people in areas such as health and education confirmed in our work and echoed by a plethora of studies such as those edited by Bryne et al. (2020). In terms of health, the recent COVID-19 global pandemic has disproportionately impacted the Black population in Britain, with Black Caribbean females among the highest death rates, twice that of their White counterparts (Office for National Statistics, 2020). Unfortunately, similar findings are reported among African heritage women on both sides of the Atlantic (Drew et al. forthcoming). The explanations for inequities in COVID-19 in Britain have been attributed to institutional and structural racism shaping social and health outcomes (see Public Health England Report: *Beyond the Data: Understanding the Impact of COVID-19 on BAME Groups*, 2020). There is no lack of education research, as will be discussed throughout this book. In an open letter, education researchers expressed concerns with the selective and distorted use of academic research in the Sewell Report and its claim that education is 'the single most emphatic success story of the British ethnic minority experience' (p. 55). Academics criticise the Report for overlooking the substantial evidence in education research that has demonstrated how structural, institutional and direct racism works in sites of education.

The Report states 'that the root of advantage and disadvantage for different groups are complex and often as much to do with social class, "family" culture and geography as ethnicity' (p. 10). We repudiate the Report's claim because conclusions drawn based on comparisons of different minority ethnic groups can be problematic without robust analyses of various groups' histories, geopolitics, economics and social contexts. In the words of the Report, 'We found that most of the disparities we examined, which some attribute to racial discrimination, often do not have their origins in racism' (p. 11). Fragmented outcomes for Black and Brown people require an intersectional analysis. Racial barriers may have declined for individual upwardly mobile minority ethnic groups who are also divided by class – similar to the White majority ethnic group. Hence, social mobility for some minorities, on the surface evidences the declining significance of race (Wilson, 1978). We argue that for Black women as a group, the disparities can be assigned to racial discrimination. Variables of class and gender combined do not sufficiently explain why Black women collectively experience challenges in domains such as the labour market, even accounting for class and gender, comparable to their White counterparts of the same social class status and gender. The role of class cannot be invalidated (Reay, 2017; Erzsébet and Goldthorpe, 2018), but the abundance of research referenced throughout this book confirms that 'race' is the most salient factor influencing adverse outcomes for Black females. As Ladson-Billings and Tate (1995) remind us, class and gender are not unimportant but rather, as West (1993) purports, race matters, confirmed by Smith (1993, p. 76), who emphasises that 'blackness matters in more detailed ways'. In other words, 'Blackness' is skin deep and moves class out of the equation, inculcating anti-Black racism. Anti-Blackness, in particular, centres the discussion.

BLACKNESS AND WHITENESS

'Blackness' remains a contested site because of the legacy of slavery and colonialism (Fanon, 1952/2021). In addition, Blackness relating to Black female bodies is also imbued with notions of colourism or shadeism. The physiological approximation to Whiteness (Davis, 2011) and anti-Blackness become internalised by Black women, sometimes resulting in ambivalent behaviours (Bivens, 2005). Any discussion on Blackness inevitably entails problematising Whiteness. As Leonardo (2002, p. 31) explains, Whiteness is a discourse on race, whereas the category White people marks a socially constructed identity, usually identifiable by skin colour.

It is also helpful to understand White privilege and White supremacy, shaping White men and women advanced in critical race theory (CRT). Adams et al. (1997, p. 97) write that

> White privilege is about the concrete benefits of access to resources and social rewards and the power to shape the norms and values of society that whites receive, unconsciously or consciously, by virtue of their skin colour in a racist society.

As Leonardo (2004, p. 140) further opines, the term 'White privilege' does not elicit high levels of discomfort for White people as they are not blamed individually, nor does it imply racial hostility. In contrast, it is challenging to understand White supremacy mainly because it is associated with extreme right-wing White supremacy political groups such as the Ku Klux Klan. Understandingly, many White individuals in contemporary society disavow allegiance to groups associated with vicious racial hatred. According to Pulido (2015), while White supremacy is a complex concept, one of its defining features is the belief that White people are superior to Blacks and people of colour, a theme we will return to in chapter 2. As she goes on to say,

> Though some may question the supremacist content of such attitudes and beliefs, at their root they are predicated on the belief that whites are entitled to more, which, in turn, is predicated on the belief that they are more deserving, or 'better than other groups'. (p. 813)

The positioning of Whites as superior and Blacks inferior based historically on pseudo-scientific theories, justification of slavery, and represented contemporarily through processes such as the media (Van Dijk, 2012) contribute to the interactions of White men and women with Black women and anti-Black sentiments (Diangelo, 2018). Despite local systems with different rules, anti-Black racism is a transnational global phenomenon birthed from global White supremacy. In the case of Brazil and Colombia, for instance, Black social movements are intersectional as they underscore gendered manifestations of anti-Black racism (Busey and Coleman-King, 2020).

British research on anti-Black racism frequently focuses on the lives of men (Glynn, 2013; Shankley and Williams, 2020). Unfortunately, insufficient attention is paid to the experiences of Black women. White feminist theorists tend to focus on White women's social and economic conditions, excluding women of colour (Anim-Addo, 2014). This has led to popular Black feminist or womanist writers such as Angela Davis, Alice Walker, Tony Morrison and bell hooks, who shed light on the experiences of Black women, but their writings have been in the American context. The seminal text *The Heart of the Race* by Beverley Bryan, Stella Dadzie and Suzanne Scafe (1985) depicted the circumstances of Black women in Britain by the mid-1980s. Inevitably, the twenty-first century calls for fresh insights based on the experiences of millennials and generation Z Black females, and cross-generationally. Significantly, we intend to suggest how Black women can re-position themselves to navigate space, given their embodied racial caste-like state (Mocombe et al., 2014), regardless of their class position (Rollock et al., 2014).

Chapter 2

The Tangled Web of Blackness, *Identity* and Race

INTRODUCTION

The previous chapter examined concepts of race and racism, anti-Blackness and Whiteness. Whiteness is seen as the norm so the nomenclature of Black people in the United Kingdom and elsewhere blurs Black identities reducing heterogeneity to the falsity of homogenous Blackness.

This chapter explores the historical context of 'Blackness' using the metaphor of the 'Big House' where plantation owners held sway. The relationships which emerged in this context are detailed, and parallels are drawn to contemporary interracial workplace power dynamics. Typologies of the strategies adopted by house slaves are analysed and related to examples of how Black people attempt to cope with the difficulties they face in today's workplaces.

The behaviours of White women and Black women and their relationships are deconstructed, starting with their interconnected lives in the plantation 'Big House'. The mutual distrust emanating from this background is elucidated and linked to the challenges faced by Black women in contemporary society.

Black culture and multiculturalism are described, and the emergence of shifting terms to categorise Black people is charted and analysed. The historical influences which have shaped notions of Whiteness and skin-colour hierarchies are detailed and linked to colourism in contemporary society. White reluctance to acknowledge the diversity of Black identities is also explored alongside the complexity of class and Blackness.

UNDERSTANDINGS OF RACIAL ETHNICITIES: THE HISTORICAL CONTEXT OF 'BLACKNESS'

The impact of the historical backdrop of transatlantic slavery on contemporary attitudes to Blackness is now analysed. During the transatlantic slave trade from the fifteenth to the nineteenth century, Europeans forcibly took Africans from their homelands and sold them as slaves to work on the plantation fields of the Americas, the so-called 'New World'. Typically, a plantation is a large-scale agricultural estate that specializes in cash crops where labourers are paid, but in the plantocracy or slave regime it was dominated by White slave owners. These slave owners formed the ruling planter class who profited enormously from the free labour of Black chattel slaves.

THE TANGLED WEB OF BLACKNESS IN THE 'BIG HOUSE': A METAPHOR

The core of this book is a set of strategies for managing sophisticated and everyday racism. The 'Big House' metaphor is central to the development of our understandings of Blackness, identity and race. The metaphor is used to explain the interplay of race with colourism and gender. The characteristics of racism in the plantocracy persist in contemporary society, so it is helpful to draw a parallel between them and the challenges which continue to confront Black minorities.

The 'Big House' on plantations was the home of slave owners or their plantation overseers and was the site of the emergence of a societal structure built on racist foundations. The term the 'Big House' was coined by the slaves themselves (see, for example, Vlach, 1993). This complex hierarchical society emerged because the 'Big House' was a hotbed of the interplay of Black-White relationships. The resultant patterns of the abuse of power and the suffering and resourceful opportunism of its victims are crucial as they have contributed to the construction of Black identities. Parallel patterns of behaviour are playing out today in our institutions; the typologies which emerged in the 'Big Houses' of the plantations still exist.

Ladson-Billings (2005) has used the 'Big House' metaphor in the specific context of the academy in *Beyond the Big House*. Other authors have examined contemporary portrayals of the 'Big House', for example in museums in the Americas (Small, 2013). The relative neglect and marginalisation of plantation cabins (occupied by so many Black slaves) and the glorification and romanticisation of life in the Big House (occupied by a few White people and their Black house slaves) are a feature of many plantation museums in the United States, reflecting the persistent dominance of White privilege in contemporary society (Small, 2013).

The plantation owner and overseer of the enslaved people used a range of tactics to dehumanise the slaves. Assaults on the bodies and minds of the enslaved exposed them to both physical and psychological trauma. The physical trauma would include extreme forms of punishment to control slaves. In addition to physical injury caused by beating, slaves suffered chronic ill health from overwork, scanty rations and insufficient clothing. In this context, the resultant psychological trauma is now termed 'post-traumatic slave syndrome' (DeGruy, 2005). Enslaved people were not permitted to appear to be thinking for themselves or to display the anger which inevitably arose from physical violence, whether being beaten or witnessing someone else's torture, increasing psychological harm.

Three groups are referred to in this chapter: the first is the group of enslaved people who worked in the field, and the second the enslaved people who moved from the field and worked in the Big House. The third group is the enslaved people who were born and worked in the 'Big House'.

COLOURISM IN THE 'BIG HOUSE'

The slaves who worked in the field were darker in complexion and treated brutally. The enslaved people who came from the field to work in the Big House would also be of a darker complexion and sometimes had an uneasy relationship with their owners. White slave owners sowed the seeds of discord among the slaves by creating hierarchies. In his memoirs, one slave wrote that 'the distinction among slaves is as marked as the classes of society are in any aristocratic community; some refusing to associate with others whom they deem beneath them in point of character, color, conditions, or the superior importance of the respective masters' (Bibb, 1968 [1849], p. 33).

Horowitz (1973) provides a useful overview of the plantocracy throughout the Americas. The heinous assault of Black women by White men resulted in Mulattoes known as 'people of colour', with female Mulattoes, as well as Black women, often becoming the mistresses of White men. The quadroon children, who had one-fourth of African blood, were the consequence of relationships between female Mulattoes who often became 'free coloured' and White men with the subsequent generations labelled 'mestees'. The people who were born, raised and worked in the Big House, the lighter-complexioned Mulattoes, were given preferential treatment by Whites and indeed Blacks. Whites saw lighter-skinned Black people as more intelligent, aesthetically pleasing and more capable of being 'civilized', but the poorest Whites still saw themselves as superior to Blacks and Mulattoes. The Mulattoes were offered positions as house servants, away from the hard work in the field, and afforded the opportunity to acquire trade skills and an education which they could use outside the plantation (Reece, 2018). In many ways, it can be argued that psychological chains have still bound Blacks to a great extent to these false categorisations, a relic of the slavery period.

STRATEGIC BEHAVIOURS IN THE 'BIG HOUSE': A TYPOLOGY

The following four strategies describe the behaviours of slaves in the Big House: passivist, complicit, activist and disruptor. These strategies were adopted by those who worked in the Big House to survive the physical and psychological aggression of slave owners especially towards women (Vlach, 1993; Fox-Genovese, 2000) (see figure 2.1).

THE TANGLED WEB OF THE BIG HOUSE

An analysis of the meaning of figure 2.1 follows.

These typologies are not in a hierarchical or sequential order, as there is much interaction between them. The *activist* seeks to obtain opportunities without any compromise. The house activist develops strategies with the

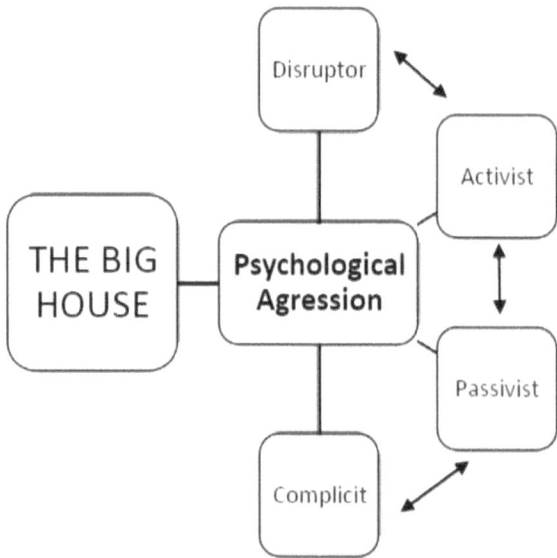

Figure 2.1   The Tangled Web of the Big House.

disruptor. The house *pacifist* spends their time pleasing the master to get what they want. The pacifist is the peacemaker and their role is to be compliant with the rules of the house. The house disruptor does whatever it takes to assist the house activist to be promoted and to receive what reflects their knowledge. The house *complicit* abides by the rules of the house without question. All these behaviours weaken the psychological aggression of the slave master and his wife.

The 'Big House' in this context is the place where privileges are distributed to enslaved people in the form of occupational status. Reece (2018) argues that slavery was more than an institution of interracial boundaries, creating and exacerbating racial inequality between Blacks and Whites; it also shaped interracial boundaries between Black people. It not only determined who was and who was not regarded as Black but also contributed to skill differences that affected occupational success post-Emancipation (Ruef and Fletcher, 2003).

PSYCHOLOGICAL AGGRESSION AND THE CONTEMPORARY WORKPLACE

One aspect of psychological aggression is called 'splitting'. Splitting is a failure to bring together the dichotomy of good and bad of the self and others, therefore the Black woman cannot be seen or tolerated as an ally but has to be split off as being all bad and the White woman all good as a way of coping with the psychological distress of her presence in the 'Big House'. Splitting is a defence mechanism or form of dissociation; for example, a way of dealing with psychological distress. The interconnecting roles generate conflicting narratives with the positions, which threatens the paralysis of the 'Big House'. When we bring the notion of splitting into sophisticated and everyday racism, it reflects the different roles in the form of the typologies which have been referred to in this chapter (see figure 2.1).

When organisations operate equal opportunities policies, they seek to address the imbalance of marginalised groups, and in the case discussed in this chapter, a Black woman. A Black person who is recruited into an organisation will be grateful for admittance, creating an unconscious or even conscious sense of indebtedness, even if they are in the organisation because of tokenism, and become an artefact or trophy for that organisation. In relation to the typologies in 'The Tangled Web of the Big House' (figure 2.1), the easiest role to adopt would be passive or indeed complicit, so as not to appear ungrateful for the opportunity to enter the 'Big House' or workplace. However, if the person is revealed as a disrupter or activist, things start to become more complex and difficult.

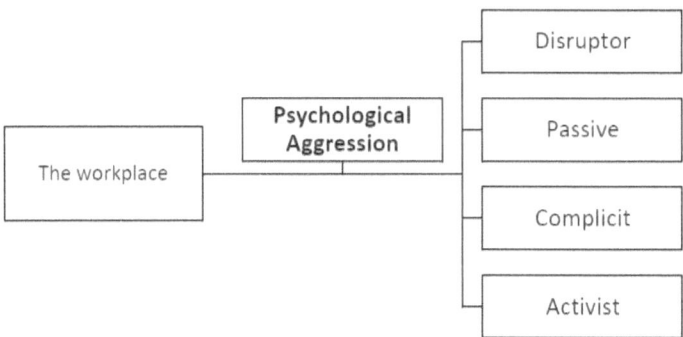

Figure 2.2 From the Big House to the Workplace: Patterns Persist. *Source*: Showunmi 2022

The 'Big House' historically reflects the interplay of Black people within contemporary society. Continuing with the metaphor of the enslaved people in the 'Big House', we can transfer the strategies they adopted to today's workplace or indeed society. The 'Big House' represents the operational behaviour that Black people have to navigate while progressing through the many levels of the House. There are still Black women who are disruptors, activists, passivist and complicit interacting today in a range of contexts. Those already in the house may be on the defensive so they can maintain their status in the 'Big House'. Their aim is to rise to an influential position, so they do not want to be disruptors. They will become complicit, steering clear of activists for fear of being tainted by those whose aim is to weaken the power of the main powerbrokers in the 'Big House', the plantation owners and overseers, or their modern-day counterparts.

There is a range of strategies that individuals utilise to accommodate the opportunities which are in sight and available. The challenge for Black individuals inhabiting Western (predominantly White) spaces is how to gain access to these limited opportunities and with what agentic means.

FROM THE BIG HOUSE TO THE WORKPLACE: PATTERNS PERSIST

The following narrative shows how the individuals who embody the roles which emerged originally in the 'Big House' still persist in today's workplace. The characters in this account with their distinctive typologies are as follows:

A key person in the story mirrors the White slave owner. He is Paul, a successful White leader. He recruits an arrogant young White male high flyer (35), Charles.

The Black supervisors are:

Karen (55), Passivist. Karen just lets things happen. Charles is allocated to Karen's team.
Angela (50), Activist. Angela could be described as the activist who creates awareness, carries the billboard and stands up for social justice.
Steven (47), Complicit. Steven empowers the White management because he is prepared to accept or even support the unjust status quo.
Donald (49), Disruptor. Donald creates alternative facts, causes chaos, upheaval and conflict.
William (45), Ambitious White Supervisor.

STORY PART 1: SOPHISTICATED RACISM[1]

Paul, 55, is White. He's the director of a large unit which is doing well under his management. He has a group of eight supervisors who ensure that all the members of each of their respective teams focus well on their work to keep up high levels of productivity.

Four of the supervisors are Black. The company prides itself on its ethnic diversity and endeavours to give responsibility to Black employees. Company leaders often highlight this.

Paul is proud to have recruited an outstanding young White male, 35, Charles, to the company. Paul is convinced he will do great things and rise rapidly to the top. He sees Charles as a younger version of himself. He allocates Charles to Karen's team. Karen is 55, and one of his best and most experienced supervisors. She is Black.

Paul has arranged a meeting with Charles to catch up after his first few weeks.

Paul: How are things going Charles?
Charles: Fine, fine.
Paul: You don't sound altogether happy. Are you enjoying the work? Is there a problem?
Charles: Well, actually there is. It's a bit awkward – but . . .
Paul: Go on, spill the beans, we're keen that you should be happy here.
Charles: I'm not sure. . . . As a matter of fact, it's Karen, I don't think Karen's the right person to be my supervisor. I don't think it's a good fit. We don't understand each other. I get on well with William, though, he would be a better fit for my supervisor.
Paul: William? He isn't nearly as experienced as Karen you know.
Charles: Yes, but . . . you know . . .
Paul: OK, I see what you mean, I'll see what I can do.

STORY PART 2: THE IMPACT OF SOPHISTICATED AND EVERYDAY RACISM ON THE BLACK PSYCHE

The following week, Charles was moved to William's team. William was White. Karen didn't mind. It wasn't the first time White high-flyers had found it challenging to be managed by a Black woman. She didn't comment or mention it to anyone.

But Angela, another Black supervisor, found out and she was furious because it wasn't usual for employees to change their supervisors.

Angela: Can you believe this Charles has been moved? When I wanted to be moved it was 'against company policy'. They only moved Charles because it was 'not a good fit'! How about that? 'Not a good fit' – with only our *best* supervisor!

She heard that Charles had been making disparaging remarks about Black footballers and taking the knee. She was on the Union and complained about Charles' behaviour. She also mentioned that she suspected that Charles had asked to move to William's team because of his attitude to Black people.

Steven, another Black supervisor, heard about Angela's conversation with the Union. He didn't like what he'd heard.

Steven: Angela I've heard you've been kicking up a fuss again. You have to stop drawing attention to yourself – to us! We're lucky to be here. We're lucky to be supervisors, considering. You need to lie low and get on with your job. Paul has every right to move Charles if that's what he wants.
Angela: Steven, I will not 'lie low' as you put it. Do you think Malcolm X would lie low? Do you think Angela Davis, or Winnie Mandela would lie low? How can we ever achieve anything like equality if we 'lie low' as you put it?

Donald overheard the conversation.

'You're both barking up the wrong tree!' he commented. 'I've heard Karen wanted Charles moved. She doesn't like arrogant young White men.'

Typical Donald. He always managed to make things worse.

WHITE WOMEN IN THE 'BIG HOUSE' AND THEIR LEGACY

Black masculinity and femininity were reconceptualised and transfigured as a consequence of the racial and gender dynamic in the Big House (Jones-Rogers, 2019). White women were enmeshed in a complex web of White male dominance. Their situation was not as enviable as might be expected because they had little agency. Despite this, both White men and women benefited from the financial capital accrued from the plantocracy system. The wealth built through the plantocracy system coupled with the hegemonic discourse of Whiteness fuelled the idea of White women as the gold standard. White women are seen as the 'ideal' of femininity while Black femininity has been rejected as Black women have been dehumanised. The rejection of the value of Black femininity in favour of White femininity persists to this day. It is a phenomenon that we as Black women grapple with every day.

THE ROLE OF WOMEN IN THE PLANTOCRACY

In relation to the earlier analysis of 'the Big House' and the plantocracy, the focus of the discussion on slavery tends to be based on White male slave owners and few highlight the pivotal role of White women (Strings, 2019). White women were key figures in the Big House, but they are often overlooked and this has to be put in context as this phenomenon is still prevalent in contemporary society.

White plantation owners, usually male, were invariably supported by White women, very often their wives. White slave owners would often inflict sexual and psychological terror on Black women who they objectified as commodities. The sexual assault of Black women by White plantation owners meant that many White women were left to devise strategies to lessen the acute trauma suffered by assaulted women and their families. This facilitated the maintenance of the status quo in relation to the owner-slave relationship. If the women had not worked to repair the worst of the damage done by these violent plantation owners, the fragile structure of the owner-slave relationship risked breaking down. The slave owners' Mulatto children as a by-product of their horrendous behaviour would inevitably cause their White wives to exhibit pent-up resentment towards both Black women and the offspring produced by this immoral union. We argue that this has produced historical memory retention (Eyeman, 2001) and is evident today in the relationship dynamics between Black and White women. This has emerged as what we term 'White women syndrome' (WWS), whereby some White women have an unconsciously adverse reaction to Black women. The Hollywood movie *Twelve Years a Slave* (2013) based on the 1853 slave memoir by Solomon Northup provides some insight into this phenomenon.

INTERRACIAL RELATIONSHIPS: BLACK EXPLOITATION AND HUMILIATION

It can be argued that the dynamics of interracial relationships, which dominated the slave era, continue even today. In the plantocracy system, the power dynamics between the enslaved and enslaver manifested themselves in exploitation and rape. Both males and females were raped by the slave master and his wife, which gave rise to a culture of sexual exploitation, hypersexuality and repression, as the slave master and his wife had to repress their desire for the African body, outwardly simulating revulsion and disdain for that same body, the object of their desire (Young, 2005). The Africans in this liminal space, however, also had to repress their own sexuality amid the discriminatory effects of their depictions as hypersexual creatures luring the enslavers into fornication and adultery (Strings, 2019). The latter, in many instances, especially among house slaves in the plantation house, led to Blacks providing sex for better treatment and privileges (clothing, time off, access to the enslaver, etc.) by and from their enslavers in the total institution of slavery (see Child, 2005, for similar views expressed by Black women regarding Black men in contemporary interracial relationships).

The docile slave acquiescing to the enslaver's advances and sexual exploitation hoped to be elevated above those who were in the fields and less desirable. The same dynamics hold true today to some extent in Black-White interracial relationships. The Black body, both male and female, is desired because of the perception of its athletic prowess and hypersexuality alongside White disdain for that same body evidenced by the killing of Black men and women in inner cities (Roberts, 1997).

The Black responses, in many instances, to these interracial relationships are no different from that of their house slave ancestors. Somehow, the interracial relationship affords Black access and privileges which Black people would not have if they were less desirable (Millward, 2010). It is not uncommon for some Black men to express a preference for White women for similar reasons; that is, a White woman can open the door to the White world of privilege (Childs, 2005). Some Black men in these kinds of relationships then demean Black women. Historically, Black women were also sexually abused by Black men as they were paired by the slave master to produce bond children for the master (Roberts, 1997).

THE BLACK WOMAN: THE MYTH OF THE SEDUCTIVE TEMPTRESS

As we continue the discussion on the devaluation of Black women and Black girls, a closer look into what is going on inside what we have called the 'Big House' is required. We have mentioned the way in which enslavement manifests itself from the historical memory of the past into the present which makes it so difficult to disentangle. There is a need, however, to add another missing piece of the jigsaw which contributes to the complexity of sophisticated and everyday racism.

The historical context also suggests that Black men were taken in by White women when they needed a shoulder to cry on and then defended them from the hands of the plantation owner (Strings, 2019). White women then became critical of Black women as they grappled with knowing and seeing what the plantation owners (their husbands or indeed fathers, uncles or brothers) were doing to Black women. The brutality and sexual violence towards Black women were seen by White women as somehow the Black women's fault (Roberts, 1997). Rooted within the plantocracy system, White men and women slave owners justified the sexual assault of Black women by White men by embracing the Jezebel stereotype (Jones-Rogers, 2019). The Jezebel stereotype characterises Black females as hypersexual, seductive and promiscuous (Collins, 2004). Black women in mainstream media are still presented in this way (Ward et al., 2018). During slavery, one of the weapons at the disposal of White women was to engage in secret encounters with Black males, as a way to hold onto their own feminine power. The sexual abuse that Black men experienced contributed to the fragility of their masculinity. Fragile masculinity refers to anxiety felt by Black men who believe they are falling short of cultural standards of manhood. Black men historically valued the Whiteness of White women embodied in the master's daughter who had access to White privilege. Black women, in contrast, were perceived as gender deviant or rebellious, cynical or controlling, a trend which has continued to this day (Stillwell and Lowery, 2020).

THE WHITE WOMAN: THE THREAT OF THE BLACK WOMAN

The distant antipathy that White women exhibit towards Black women which is indeed historical plays out in the workplace where resources are limited and Black women are seen as a threat to White women's success (Allen, 2016, p. 66). The way in which Black women have learnt to deal with the onslaught of hostility and rejection in society and the workplace is to develop resilience and strength. The archetypal strong Black woman interrogated by scholars such as Michelle Wallace (1978) remains extremely problematic as it assumes that our strength is without vulnerability. The strength is based on courage, resilience, perseverance and our will to survive. Our vulnerability is the acknowledgement of our fear of uncertainty, injustice, our need for humanity, the preservation of mental health and well-being and in some cases our dread of the loss of life.

The status of White women in the contemporary workplace is inferior to that of men. White women seek to acquire agency and resources. This echoes White women's past predicament in the Big House, where their power was circumscribed. As then, White women do not see Black women as partners in their struggle for equality. In fact, they see Black women as only Black, not as fellow women also fighting for their rights. They regard Black women as competing for limited access to recognition and resources. We coin the term WWS in order to elucidate this idea, locating its origins historically within the plantocracy hierarchy of slavery. WWS is the threat that Black women pose just by their very existence. The threat is a myth and a fallacy created by White women.

BLACK WOMEN IN THE CONTEMPORARY WORKPLACE

So how does this translate into where we are now in society and in particular in the workplace? There are countless initiatives purportedly designed to promote equality between Black women as well as White women and men. However, 'White women benefit most from affirmative action' (Massey, 2016; Bhopal, 2020). Negative consequences may sometimes result from affirmative action to address equality imbalances in society.

The following narrative illustrates the experience of Black women in the workplace. The scene takes place in a large organisation where the majority of workers are White.

> Alice is a highly qualified Black woman who has been recruited for her leadership expertise, competence and experience. When she enters the new space of this large organisation, Alice greets the people around her, but there is little response. Apart from a nod or two, it's as though she doesn't exist. The team she has been employed to manage are White British and White European. Her excitement drains away as she begins to notice that one of the team members displays an element of open resentment towards her. As she sits at her desk, there is a knock on the door. A colleague informs her that she needs to be aware that a member of her team had not been successful in the interview for the post she had been hired for. She calls a team meeting to get to know more about her colleagues. The ice breaker she has planned seems to work reasonably well, so she starts to get to know her team. However, as the members of the team introduce themselves and their responsibilities, she notices awkward body language and negative expressions which indicate disengagement. She continues to move forward with the agenda and asks for thoughts on what she is presenting. There is a deadly silence.

She is taken aback as she had not expected to be faced with such hostility. She asks if someone would like to speak up. After some time, one of the people says that they are just a part-time administrator. This encourages another person who says: 'You have been appointed as the team lead; I wish you all the best'. You are now the 5 person to be appointed to the team.

Eventually, one team member says: 'We all need to come together and make this work. Alice is our new team leader! Let's get behind her!' Another team member shares that they have a Jamaican boyfriend. The resistance is immense nevertheless.

As the team disperses, Alice overhears one say drily 'that was a good use of our time' and then laughs.

Alice steps outside the room and meets an administrator from another team who welcomes her and asks: 'Are you new?' It was the first time someone had taken the time to welcome Alice to the organisation.

After six months of hard, productive work, without support or encouragement, Alice was making headway. The administrator from the other team, the first person who had made her feel welcome, asked her to go for a coffee.

She explained the background to her recruitment. It transpired that her senior line manager (White, male, privileged and who always promoted White males like himself – perhaps unconscious bias?) had said this when a colleague pointed out that the leadership team was entirely White and male:

'Perhaps we should parachute in a BAME woman.'

Alice, as a Black woman, had been recruited because of tokenism and hired in place of an established member of the team, which was partly why her presence had initially met with such strong resentment.

This narrative illustrates the importance of including Black women in the feminist movement.

BLACK WOMEN AND FEMINISM

Much of the discussion on racism in general tends to be centred on a patriarchal frame of reference and very often White women are seen as silent colluders within systemic racism rather than perpetrators. However, Syed and Ali (2011) demonstrate that White women were willing agents in perpetuating White racial superiority. Over the years feminist literature tended to focus on White women, often ignoring interactions between Black and White women. Black women were made to choose between two characteristics which give rise to discrimination, being Black and being a woman. It is only recently that there has been more acceptance, enabling Black women to embrace being a woman and Black.

White feminist scholars have long recognised that they have regarded the feminist movement as White to the exclusion of Black women activists (see, for example, Breines, 2007). During the 1960s the early women's liberation movement was accused of being racist. Commentors, including Whites at the time and since, have consistently described White feminists' emphasis on gender at the expense of race and class as naïve, hurtful and insensitive about what it means to be a woman of colour. There was an accepted explanation for the Whiteness of the feminist movement as it was made up of women who were ignorant about racism and the problems that women of colour faced. As a result, most early feminists, even those who were radical, socialist and dissenters from the status quo, created a feminism in which Black women were unwelcome and uncomfortable in the space. bell hooks's early work which included 'Ain't I a women: Black Women and Feminism' (1981) and 'From Margin to Center' (1984) appeared at the time when many White women did not understand what the role of Black women would be in the context of the feminist movement.

BLACK CULTURE AND MULTICULTURALISM

The use of the word 'Black' has become a political term for people who identify as Black due to their African or Caribbean heritage. 'Black' was also central to the cultural movement which promoted pride in Blackness in terms of its difference from Whiteness. The Black cultural movement in North America was rooted in the music, fashion and food of the time. In contrast, being Black in Britain was more peripheral culturally, yet Black people were bursting with new-found pride that Blacks were regarded as part of a multicultural society which came to the fore from around 1970–1990. In the United Kingdom, the cities, and particularly London, are much more ethnically diverse than other parts of the country; the cities were the sites of the multicultural society.

Multiculturalism had become something that would put Britain on the map, initially a force for good. From 1965 to 1990, the Inner London Education Authority (ILEA) developed a range of successful innovations on diversity and became the envy of many countries. These initiatives demonstrated how true equality could be achieved and illustrated how diversity could contribute to the growth of the London economy.

The term 'multiculturalism' has a range of meanings. Understandings of the term in everyday use vary and can differ from interpretations in sociological or philosophical contexts. In sociology and in everyday usage, 'multiculturalism' is a synonym for 'ethnic pluralism' with the two terms often used interchangeably. One example of multiculturalism in the sense of ethnic pluralism is the collaboration of different ethnic groups; they enter into a dialogue with each other without sacrificing or adapting their own identities.

Multiculturalism has been an intrinsic part of UK society ever since it set out to establish its world-spanning empire, ranging from the small British Isles to vast parts of North America, Australia, the Caribbean and extensive regions in Africa and Asia. As many sections of British society celebrated the ways in which diversity was developing, there was an undercurrent of opposition among groups who were unhappy to see 'The Other' arriving in the United Kingdom. Many in the host community wished for things to go back to the way they had been. This unhappiness escalated in 2011 when the Conservative prime minster David Cameron announced that multiculturalism was dead. The genie had now been let out of the bottle.

NEW TERMS FOR MINORITY ETHNIC GROUPS: ETHNICITIES AND TERMINOLOGY

Cameron's announcement of the death of multiculturalism led to an unwanted and unwarranted deterioration in the way people who were not White were referred to in Britain. Terms which would not have been used previously were now becoming the norm as a way to express frustration and anger towards people who were not White. This gave rise to the ever more frequent emergence of a plethora of terms such as 'migrants' and 'Black and minority ethnic' (BAME). It was evident that much of the positive impact of beneficial work on race was about to be reversed.

Discussions as to acceptable ways of referring to people who are not White take place across the globe. In contrast, if you are White, you are simply White, no matter where you live in the world. There is an underlying assumption that Whiteness is the norm.

Although attention to terminology can be regarded as 'political correctness', it is important to minorities. The following terms are currently accepted: ethnic minorities, minority ethnic, Black and or Brown people, non-White, negro, migrant Black minority ethnic, Black minority ethnic (BME), BAME, African, Caribbean; African Caribbean, Black Indigenous People of Colour (BIPOC) and African American and Black Europeans. To complicate matters, the terms used vary from country to country. For example, the term 'BAME' is only used in Britain and recently the Anti-Racism Taskforce of the Church of England (2021) described Black people as 'UK Minority Ethnic (UKME)' or 'Global Majority Heritage' (GMH). Generally, people who are racialised as non-White have to grapple with a range of descriptions of their identity and physical appearance which they would not necessarily attribute to themselves.

It is disconcerting that the terms used to describe non-White people have been adopted with little or no consultation of the people concerned. Why does this matter? Because there are many factors which contribute to the complex entanglement of people's racialisation as non-White in a White-dominated society. For instance, if a person migrates from South America to Britain, one may assume they are White, but this is where things become more complicated. In South America, this depends on the geography of where they live. For example, the south of Brazil is essentially White while the north is Black. The population derive their identity from their side of the divide. For example, how an individual from Brazil is identified when leaving their country of origin depends on a range of phenomena such as socio-economic status, culture, class, skin tone and personality. All but one of these fit into Bourdieu's use of the word 'habitus', a concept which refers to the norms, values, attitudes and behaviours of a particular social group or social class; skin tone or colour is not included. It is not until the Brazilian resides in Britain that they are repeatedly asked 'where are you from?' The question of course invariably stems from their accent which is clearly not British. It is also likely to relate to their appearance; they are probably not White. The challenge of their skin tone disrupts the White norm.

WHITENESS

A more detailed discussion of the concept of Whiteness, White privilege and supremacy introduced in chapter 1 now follows. Whiteness can be understood through the process of its social construction. It only exists with reference to the Other who is not White. The construct of 'Whiteness' exists because the White population regards those who are not White as the 'Other'. There would be no 'White' if there was no 'Black'. Whiteness is synonymous with goodness and the 'unnamed, universal moral referent by which all others are evaluated and found wanting' (Giroux, 1997, p. 286). It is important to reiterate that Whiteness is a discourse on race. When people are described as White, this is a socially constructed identifier predicated on skin colour (Leonardo, 2002). Embedded in Whiteness is White privilege and White supremacy. The former is directly connected to institutionalised power and the privileges that benefit White people and the latter reflects the belief that Whites are superior to Blacks and other people of colour.

A further analysis of the consequences of the transatlantic slave trade/chattel slavery will enable us to better understand Whiteness, privilege and superiority, as opposed to Blackness and inferiority.

SKIN COLOUR HIERARCHIES: FROM PLANTOCRACY TO CONTEMPORARY SOCIETY

The plantocracy set the stage for a coded classification system based on skin colour with White European at the top descending to American Indian, the indigenous people of the Americas in the middle and Black Africans at the bottom. This colour-coded ranking was further elaborated through a highly developed system of concubinage and miscegenation.

The successive generations, three times removed from their African ancestry, were legally considered White, at least in the West Indies and Latin America, but not in North America where a 'one drop rule' was applied. People with one drop of African blood in their veins were known as hypodescent, according to a 1662 Virginia law. Enslavers in general did not officially recognise their mixed parentage children, of European and African descent, although they accorded them privileges that darker-skinned slaves did not enjoy. The nearer one approximated White European in appearance, the more benefits were accrued. Free-coloured people throughout the Americas disdained their darker-skinned compatriots.

There were differences to some extent between the British West Indies and North and Latin America. Wealthy plantation owners in the West Indies usually acknowledged their mixed heritage offspring and often educated these children and left them with a considerable amount of property. They were usually exempt from working on the plantation fields, were given manumission (release from slavery), owned property and were also often slave owners themselves. In North America, the free-coloured people comprised up to half the population of the 'free negro' population (around 1815–1858). While Mulattoes had been distinguished from Blacks periodically and held more property than Blacks, few Mulattoes had sufficient wealth or education to distinguish them from free Blacks. Besides, the 'one drop rule' meant that no matter how White a Mulatto or quadroon looked, they were still referred to as Negroes and both Black and Brown free people were accorded the same low status (Morris, 1996).

Racial categorisation in Latin America compared to the West Indies and North America was one of degree rather than kind. Despite Latin America purportedly exhibiting a more liberal approach to race relations, there were regressions. Cuba, for example, made several attempts to exclude non-Whites from civil society and in Brazil, 'primitive notions about "mixed breeds", were invoked to draw an uncrossable line between Whites and Mulattoes' (Horowitz, 1973, p. 515). The racial frame was on a continuum in all three geographical locations. The increasing population of Mulattoes in the West Indies caused some alarm among White slave owners, resulting in more prohibitions legally and socially for Brown people along the lines of those which had already been enforced in North America (Horowitz, 1973).

In both the West Indies and Latin America there was a distinction between Brown and Black, with free-coloured people forming an intermediate racial group. In the West Indies there was a tendency for the planter class to exclude all non-Whites from civil society, in contrast with the situation in Latin America. In Latin America, the genetic and cultural 'mixing' of Indigenous, African and European people began from initial contact, although some Europeans repudiated this practice. Labels to categorise mixed ethnicities have proliferated in the Latin American context with the word *zambo* for mixed Black and Indigenous people and *pardo* for a person of both African and European origin. Throughout the slave world, the humanity of Black and Brown people was questioned (Horowitz, 1973).

COLOURISM IN CONTEMPORARY SOCIETY

The entrenched practices associated with the skin colour plantocracy system which were legally enforced, particularly in North America, have diminished. However, lighter skin came to be viewed as an asset in the communities of enslaved people throughout the Americas, a phenomenon popularly referred to as colourism, leaving a legacy which has continued into the twenty-first century. With roots in slavery, colourism is a system of practices and ideologies which privilege lighter-skinned Black people, with facial features resembling those of Europeans, over their darker-skinned counterparts with more African-associated features (Freire, 2016). Colourism has left an indelible mark on subsequent generations of Black and Brown people in the African diaspora. Not only does colourism, with a preference for light skin, remain a hallmark for standards of beauty, especially for women, the evidence suggests that colourism is linked to other spheres of life. Darker-skinned people living in countries where the national population includes people of European descent have lower income levels, lower marriage rates, longer prison sentences and fewer job opportunities. Colourism is one of the most pernicious expressions of racism and a salient feature of sophisticated and everyday racism (see chapter 3) (Bodenhorn, H., Ruebeck, C. (2007) Gabriel, D. 2007).

WHITE RAGE

While the psychological and emotional impact of Black bondage is widely acknowledged (see Sheldon, 2016; DeGruy, 2017), the effects of 'White rage' as a set of negative responses by White people to the progress of Black individuals, discussed by authors such as Anderson (2016), remain uncharted territory. Anderson (2016) insightfully analyses 'White rage' within the political context of America demonstrated, for example, by the reaction of some White people to President Obama holding the highest office in the world, and his family residing in the White House.

THE COLLECTIVE 'OTHERING' OF BLACK PEOPLE

These examples show how the collective 'Othering' of Black people leads to an inability among the White population to appreciate the multifaceted character of Black identities, including Black women's identity as feminists. Black identities are nuanced and diverse culturally and ethnically. The premise is that the Black population is homogenous. Individuality, difference and nuance are not sufficiently accounted for.

A BLACK IDENTITY?

The concept of racism hypothesised earlier also influences ideas of Black identity, particularly in racialised countries such as Britain, Europe and the Americas, where Blackness becomes defined and redefined as it is confronted with Whiteness. Identity in itself then becomes a focal point. It is important to define the term 'identity', as it is used here within a social representation theory framework, as featured in the writings of Duveen (1993). It is based on the notion that people have a variety of conceivable identities that allow them to position themselves in different ways, in relation to the social environment in which they are placed. These differing personas which individuals enact assist in the structuring of their social world and enable them to be situated within a particular domain.

Being Black and living in a dominant White society means constructing differing personal identities including cultural, spatial and national. Defining these identities is a concern for many Black people as they can determine personal trajectories, social standing and cultural group status. As identities operate within history, our understanding of our identity or identities and their context is dependent on construction and reconstruction (Hung et al., 2010). For Hung and his associate, cultural identity is not stable but is continually shifting and fractured. In this respect, identity is fluid or in a constant state of change based on the circumstances of individuals. They note that there is no one authentic cultural identity but multiple identities centring on place, time and space. This view can be applied to the Windrush generation, the first Caribbean migrants who arrived on the MV *Empire Windrush* on

22 June 1948, at Tilbury Docks, Essex, marking the beginning of post-war Caribbean mass migration.

In addition, within the context of Britain, people from Africa and the Caribbean have distinct cultural identities. African people belong to different ethnic groups, for example, a Nigerian may be from the Yoruba ethnic/cultural group. It can be postulated that there are distinctions in the cultural and social identity of people born in various African countries marked in cultures, customs and histories. There are differences in the cultural milieu and identity of people born in Africa, compared with those in the diaspora who have been impacted by chattel slavery. In addition, there are differences between the various Caribbean islands. Moreover, a monolithic Black identity in Britain is a misnomer, for individuals tend to belong or have inherited either an African or Caribbean heritage (and in some cases both, due to being the product of union between the two heritages). The invocation of a singular homogenous Black experience, as Bakare-Yusuf (1997) stresses, 'serves to show our own complicity in a racist discourse which tries to lock Black communities in the fixity of its own construction' (p. 82).

There is another dimension which pertains to people from North Africa. In a fascinating popular article on Somalians and their 'Blackness' within Britain, Hersi (2019, n.p.) aptly explains:

> Although most, if not all, North African countries are Muslim, many of the people from these countries consider themselves Arab and not Black (many look it too). However, Somalis in the diaspora do identify themselves to be Black. I'm referring to Somalis in the diaspora because in Africa, generally people do not specify and identify with being Black. This is understandable as they are living in a society where people differentiate themselves by ethnicity and tribes and not by the colour of their skin as it would be pointless.

Hersi further recounts her experience of the subtle racism Somalians experience from their fellow non-Black Muslims. Somalian women experience Islamophobia especially if their outward headdress reflects their Muslim heritage.

It is no longer appropriate in the twenty-first century to merely posit a Caribbean background as a reference point for a Black identity in British society which was previously the case, as the African population has surpassed the Caribbean population. The African population as a whole has significantly increased over the years and according to the 2011 population census in Britain, the percentage of people from a Black African background (989,628) has doubled from 0.9 per cent in 2001 to 1.8 per cent in 2011. This group includes individuals from countries such as Nigeria, Ghana, Ethiopia, Somalia, the Congo, Zimbabwe, Uganda, Sierra Leone and Kenya. The Caribbean population is 594,825, 1.1 per cent of the population, the same as in 2001. The main country of origin is Jamaica, followed by individuals from places such as St Kitts, Nevis, Barbados, Trinidad, Antigua, Guyana, Grenada, St Vincent and Anguilla. The population for mixed Black African and White is 165,974 and for Black Caribbean and White 426,715. Again, the latter is significant because mixed heritage Black and White individuals are often assigned to the 'Black' category in policy research.

The identity of Caribbean people is complex because of the history of slavery. It is not unusual for Caribbean people to have multiple ethnicities in their family tree, and cultural identity in the Caribbean can be complex and multifaceted (see Aldred, 2005). For example, the significant South Asian population has had a strong impact on the culture in Caribbean islands such as Trinidad, although by and large the African heritage predominates in most of the Caribbean. Clearly, not all people in the Caribbean can directly relate to an African identity, but as Hall (1989, p. 75) asserts that 'everyone in the Caribbean, of whatever ethnic background, must sooner or later come to terms with this African presence. Black, brown, mulatto, White – all must look Présence Africaine in the face, speak its name.' The social and historical influence of Africa contributes to the cultural dynamic that Caribbean people experience.

Hall (2000) demonstrates the notion of an authentic Black identity as an uncertain concept because of the complexities and problematic nature of identity. He theorises that in addition to the various similar elements, there are critical points of significant difference, which constitute who we really are, or because of the intervention of history, 'what we have become' (Hall, 1989, p. 70). As he explains, 'We [Caribbean people] cannot speak for very long, with any exactness, about "one experience, one identity", without acknowledging its other side – the ruptures and discontinuities which constitute, precisely, the Caribbean's uniqueness.' From this perspective cultural identity is 'a matter of "becoming" as well as "being" ' (Hall, 1989, p. 70). Hall argues that cultural identity is context based, historical and futuristic, and it is continually developing and always in the process of change. In presenting ideas about Blackness and identity, he affirms that the third generation who was born in Britain know they come from Caribbean, are Black and are also British. As he says, 'They want to speak from all three identities. They are not prepared to give up any one of them' (Hall, 200, p. 152). Of equal importance are ideas of Blackness with regards to women which are often sublimated. As Hall goes on state,

> To operate exclusively through an unreconstructed conception of Black was to reconstitute the authority of Black masculinity over Black women, about which,

as I am sure you know, there was also, for a long time, an unbreakable silence about which the most militant Black men would not speak.

There are differences between Black communities in Britain and gender also has to be reconfigured in notions of Blackness, but shared experiences of racism in relation to Blackness are the overarching common denominator. The other point to consider is that unlike the United States, where race is seen in binary ways, the United Kingdom has a more layered texture, due to its history and the politics of race relations (Gilroy, 1987; Olusoga, 2016) combined with the impact of the class society (Tomlinson, 2013). The class dimension also has to be analysed within the constructs of Blackness.

A RACIAL CASTE IN CLASS

By the late 1940s, the African community became well-established in Britain and the emergence of a middle class was underway. Mainly men in pursuit of higher education (Killingray, 1994) were joined by their wives by the 1950s, which will be discussed in more detail in chapter 4, and from the 1960s to the 1980s onwards, an additional inflow of African immigrants to Britain occurred; there were people, many of whom were women, who came to Britain to acquire advanced educational and professional qualifications (Forson, 2007). Many Africans can be positioned as middle class in terms of their academic background and in many cases the social and cultural capital garnered from their respective homelands have benefited their offspring. The reason why some Africans in Britain have a lower socio-economic status than their educational background would suggest is based on their racial caste status (Mocombe et al., 2014). Conversely, the Caribbean population, who arrived on the MV Empire Windrush on 22 June 1948 at Tilbury Docks, Essex, marking the beginning of post-war Caribbean mass migration, were recruited as cheap labour to help rebuild Britain after the Second World War. Though many Caribbean individuals, mainly men who were later joined by women by the 1960s, possessed skills and qualifications, these were deemed unacceptable, confining them to the least desirable jobs, accommodation, income and education and thereby a lower socio-economic position. Consequently, many Caribbean people were subsumed into the lower class. Gilroy (1987) explains that the first generation experienced a loss of separate identities relating to individual Caribbean islands due to their shared experiences of racism and social class in Britain. The host community saw them collectively as 'West Indians' and working class regardless of their social status and island of origin. Thus, it can be argued that the legacy of working classness has continued to a great extent for much of the Caribbean population including women. In a sense, Black identity is regarded as implying working-class identity.

Archer's (2011) study indicates that Black British Caribbean professionals express ambivalence about occupying a dual identity of being both Black and middle class. She discusses the tensions in the idea of Black Caribbean middle-classness in the British context outlining the

> struggle between dominant discourses that conflate authentic (and 'cool'/popular) Blackness with working classness (as both imposed by dominant White society and as articulated within Black and other minorities themselves). There was ambivalence about joining a group which mainly 'functioned as a sort of pariah identity'.

In particular, many Black British people distance themselves from the negative aspects of middle-classness, such as pretence and snobbery, including the markers evidenced in the historical elites. On the other hand, as Archer also argues, not being recognised by White society as middle class despite one's social status has also impacted on the conceptions of Black middle-classness – especially for African Caribbean people. Mocombe and Tomlin (2013, p. 100) argue that

> like in the case of Blacks in America . . . constructs of identities within racialized industrialized European societies such as Britain present challenges for many Black Caribbean individuals born and socialized in Britain where the idea of middle-classness and professionalism is synonymous with being White, while poverty, the street life and Black British Talk is seen as the identity marker of so-called 'Blackness'.

Given that research on both sides of the Atlantic demonstrates that Black females are performing better academically, which impacts on access to employment and income, it can be argued that Black middle-classness is already an established norm for many African women for the aforementioned reasons and is becoming so for some Caribbean women. Research by Mocombe et al. (2016) suggests that many Black Pentecostal female Christians are excelling academically, yet this is hardly featured in British literature. Anecdotal reference suggests that they are perceived by some African Caribbean people as middle class and that can add a further complexity to identification markers of a group whose lifestyle is in opposition to perceived identity markers of 'Blackness'. In addition to the class element, it must also be borne in mind that Black women contend with both racial and gendered identities and are required to make constant changes and move in worlds referred to as 'shifting' (Jones and Shorter-Gooden,

2003), due to their double identities, a concept which will be discussed in other chapters.

SHIFTING IDENTITIES

Often, living in racialised communities such as Britain entails having limited access to the social and economic resources of society. This can then result in some Black people internalising limitations brought on by the lack of external resources and oppression. For some Blacks what is understood as 'being' Black can be seen as a script where the actors believe that they can only play a role which is reproduced through the inequities of an oppressive society (see Archer et al., 2007). In the same way that some Whites distance themselves from ideas about Whiteness and the privilege that can be accrued, some Blacks in racialised Western societies may not challenge their understanding of Blackness, particularly its restrictive manifestations. However, roles can be interpreted and reinterpreted. Ladson-Billings (2004, p. 51) captures this phenomenon well with reference to conceptual categories of race not designed as a binary but rather as she explains:

> In a racialized society where Whiteness is positioned as normative, everyone is ranked and categorized in relation to these points of opposition. These categories fundamentally sculpt the extant terrain of possibilities even when other possibilities exist. And although there is a fixedness to the notion of these categories, the ways in which they actually operate are fluid and shifting. For example, as an African American female academic, I can be and sometimes positioned as conceptually White in relation to perhaps, a Latino, Spanish-speaking gardener. In that instance, my class and social position override my racial identification and for that moment I become 'White'.

Related to shifting identities, hooks (2000) discusses the idea of these women living on the edge and developing a particular way of viewing reality. She speaks about 'looking from both the outside in and the inside out' (p. xvii) and understanding what it means to being both at the centre and the margin. Ladson-Billings and Donnor (2008, p. 373) also consider the notion of being at the margins of society from which identities and experiences are formed suggesting that racialised 'others' occupy a 'limited space of alterity', a position at the edges of society from which their identities and experiences are constructed. Rather than being regarded as a place of disadvantage and degradation, it has been argued that those excluded from the centre can experience a 'perspective advantage', as their experiences are viewed from a wider lens than the White majority are able to deploy. White people may be located in the privileged spaces of the centre, but their perspective is narrower than the Black perspective. Black British scholar Nicola Rollock (2012) extends the idea of liminality by positing that it is contextual and in a state of tension. As she states:

> The field in which racialised others are operating, the tools or resources at their disposal, the support mechanisms available to them and the relative power of other actors present within the social space or field fundamentally impacts and brings into awkward tension the extent to which occupying a site in the margins becomes advantageous. (p. 66)

The heart of the matter is only beginning to unfold. The deleterious experiences of Black women have affected their mental well-being. Black women move in worlds that require constant adjustments to racial and gender identity, the focus of the fascinating work of Jones and Shorter-Gooden who discuss the role of shifting: 'From one moment to the next, [Black women] change their outward behaviour, attitude or tone, shifting "White" then shifting "Black again" ' (Jones and Shorter-Gooden, 2003, pp. 6–7).

There is a juxtaposition of existing in both White and Black worlds. W. E. B. Du Bois (1903) first coined the term 'double consciousness' to describe Blacks operating with a double identity, one part being the authentic Black self and the other accommodating and enacting the perceptions of Blackness, in other words the push towards White culture while simultaneously pulling away from it. For Black women, the strong archetypal reference has not allowed them to display authenticity because the strong Black woman syndrome has become self-fulfilling and has possibly impacted on their authentic individual identity.

SUMMARY AND CONCLUSION

In order to unpeel the layers of the nomenclatures specifically for Black people, it was imperative to situate the issue through a historical context which was discussed with reference to slavery. The 'Big House' as a metaphor in the plantocracy system was important in locating the interplay between Blacks and Whites and the antipathy exhibited towards Black women by White women. Sophisticated and everyday racism was the term coined to describe how racism often manifests itself in the British context. Discussions on racism inevitably entail exploring Blackness and Whiteness and the formulation of a Black identity. However, in many situations, the identities ascribed to Black individuals are conferred by the dominant White group as described in this chapter. In addition, African and Caribbean heritages differ in marked ways which influence the fluid parameters of identity. Shifting identities for Black women entail living on the edge of society, where women's identities are constructed.

The chapter has mapped the tangled web of Blackness, showing how White people have created hierarchies of Blackness through colourism and disregarded the complexity of the identities of Black minorities in the United Kingdom and across the globe. The importance of the patterns of the exploitation of enslaved Black people with reference to the 'Big House' has been underlined by identifying parallels in contemporary settings. Circumstances in which Black people have less chance of prospering than White people persist in contemporary workplaces and indeed across all sectors of society.

NOTE

1. Requesting a White supervisor because you think a Black supervisor 'isn't a good fit', comes from examples of micro-aggressions supplied by Forbes. https://www.forbes.com/sites/stephaniesarkis/2020/06/15/lets-talk-about-racial-microaggressions-in-the-workplace/?sh=86da3af5d283

Chapter 3

Sophisticated and Everyday Racism
What Does It Look Like?

Malcolm X (1965) said, 'I am not a racist. I am against every form of racism and segregation, every form of discrimination. I believe in human beings, and that all human beings should be respected as such, regardless of their color.' Malcolm X's declaration is integral to the aim of this chapter: to identify what sophisticated and everyday racism is and how it manifests itself in daily life. Before detailing various manifestations of racism, an examination of background is essential. This is because this chapter will pose difficult and uncomfortable questions, many of which may not have been broached in this way before.

Before examining sophisticated racism in detail, I would like to acknowledge the value of a series of discussions with colleagues, in particular the contribution of Stephen Hancock. His rich insights have added value to our understandings.

The first phenomenon which I would like to examine is what I term 'sophisticated racism' (Showunmi, 2018). This term sheds light on the diverse forms of racism which people face depending on the communities they belong to and identify with. Examples of sophisticated as against raw racism will act as a vehicle to deepen insights into the lived experiences of Black people.

SOPHISTICATED RACISM

Definition

Sophisticated racism is based on systemic structures designed to promote racism while disingenuously appearing to promote anti-racist or equitable policies. The perpetrators would not want to be accused of racist behaviours and they pay lip service to condemning racism. Sometimes this form of racism is unconscious and subconscious.

The impact of mental schemata is important here. These represent how events are recalled in the mind. Mental schemata are shaped by a person's political and cultural background. When used in the workplace, they shape and disguise racist behaviours. They convince the perpetrators of sophisticated racism that their actions are intended to be beneficent.

First, for example, the proliferation of Diversity, Equity, and Inclusion (DEI) offices in corporate and educational institutions are seen as a platform for anti-racism. A critical examination of the power and influence of a DEI office, however, reveals that the position has a minor influence and little if any voice in major decisions.

Second, sophisticated racism supports a disposition that uses a false belief in anti-racist ideals to hide interest divergence. The notion and policy of Positive or Affirmative Action was supposedly designed to engage minoritized people in equitable work environments. However, such policies have overwhelmingly benefited White women and thus increased White wealth. Sophisticated racism is a form of racism which is pervasive yet invisible. It is deliberate yet unconfrontational, and it exploits 'political correctness' to gain societal benefits and privileges.

Third, sophisticated racism stems from a deeply ingrained and acute sense of privilege and the othering of Black people which is not openly acknowledged. For instance, the wearing of a racist brooch depicting a Black person (a 'Blackamoor Brooch') by Princess Michael of Kent when she met Meghan Markle in 2017 was based on a brazen and acute sense of privilege. This purportedly indicated blissful ignorance of the distress that such images cause Black minorities.

A fourth and final characteristic of sophisticated racism is the shielding of racist intent behind complex ideals. One such ideal is liberalism. The promotion of social welfare, openness to multiple perspectives and civil liberties to lessen racism is complex and is actually devalued by the fact that the adherents of liberal and neoliberal ideology hold on tightly to their privilege while denying those privileges to those they are supposedly supporting.

The term 'woke' is relevant in this context. It means becoming aware of racism and social injustice and remaining alert to inequalities. The sections of society which espouse a 'woke' ideology stop short of introducing policies which promote equality in their own environment. They are happy to criticise shortcomings in workplaces and communities which are not their own. If they implemented initiatives which resulted in equity for ethnic and racial minorities, that might lessen their own chances of progression and success. The impact of sophisticated racism is to create barriers for the career progression of Black people.

Those who claim to be 'woke' may be asked to explain why their behaviours are in fact evidence of racism. In such a situation, they may respond defensively and say something like:

'I didn't know, I was just trying to help.'
'It's not easy for us' (meaning White people).

They distance themselves from their sophisticated and everyday racism. They are thoughtless and oblivious of the impact of their behaviour.

Another concern is the sophisticated racism which occurs between minority cultures. Shadism (how dark your skin is), as distinct from your ethnicity, is central to how people of colour regard themselves. White privilege and access to it is unattainable for those who are Black because of the darkness of their skins. Belonging to the Whiter side of society is likely to appear to afford more access to privilege than belonging to Blacker groups. The benefits of assimilation into Whiteness outweigh the benefits of being seen as Black.

For this reason, inclusive notions of Blackness, encompassing all those who are not White, appear to Brown (Asian, Latinex and/or Puerto Rican) people to prevent them from accruing advantage from the lighter shade of their skin. The epithet 'Black', they believe, should be reserved for African and African Caribbean communities. Asian communities seek to avoid anything which risks subsuming their non-Whiteness with Black communities.

The practice of trying to pass as White is known as 'passing'. This is explored by Larsen (1929) in her book which examines the lives of two women. One hid her African American heritage and married a White male while the other continued her life as an African American in her own community. The book added a new dimension to the discussion of race, class and gender, initiating the notion of self-identities. Since the late twentieth century, *Passing* has received renewed attention from scholars because of its close examination of racial and sexual ambiguities and liminal spaces. This issue will be discussed in a forthcoming paper.

The patterns of behaviour outlined in this chapter are enacted through what Showunmi (2018) coins as sophisticated racism which describes the shielding or 'smoke-screening' of racist epistemologies (see earlier definition).

Figure 3.1 demonstrates the characteristics of sophisticated racism.

THE SOPHISTICATED RACISM FRAMEWORK

The Framework

Shielding of Racist Ideals
- Covering up racism by pseudonym liberating ideals and action

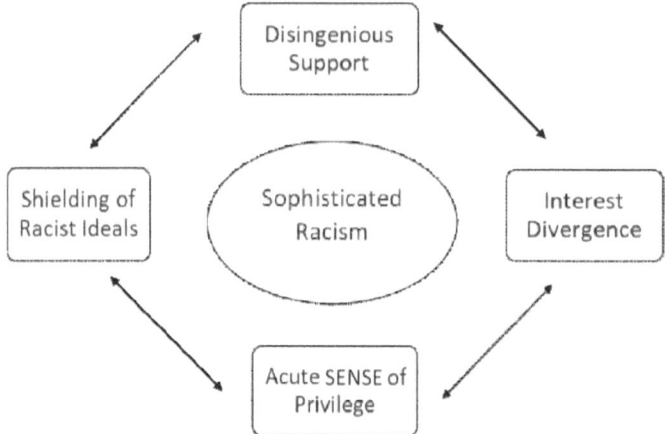

Figure 3.1 The Sophisticated Racism Framework.

Acute Sense of Privilege
  ◦ Desperate need to be superior
Interest Divergence
  ◦ Supporting *just* causes for social and personal benefit
Disingenuous Support
  ◦ Insincere intention towards the diverse other

EQUITY AND DIVERSITY

The concept of equity explores the engagement of policies and actions that support equitable opportunities for marginalised people to develop and contribute to society. Diversity refers to a range of intersectional concepts that make up a person's identity. The notion of diversity in public spaces limits identities to race, gender identity and sex. Equity and diversity then become a smokescreen for racism as it provides a space for those who lack racial and cultural competence to relegate all things equity/diverse to a particular person or place.

Ahmed (2012) discusses how diversity practitioners have created conditions that allow sophisticated racism to develop, paralysing their racist policies and procedures. Organisations have often lost a sense of the rationale for equality initiatives. The language used is so muddled that employees are left to operate under sets of dysfunctional guidelines. Instead of lessening the impact of racism, diversity practitioners have created a fertile breeding ground for sophisticated and everyday racism which contributes to stress and trauma among minority groups.

THE EXPERIENCE OF RACISM

The experience of racism differs. When you experience racism in the rural parts of the UK, for instance, it will be very different from the experience of the Black population in cities.

RAW RACISM IN CONTEMPORARY SOCIETY

Over the years, an ever-increasing volume of work has been produced to enable the reader to distinguish what racism is, and indeed what racism is not. However, there has been much less discussion of the deeper nuances of racism and how it manifests itself across individuals' daily lives. Why is this? One factor is that racism as it is experienced in rural communities (Garland and Chakraborti, 2003) is very different. It is a raw experience compared with the more subtle examples of everyday racism met by those who live in cities. The victims are often left unsure if what they are experiencing is discrimination. Furthermore, many struggle with the vocabulary and language to describe what they have witnessed. Seemingly innocent comments are a reminder that one is seen by some as an outsider. Rural racism is more open and direct. There are no elaborate circumventions to hide the blatant racism which is exposed in rural environments. When I walked into a restaurant in the country to meet friends, I noticed that silence had descended on the whole room. It was not until the next day that my friends explained that people were puzzled by the way I spoke which is not what they saw as 'traditionally Black'. Sophisticated racism (see figure 3.1), in contrast, actually protects racist epistemologies by creating a smokescreen of complex ideals and worldly experiences couched in liberal ideology.

Racism has come to be regarded as the problem of the individual; the same applies to people with other characteristics related to equality and inclusivity, such as gender, disability or LGBT+. When a Black person is given the silent treatment or the sly look, it is difficult to explain, as only the individual it has been directed at is in a position to gauge its significance (see Di Angelo, 2011). There is no escape from the sense of unease that results; the feeling gnaws away at your soul.

SOPHISTICATED RACISM IN A SCHOOL CONTEXT

A 16-year-old Black girl volunteered to show prospective parents and their children round her school. She was very pleased to be selected to be a guide.

The other volunteers were one pair of White girls, one pair with an Asian girl and a White girl and one pair with a Black girl and a mixed heritage girl.

The teachers directed the parents to the girls. The Black girl and her partner stepped forward and greeted them, but they all without exception (including Black, mixed heritage and Asian parents) simply smiled and went on to the other pairs, that is, the White pair or the Asian and White girl. The popular guides were excited because they had shown so many parents round the school, as indicated by the number of 'visitor' stickers which had been allocated to each group. When the White girls went on their break, some parents chose the mixed heritage partner of the Black girl to show them round the school. The Black girl had been unable to guide a single group round the school. Her sheet of stickers was still complete. When she mentioned this to the other guides, they didn't understand that she had not been chosen because she was Black.

When recounting this experience to her mother, the Black teenager commented:

'This is sophisticated and it's racism.'

This encounter highlights White privilege and unwitting racism. As a teenager, the parallel to the White privilege experienced by Black women in the 'Big House' on the antebellum plantations is relevant here. As a Black girl, she was invisible.

SOPHISTICATED RACISM IN THE ACADEMY

More narratives to illustrate what is meant by sophisticated racism follow. The first takes place in the context of the merger of the small higher education institution with a large, successful top-ranked university. This prospect seemed to me to offer countless opportunities for collaboration, and I was eager to benefit from this exciting new environment. This was particularly important to me in the area of gender and sexuality. Our aim was to seek ways of working on these issues involving academics and doctoral students across the university.

Together with two colleagues, I created some ideas around intersectionality and planned an initial session. We decided on a speaker and identified people to invite, with a date and time. During one of many conversations with a colleague from my institution, I realised that she was anxious that the merger might threaten her role and status. She feared losing students and research opportunities. I was not anxious, as I saw the merger as of great benefit to all of us. This colleague from my own institution told me that 'Mandy' (not her real name), our contact at the university, had asked, 'Why is she involved? What does she know about gender?' Although this shocked me, the sense was that Mandy's suggestion that I should be excluded was unimportant, Mandy hadn't thought it through.

Sometimes in academia, we have particular specialisms which make it natural for us to work on our own. However, my area has always been gender, race and identity. Mandy's questions, possibly a prelude to excluding me from the collaboration, appeared to me to be deliberate, and designed to ensure that these engaging new areas of work should not involve me as a Black woman. All the other individuals involved with gender and/or sexualities were White women and men. Mandy's questions suggested that she believed that this was not an area where my participation was needed. She was asking herself: 'Who is she, to be leading on this opportunity, when so many other (White) people show potential? They should be leading on this.'

This was not the first time I had encountered this type of attempt to exclude me. What is actually happening here, is it 'Whiteness' or is it racism?

Sara Ahmed (2007) and many others (Robin, 2011; Mirza, 1997) suggest that Whiteness can be approached through the lens of phenomenology. Ahmed describes Whiteness as an ever-present and ongoing, unfinished history, which orientates bodies in specific directions, affecting how they take up space and 'what they can do'. Whiteness must be discussed alongside racism, as the two are intertwined.

How is this relevant to 'Mandy's' question: 'What does she know about gender?' We are purportedly academics, seeking opportunities to make a difference through sharing thoughts and ideas. There is a dark shadow lurking in the background. It is unexplained White privilege. It is invisible, hidden from plain view. As a Black person whose legitimacy was questioned, I was left with a sense of anxiety and uneasiness. This sense cannot be shared but is swallowed like a bitter pill. This is sophisticated and everyday racism suffered in silence. For me, it was not enough to be an established feminist. From the White perspective, more needed to be done to keep me outside in the cold. There was no welcoming arm to include me in the warm collaborative community, as I constituted a threat. Being Black was enough to deal with. However, being Black and a woman – well, my inclusion was really overstepping the mark and regarded as potentially impoverishing the community. There was only so much space around the table and at this particular moment, the essential was enabling White women to capitalise on the merger so as to benefit people like themselves (White).

The struggle lay in appearance, in what was visible, Blackness, which was more important than gender. How could a Black person understand what it is like to be a woman? Gender issues are for White women, and it is essential that the waters aren't muddied by another issue. Focusing on Black to the exclusion of other issues would, of course, make life so much easier, but it would not be presenting reality.

As a Black person in the midst of such events, you are prevented from thinking analytically about why the questioner, 'Mandy' felt it was necessary to question your legitimacy as an academic with expertise on gender. The lack of recognition of your academic credentials strips you of your identity. It reduces you to what is regarded as your main characteristic. You are nothing beyond Black.

Much has been written about accepting Black women as women (see, for example, bell hooks, 1981). Most people only see the colour – Black – and disregard the fact that the Blackness is present together with being female. Black women appear to be gender neutral. Their sexuality is dehumanised as Black women emerge as sexualised and exotic or loud and/or aggressive. Black women are women who Whites have been unable to tame to fit into White establishment expectations. The phenomenon of being an accepted member of the establishment is described as admittance to 'the Big House' in chapter 2.

It was actually rather absurd to question my entitlement to join the discussion on gender, doubting what I had to bring to the academic community, in full knowledge that my research interest was focused on Black women. Why did this happen? Was the questioner doubting my academic expertise in the area or was this actually a question about whose knowledge was acceptable and regarded as worthwhile?

I now examine what I have called 'White women syndrome' (WWS) in more detail. WWS is the unnamed feeling many Black women experience in relation to White women if they, as Black women, are getting too close to the 'pot of gold', recognition and reward for success. Only limited resources are available, and these have been earmarked for White women only. Recognising this helps to position the way everyday racism can be overlooked. Unexplained insidious behaviour often originates from a fear of the loss of privilege and elements of unwelcome behaviour come together here to generate a strong force field which results in sophisticated racism.

Because White women benefit from White privilege, they want to safeguard their advantageous status. This can lead to White women turning to the bullying and harassment of Black women who appear to pose a threat to White women's progression in society.

We have seen in chapter 2 that ideals of feminine beauty are traditionally White rather than Black. White women exploit and manipulate their femininity and flaunt their Whiteness and privilege by denigrating Black women's experience, knowledge and skills. They do not want to share the limited space for professional success with Black women, which produces a spider's web of jealousy and resentful behaviour that emanates from White women's own sense of insecurity.

Sophisticated and everyday racism takes many forms, including patterns of behaviour, exclusion, lack of knowing, silence, subtle behaviours and stereotyping. The term 'casual racism' has begun to gain traction. This means making seemingly friendly comments such as 'Where are you from?' or 'Your type of eyes are good for eyeliner' or even 'I love your hair! May I touch it?' The first suggests that the questioner believes Black people do not belong in the country because of their ethnicity. The second focuses on the difference in a Black person's appearance. There is an underlying sense of White as the norm.

An example of my experience of everyday racism follows. The conversation took place in a lift.

Me (to man already in lift): Good morning
Man (looking up at me): Good morning. Thank you for your PhD thesis. I haven't had time to read it yet, but it looks very good.
Me (surprised): I don't think it could have been my thesis. I'm an academic here, and I handed in my thesis many years ago at another university.

We approached our destination, the sixth floor, where we both stepped out of the lift. He scuttled away with a red face and I went to get my lunch.

As you start to digest this story, you may wonder why I've included it. There are several reasons. First, there is the perception that I was a student and not a colleague. Of course, this mistake can be easily made because a high percentage of academics are White and male. However, there is also the confusion resulting from the perception that one Black person looks the same as another. This is often a classic introduction to everyday racism, supported by Maylor (2009) in a paper entitled 'Is it because I'm Black? A Black female research experience'. In this paper, Maylor describes how a PA presumed she was a parent, although she had introduced herself as Professor Maylor, a researcher, when she was at a school to do fieldwork, with an appointment to speak to the Head Teacher. Maylor's introduction had been ignored.

Both these examples raise the issue of why it is that people who are Black:

1. Need to be questioned
2. Are automatically regarded as having a lower status.

These are both examples of the subtlety of the manifestations of racism. There are many instances of the challenges faced by Black people in the professions and in leadership roles. They are seen as the 'Other', as Black, and as such they are expected to belong to an underclass. Black barristers are assumed to be offenders, Black school principals are assumed to be administrators, so parents ask to speak to the principal when they already are.

RACIAL TRAUMA

The constant and repeated questioning of what is happening to you in your environment as a person of colour can lead to trauma triggered by racism, racial trauma. Racial trauma is the result of persistent racism, racist bias and exposure to racist abuse in society. Racial trauma can affect many aspects of a person's life, including the ability to form relationships, concentrate at school or in professional life and feel safe. Degruy (2007) Hancock, Showunmi, Lewis (2021) and many others have written on racial trauma. It is widespread among marginalised groups, including Jewish communities. It is particularly common among Black people in the United States and the United Kingdom, as the majority have experienced racism. Globally, media depictions of racism, such as police violence against unarmed Black people, may also trigger racial trauma. DeGruy's work examines post-traumatic stress disorder (PTSD), which she calls Post-Traumatic Slave Disorder, as it is more frequent in Black groups than among White people. Black people in the United Kingdom and the United States (The McGregor-Smith review 2017) are around five times as likely as White people to report unfair or discriminatory experiences in everyday life.

RACIAL MICRO-AGGRESSIONS

The notion of 'racial micro-aggressions' has emerged and become common over the past ten years. Sara Ahmed (2012), in her book *On Being Included: Racism and Diversity in Institutional Life*, describes the term 'diversity' as overused, and often out of context. The same could be said of 'racial micro-aggressions'.

Derald Wing Sue et al. (2007) discuss what is meant by 'racial micro-aggressions' in everyday life:

> Racial microaggressions are brief and commonplace daily verbal, behavioural, or environmental indignities, whether intentional or unintentional, that communicate hostile, derogatory, or negative racial slights and insults towards people of colour. Perpetrators of microaggressions are often unaware that they engage in such communications when they interact with racial/ethnic minorities. A taxonomy of racial microaggressions in everyday life was created through a review of the social psychological literature on aversive racism, from

formulations regarding the manifestation and impact of everyday racism, from reading the manifestation and impact of everyday racism, and from reading numerous personal narratives of counsellors (both White and those of colour) on their racial/cultural awakening. Almost all interracial encounters are prone to microaggressions.

Derald Wing's taxonomy of everyday racism underlines the variety of adverse events which occur on a regular basis in the lives of Black people. Micro-aggressions therefore have profound implications, and we must acknowledge that they manifest themselves in everything we do. TV reality shows highlight how Black people are harassed in the course of everyday tasks. Black shoppers, for example, are monitored by security as they browse in shops. Even more sinister, as certain groups feel a loss of power or dominance, they depend on racial profiling to defend their actions. Racial profiling is the act of suspecting or discriminating against a person on the basis of their ethnicity or religion, rather than on individual suspicion. Profiling is not challenged.

The police have many excuses for targeting Black people for stop and search. A recent example occurred when a White teenage boy was out with a group of Black and Asian friends. They were stopped by plain clothes drugs police. The police searched his friends but not him. The White boy was profoundly shocked. He felt he was experiencing discrimination in action. Profiling of Black people is common; they are the powerless passive victims of profiling – it is done to them. It has become a phenomenon which contributes to everyday racism, although this can be presented as an unintended consequence of profiling.

UK COMMISSION ON RACE AND ETHNIC DISPARITIES: THE REPORT

Despite the examples of everyday racism in this chapter, if we were to concur with the conclusions of the recent UK Report (2021), we would accept the implication that racism is imagined rather than real. Evidence shows that repeated experiences of discrimination impact negatively on victims' wellbeing (Combs and Milosevic, 2016). Individuals, whether children, young people or adults, do all they can to assimilate and be accepted by the White majority. They are repeatedly rejected, which has a long-term damaging effect on their mental health.

The fictions in the report on Race and Ethnic Disparities were revealed by the November 2021 hearing of evidence provided by Aseem Rafiq on the discrimination and resultant psychological trauma he suffered as a cricketer in the Yorkshire team. Initially, he was reluctant to accept that he was the victim of racist behaviour. The following are quotations from his testimony:

I didn't want to believe it. I reported it as bullying.
All I wanted was acceptance.
Was it racism?
Should I have called it out?
If you speak out, your life is made hell.

Instead of acknowledging the true situation and accepting that everyday racism exists as a salient feature in the lives of Black people, there has been a surge in nationalistic behaviour and a desire to defend what White people believe is their heritage. This links back to the reluctance of White academics to admit Black people into the academic community (see, for example, Bhopal 2015 and 2018). Black people do not conform to the White academics' stereotypical perception of what an academic should be.

WHITE SUPREMACY

The cumulative effects of sophisticated and everyday racism validate the notion of White supremacy. Much discriminatory behaviour is rooted in White supremacy. White supremacy is the belief that White people are superior to people of other 'races' and should therefore dominate them. This is related to skin tone and class and to the inability or refusal to recognise the rights, needs, dignity or value of people of a particular race or geographical origin. Racism entails the devaluation of traits of character or intelligence which are regarded as 'typical' of particular ethnic groups. The characterisation of certain ethnic groups as sharing specific negative traits is erroneous but widespread among White supremacists. The acceptance of the superiority of one race leading to their dominance of another continues to generate hostility across society. The denial of this state of affairs leads to repeated patterns of disbelief when complaints relating to discrimination are made. 'Surely you're imagining it!' is a common reaction (Showunmi, 1995).

REVERSE RACISM

'Reverse racism' has recently attracted a lot of media attention, especially where there has been a high-profile case of everyday racism. White people often resort to reverse racism when people of colour call out racism and discrimination or create spaces for themselves which exclude White people. Blay (2015) states that reverse racism originates from White people's desire to prove that people of colour 'don't have it that bad' (cf. UK Commission on Race and Ethnic Disparities: The Report 2021). The contention is that only White people are put at a disadvantage or are targeted because of their race. It is almost as if there was a competition to see which 'side' wins in terms of disadvantage on grounds of race. It's akin to a 'Racism Olympics' and is patently a distortion of the truth.

A recent onslaught on everyday racism involves Megan Markle and the way the media portrayed her in comparison to her sister-in-law Kate Middleton. The person who claims something does not feel right very swiftly becomes the problem. The focus shifts from the victim to the oppressor. Both Martin Luther King and Malcolm X spoke to both the oppressors and the oppressed in their speeches to civil rights crowds in the 1960s. Both were assassinated when they became a threat to the establishment. Malcolm X in particular learnt to address both the oppressors and the oppressed in the same speech at the same time. In doing this, he would instil fear into the hearts of the powerful and erase it from the psyche of the powerless. A famous quote is,

> I believe that there will ultimately be a clash between the oppressed and those that do the oppressing. I believe that there will be a clash between those who want freedom, justice and equality for everyone and those who want to continue the systems of exploitation. (Malcolm X's speech at the Militant Labor Forum, New York, May 1964)

STEREOTYPING

Stereotypes will now be discussed. Stereotypes have been constructed to justify the positioning of an individual as the cause of a problem. Black people may find themselves unable to gain acceptance, or admittance to a particular group, even though they do all they can to fit into the required mould. They repeatedly try to reinvent themselves, which is an exhausting and soul-destroying experience. During this journey, there is frustration, hurt, pain and emotional fatigue, including on the side of the excluder, but especially on the side of the victim of stereotyping. The oppressor generally believes misguidedly that they are only acting on the basis of facts.

This is an example of stereotyping. A Black administrator was recently asked to supply members of a research project team with sandwiches as they would not have time for a lunch break because of back-to-back meetings. A manager mentioned that a tray would be needed as so many items were ordered. A White female professor commented:

'A tray? I imagined you carrying the food in a basket on your head!'.

A range of assumptions underlie this comment. Is this an example of unconscious bias because an administrator is regarded as a low-status role? What are the symbolic messages behind this comment? What was the person thinking of? Was the professor unaware of the implications of what she had said? Did she experience a momentary vision of the exotic, which perhaps took her back to a childhood experience, such as a character she had seen in a book or film? Stereotyping and projecting can give oppressors a momentary feeling of security. They put themselves into a space that allows them to feel comfortable, imagining they appear to be an acceptable and liberal-minded person.

This approach to projecting onto others is actually a form of violence which is not to be taken lightly. We could analyse this in psychological terms and make a range of excuses for such behaviours.

How often does the victim of everyday racism have to suffer such experiences before the oppressor understands what they are doing? It is easy to suggest that most people are 'really very nice' and would feel mortified if they unwittingly offended someone. An oppressor may genuinely believe that what they observe is 'fact'. They may, for example, say all Black people do 'X', or buy into the many assumptions about the portrayal of Black individuals.

People who have been stereotyped to 'fit' the oppressors' image would have taken on the role to shield people who have experienced unfair treatment. Many such roles are hidden, such as ensuring policies include the voices of people who are not White. More Black people need to become involved in activities and initiatives across communities and organisations so Black voices are heard.

Stereotypes are real and significant. They come from both Black and White communities. It can come as a rude awakening when you find yourself having to acknowledge that long-held beliefs based on stereotyping are wrong. Both Black and White people can develop misconceptions in relation to stereotypical attributes ascribed to a range of Black or White groups.

Stereotyping is complex. Individuals do not fit into neat groups. You could be visibly Black but you may not have grown up or lived in a diverse community. To Black people and others who are not White, your behaviours could appear to be 'off key' and not what they expected. You may 'act White' which is a term used by many scholars, particularly in the United States. The term has been widely applied to Black people who are perceived to betray their culture by conforming with the social expectations of White society. Success in education (depending on cultural background) can be seen as 'selling out' and being disloyal to one's own culture.

The notion of 'acting White' is controversial because it excludes Black people who were raised in homes with parents of a different ethnicity because of adoption. They may then be socialised as White. As discussed by Showunmi (2018) these individuals experience everyday racism from both Black and White people. What you see is not what you expect, which is confusing. Both Black people and White people have a fixed narrative, so problems occur for a person who does not fit that narrative.

Another example follows. During the 2020 lockdown, a colleague kept their hair natural. Before virtual meetings, she would carefully put her hair in a top bun, and sometimes wrap the bun in a scarf. By November, she was getting bored, so she put in some braids. Our Christmas party was on Zoom, and when she logged on, a White colleague said,

> 'Oh, "Nina" (not her real name), I'm glad you've been able to get your hair so neat. The last time I saw you, it was so wild!'

This person was a professor who spent most of their time working in East Africa, probably surrounded by Black women. This is another instance of speaking without any thought of how that comment would be received.

Stereotype threat manifests itself in both the aforementioned narratives about the two professors. Stereotype threat is the threat of being viewed through the lens of a negative stereotype or the fear of doing something that would inadvertently confirm that stereotype (Steele, 1999). Stereotype threat refers to being at risk of confirming, as a self-characteristic, a negative stereotype about one's social group (Steele and Aronson, 1995).

As we continue to deconstruct and add to our insights into the meaning of sophisticated and everyday racism, we should include the notion of stereotype threat as a transferable term that could be used in society and in the workplace.

I will now introduce the notion of Whiteness and how it contributes to the ever-present pain and racial trauma experienced by so many who are not White.

WHITENESS

Why do majority ethnic groups feel entitled to comment on the characteristics of minority groups, be they Black, Asian or 'Other'? When insensitive comments are criticised, the reaction is to plead ignorance. The defence of ignorance is weak, but also dangerous, as it can be followed by assertions of inclusive and tolerant liberalism.

Why is it that White people are able to believe in their entitlement and superiority? They claim that they never intend to be racist. They are not self-aware or critically reflective in relation to their racist behaviours, so that, as the White majority see it, they can be exonerated from blame. They are mortified when confronted with their own racism or faced with the suggestion that they might indeed be racist.

Sara Ahmed's (2007) paper on the phenomenology of Whiteness provides us with an interesting standpoint as she considers Whiteness as involving a form of orientation. Orientations are about a starting point.

So how does this help us gain a better understanding of the way Whiteness involves orientation? Whiteness is reproduced by being seen as a form of immovable status, as if it were a complex of persons, cultures and places. Whiteness becomes, you could say, 'like itself' akin to a form of family resemblance. Similar to privilege, it is invisible to those who have it. It is no accident that race has been understood through familial metaphors in the sense that 'races' come to be seen as having 'shared ancestry' (Fenton, 2003, p. 2). Ahmed suggests that race 'extends' the family form; other members of the same race are 'like a family'.

EVOLUTION: FROM EVERYDAY RACISM TO SOPHISTICATED RACISM

The struggle faced by the Windrush generation is illustrated in the following account based on the experiences of Carol's mother. Her Jamaican voice (Jamaican Creole) is captured in the account.

> Bwoy dem did do we some tings. Wat we did have to go tru. Some a dem did tink sey we did have tale. Daf beggars. We couldn't fine nowhere fi live. Most a di landlord dem put up sign which sey no dog, no Irish and no Black. We have to live in a one room, everyting in a one room and punch gas, put shilling in a de meter. When me did train up some a de White women dem fi do de work afterward dem get rid of mi. Wen you go to dem church, some a dem tell you no fi come back again. You tink a one ting we go tru. When de White women go to de toilet and smoke for a long time, the supervisor didn't sey anyting to dem but when it was de Black dem you hafi go to de toilet quick quick in 5 minutes otherwise de supervisor will come in a de toilet an tell us fi hurry up. Bwoy we go true some tings.
>
> Boy we went through a lot. What we had to go through. Some of them (White people) thought that we had a tail attached to our bottoms. We could not find anywhere suitable accommodation. Most of the landlords had a sign that said 'no dogs, no Irish and no Blacks'. We had to live a single room. We had everything in that room. We had a gas metre and had to put a shilling in it. When I trained some of the White girls to do the job that I was doing, they got rid of me afterwards. When you go to church, some of them (vicars) told you not to come back. We went through a lot. When the White women went to the toilet to smoke cigarettes, they were allowed to stay in the toilets for a considerable time.

We on other hand could only stay in the toilet for 5 minutes and the supervisor would come and tell bus to hurry up. Boy we really went through a lot.

Carol's mother is part of the Windrush generation which centres on the years when Caribbean people relocated to find work in Britain along with people from other former colonies and Europeans. For more detail on the experiences of Black women during this period, see Evaristo (2018) and Bryan et al. (1985). The arrival of the MV Empire Windrush on 22 June 1948, at Tilbury Docks, Essex, marked the beginning of post-war Caribbean mass migration and an arduous journey culminating in the Windrush scandal of 2018. The Windrush scandal involved British subjects who had arrived from Caribbean countries before 1973 and who were wrongly detained, denied legal rights and threatened with deportation or wrongly deported by the United Kingdom's Home Office.

Steps have since been taken that appear to represent efforts to lessen the impact of racism. However, it is evident from the recent unjust treatment of migrants from the Caribbean and from the examples of sophisticated and everyday racism in this chapter that much more needs to be done to eliminate all forms of racism.

SUMMARY

The aim of this chapter has been to develop our thinking through the application of theories of racism and the analysis of short narratives. This has enabled us to recognise and deconstruct diverse manifestations of sophisticated and everyday racism, deepening insights and heightening awareness.

Chapter 4

The Language Style of Black Women and Its Implications for Education and Work

During slavery, Black people in general, and Black women in particular, carved out a space within it to develop strategies to manage the sophisticated racism of the Big House. The Creole Language and communicative discourse of Blacks, in opposition to the language and communicative discourse of the master, was one such strategy. Language functions as an identity marker and expresses power relationships. For Black women, it is often utilised to manage daily encounters of sophisticated racism, associated with being both Black and female in the Big House or organisation of work.

LANGUAGES OF BLACK WOMEN IN BRITAIN

Black women throughout Britain speak several languages, including the many African ones such as Yoruba, Hausa, Igbo, Twi, Lingala, Swahili, Zulu and European languages, for example, French, Portuguese and Spanish. Many are multilingual. Apart from African or European languages, pidgins such as Nigerian or creoles like Kri, the official language of Sierra Leonne, are spoken frequently by respective African women in the United Kingdom. Tomlin's (1999) work highlights that people/women from a Caribbean background speak a Caribbean creole, unique to their country of origin, for example, Jamaican, Kittitian and Dominican. Creoles are seen as a dialect, a social variety of a standard language such as English, but from a linguistic standpoint, they can be viewed as languages in their own right. Jamaican Creole (JC), popularly known as Patois, pronounced as 'patwa' is most common in Britain. Developed from the contact situation between West African slaves and British slave owners in the Caribbean where new dialects or creoles emerged, it is the dominant mode of communication in Jamaica and was transported to the shore of Britain, primarily by the Windrush migrants.

AFRICAN WORLD VIEW AND ETHNOGRAPHY OF SPEAKING

The common linguistic-cultural heritage of Black women from the diaspora lay in Africa and the institution of slavery. Despite the substantive differences in African societies (Zeleza, 2006) and the obstacles the African slaves experienced in maintaining their traditional cultures and languages, there are some underpinning commonalities, certainly in West Africa, the landmass from which many of the slaves came. As Levine (1977, p. 4) eloquently states:

> Though they varied widely in language, institutions, gods, and familial patterns, they shared a fundamental outlook toward the past, present, and future and common means of cultural expression, which could well have constituted a basis of a sense of common identity and worldview capable of withstanding the impact of slavery. We must be sensitive to the ways in which the African worldview interacted with that of the Euro-American world into which it was carried.

A world view is an orientation mindset or perception of the world that shapes how a group lives and is fundamental to their values and culture. Simply put, it involves thinking, believing and behaving. There is no distinction between the sacred and secular or the spiritual and natural world in the traditional African world view or philosophy. They are both inextricably linked into a holistic and harmonious system where individuals interact with the supernatural and their ancestors (Mbiti, 1990). Community solidarity rather than excessive individualism is also a vital feature of the African world view. Enslavement did not wholly eliminate African sensibilities, and there are retentions in the culture and language of Black people in the diaspora, albeit reconfigured under conditions of extreme brutality.

Regarding language, scholars such as Smitherman (1977) and Tomlin (1999) convincingly demonstrate that African retentions are most prominent in the style of speaking. Style of speech forms an integral part of the two dimensions of language: linguistics which examines areas such as lexis (words), phonology (sounds) and syntax (arrangement of words grammatically), and the stylistics, which examine how these different elements are combined to create a variety of effects. The term 'African communication system' (ACS) describes the style of speech found in Africa, which is retained by people in the Caribbean, the Americas, Britain and elsewhere (Tomlin, 1999). The stylistic features include a range of linguistic devices such as call-response, whereby comments from the listener punctuate a speaker's statement; repetition, which is repeating a phrase or sentence; and overlapping voices, where two or more individuals seemingly speak at the same time (see Tomlin, 1999, for a detailed discussion of these elements). A critical area of stylistics is the presentation of self and racialised discourses concerning how Black women present self is discussed in this chapter. The chapter also outlines the non-verbal characteristics of the style of speech among Black females as they can potentially cause conflict in interracial interactions.

Writers have viewed the study of language in the African diaspora from the 'ethnography of speaking', drawing attention to language behaviours in context rather than linguistics or language structure. Hymes's work (1972, p. 2) provides a useful framework for this approach: 'Ethnography of communication ... cannot take linguistic form, a given code, or speech itself, as frame of reference. It must take as context a community, investigating its communicative habits as a whole.' Early research based on an ethnographic approach generally failed to present the voices of Black women in the discussion and when they did, linguistic depictions of Black women as 'surely' and 'flagrant' were unflattering and one-dimensional (Morgan, 2002, p. 85). Even more alarming is that in credible writings such as those found in Kochman's (1981) work, Black women are seen as objects in conversations with sexual undertones. As (Morgan, 2002, p. 860) goes on to state,

> In contrast to stereotypes of the dominant, submissive and subversive, emasculating, uncaring Black women feminist psychology and linguistic theory have stereotyped middle-class White women as indiscriminate 'people pleasers', concerned with harmony, being accepted and so on in life and in conversation.

Analyses of the stylistic features of the ACS utilised by Black women is evidenced by Mitchell-Kernan's (1971) excellent ethnographic study, providing rich data on the linguistic resources and style of African American women compared to men. Similarly, Tomlin's (1999) study charting the stylistic components of both women and men documents African diasporic communities, including the Black British context.

BLACK BRITISH TALK AND THE COMMUNICATION STYLE OF WOMEN IN THE AFRICAN DIASPORA

In addition to the languages spoken by African females in Britain, there is a uniquely stylised way of communicating among young Black British people, crossing the ethnic spectrum in cities such as London (Hewitt, 1986; Rampton, 1995, 2010). Interestingly, this stylised talk in inner London has been referred to as 'Multicultural London English' (Kerswill and Sebba, 2011); it is popularised in the media as Jafaikan (fake Jamaican) because of its JC features and satirised by the comedian Ali G (Sacha Baron Cohen). Kerswill and Sebba have focused on the fusion of JC, 'African Englishes', Indian English and a range of inter-language varieties spoken alongside London English.

Tomlin and Bryan (2009) call the hybridity of speech among young Black people, Black British talk (BBT). Young people call it speaking 'slang'. Interestingly, young women across social class boundaries also speak BBT. Moreover, BBT encompasses the respective local accents and varieties of English and has vestiges of the phonology or sounds and vocabulary of African American Vernacular English (AAVE) (Tomlin and Bryan, 2009), due in part to the influence of the African American urban Hip Hop culture (see Mocombe et al., 2017). In BBT, the semantic meaning of certain words and phrases are re-created, which do not form a part of the matrix of the standard language. For instance, phrases such as *ride or die are used*, meaning a person who remains loyal to their partner or friend at any cost, and *popping* or *slaying* to denote someone fashionable. BBT often involves a degree of code-switching from standard English (SE) or the local variety to a pidgin, creole or BBT. Code-switching when a speaker alternates between two or more languages or language varieties (in this sense dialects) can be seen in an example of an extract from Esther Bonsu-Liburd, who discusses the importance of being in a state of relaxation when interacting with a potential mate:

> EB: You chill, you show, you flex [BBT flex means relax]. If he likes it, come tune [JC meaning let us talk together] come talk to my pastor or father maybe he might put a ring on you know. If not park youself somewhere else [JC means literally sit down or in this instance go elsewhere] there's a king on his way and you're holding up the chair yeah [yeah is a BBT expression]. There's a chair over there for Penelope but this chair is for the king, and that's for brothers too.

Apart from BBT, Esther speaks the Ghanaian language of Twi and uses JC due to her relationships with individuals from a Jamaican heritage.

PRESENTATION OF SELF: CULTURAL AND LINGUISTIC AMBIGUITY

Language style can be viewed much broader than merely how different components of speech combine for effect as it also involves the presentation of self and the functionality of types of communication. It is worthwhile at this point to draw on Reisman's (1970) study of creole speakers in Antigua. Reisman sees the use of creole as related to the duality of cultural and linguistic ambiguity, that is, the function of creole and SE. The former expresses the African culture and the latter English. The use of creole is associated with low status and denotes relaxation while SE, formality. This context can be applied equally to the British one. An increase in creole for the second and BBT for the third and fourth generations manifests during moments of relaxation, expressiveness, involvement and unrestraint. Reisman observes that SE is perceived as maintaining order, decorum and quietness and used non-confrontational. However, order and decorum can be viewed as social constructs, and euro-centric notions often inform discourses on behaviours revealing the dominant hegemony. Caribbean cultures are often characterised by an underlying set of conflicting cultural values, one echoing relics of colonialism the other Africanism (Tomlin, 2019). As Reisman (1974) explains, passionate discourses involving 'quarrelling' or argument break the norm of constraint and establish a connection between arguments, creole and noise. Both creole and arguments are referred to as 'making noise'. He observes that Caribbean speakers seem to take great pleasure in making noise, but he uses the word noise in the Elizabethan sense to mean the noise band of musicians or melodious sounds as opposed to the mere loud or disorderly component. He calls this contrapuntal in the sense that each voice has a tune that is maintained and that the voices often sing independently at the same time. As the Barbadian writer George Lamming so eloquently puts it: 'So I made a heaven of noise which is characteristic of my voice . . . an ingredient of West Indian behaviours' (1960, p. 62). Within in-group conversations between Black females in the diaspora including Britain, the contrapuntal dynamics of 'noise' is prevalent and linked to sound and motion. As early as 1929, Martha Warren Beckwith aptly stated that Jamaicans express their inner life through sound and motion (Surcliffe and Tomlin, 1986), suggesting the African world view of a spiritual world composed of interactive forces (Tomlin, 2019).

PRESENTATION OF SELF: *THOSE LOUD [SILENT] BLACK GIRLS*

Developing on the area of noise concerning Black females, Evans's (1988) seminal text, coining the phrase 'those loud Black girls', has been the framework for subsequent analyses of Black females in the area of 'loudness' pertaining to education. Working as an African American social studies teacher in several inner-city secondary schools in London, she writes of those loud Black girls:

> In staffrooms [of the schools] a common cry to be heard from White teachers – usually women, for male teachers seldom revealed that everything for them was not firmly under control – was, 'Oh, those loud Black girls!' This exclamation was usually followed by the slamming of a pile of folders on to a table. . . . The words were usually uttered in response to a confrontation in which the teacher's sense of authority had been threatened by an attitude of defiance on the part of a group of Black girls in a classroom or corridor. The girls' use of Patois and

their stubborn refusal to conform to standards of 'good behaviour', without actually entering the realm of 'bad behaviour' by breaking any school rules, was exasperating for many teachers. The behaviour of the girls could be located in the outer limits of tolerable behaviour, and they patrolled this territory with much skill, sending a distinct message of being in and for themselves. (Evans, 1988, p. 183)

Koonce (2012) argues that these teachers were not necessarily remarking on the volume of the girls' speech (see Mitchell-Kernan, 1972, on loud-talking), but they were incensed at the insubordinate attitudes of the girls. It could well be that Fordham (1993) believes that 'loudness' is a metaphor for the 'nothingness' of Black women and that loudness is a subversive tool of these women. Therefore, loudness can also be seen as Black women's commitment to being visible as culturally specific women. In Griffin's (2012) study, Black women also self-construct their style of speech as direct and assertive to counter stereotypes and show proficiency in environments where they are in the minority. African American women in Bell and Golombisky (2004) project used language as a form of resistance to embody their Black femininity in the classroom setting that made them feel invisible. Students valued 'dynamic talk', or speech that fosters confidence in the speaker. These women performed their Black womanhood by unequivocally being forthright and appending their voices into classroom discussions through feedback or co-signing as discussed earlier, for example, 'mhmm' and head nods. Loud laughter was also used as a sign of communication. As well as dynamic talk and non-verbal cues, words were employed as a marker for Black women's social identity and unique experiences. Tomlin (1999) finds similar speech patterns among some Black British women in the British context (Tomlin, 1999).

However, the issue of loudness can be interpreted in other ways. As Caraballo (2019, pp. 1293–1294) asserts:

What does it mean to be 'loud'? Loud in comparison with what or whom? Like other qualifiers, 'loudness' is arguably relative, and, therefore, 'being loud' does not mean much as a term on its own, although it takes on a host of meanings when we consider with whom the loud person is being compared . . . in mainstream western societies, the notion of being loud conveys a sense of excess, whether that excess may be one of volume, behaviour, or style.

Lei (2003) affirms that Black girls use loudness to express themselves and for enjoyment. Comparatively, Caraballo (2019) points out that being loud for her Latinx students is a general cultural trait that the students themselves deem appropriate. Citing Fordham's (1993) 'loud Black girls' study, Caraballo further explains that being loud goes against educational and professional behaviours deemed appropriate and expectations assumed to be impartial and the norm. Describing herself as a first-generation Cuban American, she negotiated being positioned as 'loud' due to her cultural and ethnic background irrespective of whether or not she identified as a 'loud girl'.

Loud females represent the diversity of gender construction in euro-centric contexts and the desire to suppress that diversity, leading to sophisticated racism. In the British context, Black females are often seen as volatile and aggressive (Connolly, 1998). It must be borne in mind that historically, gendered roles were not distinct due to the context of slavery. Consequently, emotional qualities traditionally assigned to successful men relates to the threat Black women pose, which further casts them in the mould of a racialised other. Lei (2003) asserts that in both education and the larger society, Black females are disciplined to contain and manage themselves due to the negativity associated with 'loudness' so as not to threaten White supremacy and dominant masculinity.

Notable scholars such as bell hooks (2015) view loud-talking among Black women as a different set of cultural values and the performance of power. As hooks correctly explains, the voices of Black women, who, in their speech acts, are commanding, threatening, fussing and so on, are not considered as important compared to an authoritative male such as a church minister. hooks (1994) contends that the most appropriate way to resist powerful oppressors is to break the silence by using an audible voice. She believes that women can speak against any form of hostility by speaking in a direct way to those who have the power to oppress and dominate individuals. Silence, hooks argues, is a sign of women's submission to patriarchal authority and speaking in a voice that is liberating allows Black women to obstruct social domination. In relation to silence and patriarchy, it can be argued that there are complex gendered relationships for women who are committed Christians, as spirituality has significance for these females. Such women comply with patriarchal authority in sacred space, for men tend to be leaders in the ecclesiastic domain, a view alluded to above by hooks. Though African Caribbean and African American women often disrupt patriarchy by wielding some influence, due to the high numbers in the church setting and through the activities in which they engage (see Toulis, 1997, for a discussion on the Caribbean and Butler, 2007, for America). 'Church women' present themselves in a layered manner. Therefore, 'loudness' may not be an attribute embraced by church women, but that is not to say that they are silent. Their relationship with God helps shape their identity and persona, which may in some cases counter the stereotypes of loud, sassy, finger-snapping, assertive and so on, Black women, as Linton and McLean (2017) document in the Canadian literature about their Jamaican female students. Equally, we have observed differences in the posture of women from some parts of continental Africa who are neither loud nor silent but their presentation of self depends on the situational context.

However, in the Bell and Golombisky (2004) study, silence is a communicative strategy employed by some Black girls to guard against the anger and hostility that they perceived are aimed at the loud girls. Silence on their part is an effective strategy to deflect the anger and hostility of teachers and peers. Moreover, Evans, the originator of the loud Black female theory, describes herself as quiet because of the perception of her status as a minority and her parents' preparation for a future career in teaching. Fordham (1990) views high attaining Black females as using strategies such as silence, impersonating male image symbolically in self-presentation including voice, thinking, speech pattern and writing style when formally interacting with their teachers in the classrooms and so on. She does not see silence as acquiescence but rather a rebuttal to the image of nothingness ascribed to Black women.

The presentation of self, regarding issues of loudness and silence and how that is conceptualised for Black females, along with other historically oppressed people, also reveals Du Bois's 'double-consciousness'. This centres on the notion that Blacks have the burden of displaying two selves, one that is acceptable to dominant society and one that desires to be their authentic selves. Linked to this is Fordham's (1993, p. 4) term gender passing for coexisting in terms of imitating White males and females, which is oppositional to the literal image of the marginalised or 'doubly refracted other', implying impersonation, acting as if one is somebody else. She explains that to 'be taken seriously' for Black women involves transforming their identity so that their persona makes them appear less female. This shifting persona reflects and highlights socially defined maleness. Added to this is the good girl/bad girl dichotomy located in White womanhood or rather White middle-class womanhood, seen as the universal norm. Evans-Winters and Esposito (2010) posit the social construction of Black females as being dark, sinister, raunchy, belligerent and so on, in direct contrast to the Whiteness of maleness and femininity. Black women are consistently presented with universalised images of White euro-centric womanhood, such as body image, communication patterns and styles of interacting, thus compelling some Black females to silence or gender passing. Black females who do not conform by choosing to portray their entire cultural identities are often on the outskirts of academic spaces (Morris, 2016), while those who are silent and conforming are embraced. It can be argued that there are no strict dichotomies and in fact, there is shifting and inner conflict as eloquently expressed by Taliaferro-Baszile (2006) who self-reflects on her battle between the 'real me' that was tied to the Black culture and consciousness and the 'good school girl' who acted accordingly in order to succeed. However, it can be postulated that the good schoolgirl in racialised Western systems is a role that may be difficult to enact consistently due to the pathologising of Black females. There is no universal script for the presentation of self among Black women, for they are as diverse as the context within which they are located geographically across space and time, and our discussion is primarily confined to those living in diasporic communities such as Britain and America.

NON-VERBAL AND PARALINGUISTIC IN EDUCATION

Features of the ACS include distinctive non-verbal or body language paralinguistic behaviours, or aspects of speech not involving words such as 'hmhm'. Differences in non-verbal styles also form an important area of discord between White educators and Black female students. The differences between the communication of Blacks and Whites, particularly in relation to schooling, are reported in the British literature (see Callender, 1997; Tomlin, 1999). Black students in general often receive disproportionate punishment located in negative interactions mediated through non-verbal communication. The body language of young Black people is often interpreted as anti-authoritarian, insolent and rebellious (Nottingham Advisory and Inspection Service, 1992). Koonce's (2012) study on talking with an attitude (TWA) focuses on the body language of African American women marked by voice inflection, flipping fingers and head movement. The rolling of the eyes and one hand or hands on the hip/hips are also a part of the body language matrix of some Black women.

A practice that deserves some attention as it is also a source of conflict in interracial educational settings in Britain is known as 'kissing teeth'. Kissing teeth, also called 'sucking teeth', is prevalent in many West African and Caribbean communities. The best way of describing it is where a distinctive sound is made with the teeth followed immediately by pursed lips. Kissing teeth has several functions depending on its use. It can demonstrate, for example, anger and annoyance aimed at others or self-deprecation if a task is proving to be difficult. Rickford and Rickford (1976, p. 308) find evidence of sucking teeth in various African languages such as Yoruba, Temne, Igbo, Cameroon Pidgin and Caribbean creoles. They suggest that kissing teeth is an African retention among Black people in the Caribbean. Callender (1997) notes its widespread practice among Black British people. Colleagues have reported Black students using paralinguistic features such as 'kissing teeth' or 'sucking teeth'. More recently, a BBC report by the education and social affairs reporter Hannah Richardson (2020) emphasised kissing teeth among the reasons for the disproportionate levels of exclusions among Black pupils. Kissing teeth can be a form of racial oppression if the student is not being insolent or aiming it at the adult teacher or educator. One White male academic colleague recounted a Jamaican female student 'smacking the lips', as he described it. Apparently, she was displeased about the explanation for the grade he had given her on an assignment. I confirmed to the tutor his interpretation that the behaviour in this instance was intended to display contempt.

The communicative process is the main area where conflict arises between White tutors and Black students in the educational environment. There is often miscommunication due to cultural and language differences. Some White tutors may be anxious about confronting and challenging offensive behaviours from Black students because of fear of being labelled a 'racist'. Black students who embrace certain cultural forms as signifiers of identity may desire at a conscious or subconscious level, reaffirmation of facets construed as 'Black culture', even those features that are used in unconstructive ways (Archer et al., 2007). Sometimes negative manifestations of behaviours are more rooted in the diasporic community's experiences of racial oppression. For instance, in the context of Africa or the Caribbean, a student 'kissing their teeth' at an educator would be considered as gross disrespect and receive strong censure from educators, peers and parents, particularly as educators are held in high esteem. It can be suggested that the inappropriate use of Black cultural or language styles within White majority settings such as education can be interpreted as a form of resistance to sophisticated racism. There are several communicative strategies utilised as Black women's agency not only in the realm of education but also in the workplace.

COMMUNICATION STYLE IN THE WORKPLACE

Increasingly, communication scholars have provided autoethnographic studies of racial and gendered identities and analysed the ways such interconnecting identities are lived in everyday experiences or encounters and the importance of supporting those experiences with research (Scott, 1995; Houston, 2002; Griffin, 2012). It is critical to focus on the communicative strategies employed to negotiate identities in their lived experiences of occupying the duality of Black womanhood within euro-centric spaces such as those in the British context. Generally, there remains a dearth of academic writings on the language strategies of Black women in cross-cultural communication. Scholars such as Houston and Scott (2006), Scott (2017) and Davis (2018) provide accounts of African American women's communicative strategies. In the British context, studies of cross-cultural elements have not tended to be gender specific (Hewitt, 1986; Rampton, 1995; Tomlin, 1999).

A valid theory is the co-cultural theory, which examines the communicative practices of traditionally marginalised groups. The fundamental premise of the co-cultural theory is the assumption that 'to confront oppressive dominant structures and achieve any measure of "success", co-cultural group members strategically adopt certain communication behaviours when functioning within the confines of public communicative structures' (Orbe, 1998, p. 11). According to Davis (2018), Black women utilise many communication strategies to resist dominant hegemony. As she further explains, Black women can use these strategies to

> subtly redefine – and perhaps even transform – their inferior place. By recognising the catalytic quality of their communication and its potential to subvert exaggerated definitions of Black womanhood, Black women can use various communication strategies to demonstrate that culturally imposed images hold little truth and can actually set the conditions for their resilience. (p. 305)

In the workplace, particularly in Britain, Black women are often in a subordinate position reflective of their racial caste status. Davis (2018, p. 307) rightly asserts that

> confronting oppressive forces might be difficult to employ in situations where women's livelihood and well-being are threatened by people such as supervisors and clients with greater organisational and social power. Unlike in academic and relational environments, Black women's 'disruptive' behaviour in the workplace can result in long-term financial and professional consequences. These reasons might help explain why many Black women professionals in research studies used resistance strategies that were more inconspicuous.

Davis highlights some of these resistant discourses in the workplace. Studies demonstrated that Black women found ways to make their voices non-threatening yet audible. In Parker's (2002) research, for example, Black female managers used indirect communication to diffuse conflict in the workplace to appear less threatening to their White male colleagues. This also entailed maintaining standards of excellence in their work-related performance instead of communicating their values to their peers. Others expressed themselves in unassertive, humorous or tentative ways to change working situations that could potentially be restricted. Their unassuming manner accommodated their White male colleagues and allowed them to feel more at ease processing and accepting the women's view. Non-threatening resistance strategies took many forms. Avoidance was identified as a vital strategy in Shorter-Gooden's (2004) qualitative study of Black women's coping strategies. One participant in the study explained that she was quiet and professional and never expressed her true feelings, including any anger. Some participants in the study avoided topics centred on racial issues such as Black cultural heritage and values. Others avoided confrontation altogether by leaving jobs that unfairly privileged their White male peers. These strategies are all suggestive of the broader view of communication styles that these women chose to embrace. Scott (2017) uses the term 'crossings' to go into and operate in White spaces. As she explains:

> In our lived experiences across generations, we found strategic language use is part of the 'gift' and critical to crossings. We also discovered identity implications as we 'shift' across borders into predominantly White environments and back into our Black communities where language is perceived as a marker of racial solidarity. (p. 119)

Critically, some Black women adapted their speech style to the environment by code-switching. Individual women shifted from AAVE, spoken in the company of other Black women, to standard American English, used in the professional context.

Young Black women in Britain also often code-switch from BBT to SE. Anecdotal reference indicates that women tend to use pidgin, creole or BBT, where there are large numbers of Black women in work environments such as the social and healthcare professions and the local government. In the professional context of Britain, unlike America, there is no Affirmative Action, a set of laws, policies, guidelines and administrative practices aimed at dismantling discrimination. Significant numbers of Black women in Britain are confined to the lower echelons of the work environment. Even those who have achieved some degree of success in their career may never be promoted to the highest managerial positions for varied reasons, including sophisticated racism. This is the case for some Black African women whose educational qualifications tend to be incompatible with their professional status. In other words, they are overqualified for the jobs with which they are employed. There may be cultural and linguistic ambiguity among African Caribbean women, particularly for the second and subsequent generations, whose forebears came from slavery and then post-colonial societies, cited earlier by Reisman. The Caribbean communities are mainly confined to urban working-class areas and the second and third generations are only beginning to make substantial progress in some professions. While they have a rich oral tradition, they may not have the transferable language skills because of their exclusion and lack of social and economic participation in mainstream British society. In Britain, accents and dialects are linked to social class (Trudgill, 1990), which can be theorised. This affects the degree of cultural and economic capital acquisition (Barone, 2006). Thus, there may be less pressure in the British context for some Black women to make these adaptive modifications in their communication style.

There has been an increase in the migration of Black professional women to Britain, including nurses, doctors and lawyers from Nigeria, Zimbabwe and Ghana engaged in international migration; they have taken advantage of enhanced employment prospects (Forson, 2007) and adjusted to the British working environment. Nevertheless, such individuals can still be at a disadvantage and operate using different communicative strategies concurrent with their country of origin. British prejudice regarding 'foreign accents', and subtle cultural communication barriers can implicitly preclude these women from career promotion. One such barrier of communication that can arise for both African and African Caribbean women is private and public talk. In most Black cultures, disclosure of one's personal life or 'business' to individuals with whom you have not formed a close relationship is frowned upon (see hooks, 2015, for the African American context). Privacy and being frugal about disclosing the content of specific confidential topics in communication is both desirable and acceptable. We have observed this phenomenon among many Black women in Britain. As [Author B]'s Jamaican mother says, *'mi no like anyone a question me'* (I do not like anyone interrogating me). This can have implications for individuals working in the social health care profession, who may not wish to probe into conversations perceived as contravening privacy. In fact, [Author B] explained to a White colleague at a British university that her Nigerian trainee social worker was not uncooperative in not wishing to extend the boundaries of communicating with clients. On the contrary, the trainee maintained a cultural stance of the client's right to privacy in communication.

Another strategy employed in the Shorter-Gooden study is what she refers to as role flex, or modification of non-verbal behaviours supplemented by dress sense to adapt to the dominant professional culture. Butler's (2007) illuminating study of the role of dress among African American women in the Church of God in Christ (COGIC) reveals the idealised 'holy' woman represented in dress and deportment as a response to the racialised climate of the society. Similarly, in Britain, there is an unspoken rule among Black women that one should be presented well in terms of dress style in professional contexts to bolster confidence also aimed at countering racism. Having said that women in Black majority countries take great pride in their appearance.

Of significance in the Jones and Shorter-Gooden's project (2002) is the excessive attention Black women give to their actual behaviour and how others perceive them. For instance, one respondent, aware of her interactions, took a great deal of care in her approach to deflect any negative responses from others. Even though code-switching and role flexing are vital in the workplace, both strategies can signify that the perceived essence of Black womanhood is antithetical to professionalism, and this in itself is an insidious form of racism. Shifting to acceptable communication styles in the workplace can allow some women to avoid criticisms of their culturally specific deportment and ways of communicating (Jones and Shorter-Gooden, 2003). On the other hand, some Black women's communication strategies in the workplace can be misinterpreted as embodying the 'good girl' performance that is being amicable, respectful and submissive, which unwittingly can feed into passive compliance of their domination and unwittingly attract more covert forms of racism. In spite of this struggle, language and communicative discourse provide a mechanism to analyse how Black women position themselves in education and the workplace to counteract sophisticated racism.

Chapter 5

Challenges Hindering the Success of Some Black Women

Education, Parenting and the Labour Market

Reynolds (2001) interrogates the discourse of the global bond of Black women hinged on their collective history of racial injustice, trauma and marginalisation. She maintains, given, as we see it, the emergence of the pacifist, disruptor, activist and complicitor identities that would develop out of the Big House, that these facets are an outmoded approach to 'contextualising' the lives of Black women. Still, she recognises that 'this underlying assumption of oppression and collective history based on struggle, pain and marginalisation is still central to debates' (p. 596). In her research Reynolds demonstrates, as we have done here with language and communicative discourse, how Black women reconfigure the status quo in domains such as employment through agentic means such as mobilisation. Nevertheless, it can be argued that despite Black women's agency in language and communicative discourse, discussed in the previous chapter, the shared collective experiences of being Black women in the Western world is fraught with challenges in other institutions such as education, household and the labour market, to say the least, and resonates with other women of colour throughout the diaspora. The obstacles impeding the success of some Black women are replicated in North America, for which ample research exists, and is also symptomatic of diasporic communities in other geographical locations such as the Caribbean and Brazil.

The ways in which success is defined is critical and maybe somewhat nebulous even though its manifestations are evident in certain individuals. For instance, no one would doubt that the following women are highly accomplished individuals: Diane Abbott, member of parliament, Maggie Aderin-Pocock, space scientist and science educator from the United Kingdom, media mogul Oprah Winfrey and former first lady Michelle Obama from the United States. In general, fewer women than men are seen as successful based on the standard criteria, often linked to phenomena such as wealth, power or influence and social status often framed in terms of a social hierarchy. Acquisition of education related to the labour market is also understood as a foreground in success attribution. Bostock's (2014) in the *Meaning of Success* challenges traditional understandings and points to an evolving definition educed from her research of 'successful' women working at Cambridge University. Her study, based on interviews and questionnaires, revealed that

> personal success or acknowledgement was most valued when it came as a by-product or consequence of having got something important done, or as a result of having contributed to others' achievements. Similarly, influence or power was often embraced, but only in so far as it enabled a person to instigate an important change. (p. 9)

The ability to collaborate in a team and produce high-quality work was seen as components of success. In addition, it was incumbent on developing other individuals as opposed to aggrandisement gained from personal promotion obtained through fierce competition. The women viewed success from a broader perspective embracing the family and pursuing various activities and interests. The successful women identified in the Cambridge project represent very few females of colour and exclude those of African heritage, evidenced by the photographs of the women in the actual text. Moreover, the research reflects other publications such as Coleman's (2012) study of senior women leaders across sectors that also omits Black females.

Diverging from merely traditional assumptions of success, as exemplified by Bostock, we seek to posit a nuanced approach pertaining to Black women that includes conventional ones by encompassing a broader spectrum based on a conceptual frame also entailing the historical backdrop. In addition, these women's lives are shaped by a number of forces impacting the totality of their well-being psychologically, socially, politically, academically and employability. Despite the narrative of the strong Black woman contested in Michelle Wallace's seminal and eloquent book (1978) *Black Macho and the Myth of the Superwoman*, some of these women face insurmountable obstacles and, as will be discussed in the chapter 6, and are suffering silently. Let us first consider predictable indicators of success such as education as this is the primary conduit between family, community and society and the step into employment, which implicates well-being.

EDUCATION

In the realm of education, Mirza (2009, p. 1) poses the question, 'why is that those most committed to education often struggle the most to succeed?'

She argues that the strong desire for education evidenced in Black women's agency allows one to explore the real meaning of education, which should be a transformative tool. Education in several ways is the path that often leads to success and has been a key motivating factor for Black women's academic gains, especially in higher education which will be the basis for this part of the chapter. According to the figures on progression in higher education by the Office for Students (2020) in Britain, the most significant undergraduate entrants for 2018–2019 was from the majority White ethnic group with 71.2 per cent and the remainder from a minority ethnic background. The majority of entrants, in general, were female (56.1 per cent). It is difficult to give a precise figure of Black female students as British studies do not always provide numbers regarding individual ethnicities, and even when they do, they do not consider gender. For example, Ivy's (2010) quantitative survey of 427 sixth form colleges of 18-year-old students in Leicester found the most considerable growth in applications for the 2006 and 2007 intake came from Black students; these were mainly Africans whose number was more significant than Whites for the last five years. Ivy's study (2004), which provides both ethnic and gender specifications, confirms Connor et al.'s earlier survey that reports the high participation rates of Black women in higher education. Of the total 127,700 entrants, aggregated and based on ethnicity, a total of 70 per cent African Caribbean women attended university, twice that of African Caribbean men of 36 per cent, which were slightly higher than White males, 34 per cent. A similar finding occurs for African American women who graduate at twice the rates of African American men and these women enrol at college at the same rate as White men (Mocombe et al., 2016). Evidently, African Caribbean and African American women are making academic strides. While access to higher education in Britain is not the issue for many Black women; the African Caribbean group tend to be concentrated in less prestigious universities (Noden et al., 2014). In contrast, Ivy (2010) points to Africans as more likely to apply for and be accepted at top universities. Given that his study was also based on roughly equal numbers across the genders, we can infer that African women are also more likely to attend top universities than their Caribbean counterparts. A different pattern also emerges for the African group, where 75 per cent of women and 70 per cent of men participated in higher education. Worthy of note are the findings of the collaborative Manchester University and Joseph Rowntree (2014) joint study that Black Africans are among the highest attaining degree holders after the Chinese and Indians; significantly, of all ethnic groups, 'Black African people were the least likely to have no qualifications' [including women] (p. 2).

The Office for Students (2020) indicates that the proportion of White postgraduate entrants has declined concerning postgraduate studies. For example, in 2010–2011, 80.9 per cent of postgraduate entrants were White compared to 74.4 per cent in 2018–2019. There has been an equivalent increase in non-White students. During the last eight years, Black students had the most significant increase in postgraduate entrance, rising from 5.8 per cent of postgraduate entrants in 2010–2011 to 8.1 per cent in 2018–2019. Given our previous discussion on the high participation rates of Black females, we can deduce that there is a reasonably high probability that they are more likely to continue with postgraduate studies. Interestingly, African American women account for 63 per cent and 71 per cent, respectively, of the number of graduate and professional degrees awarded to all African Americans (Mocombe et al., 2016). In fact, according to these researchers, both African Caribbean and African American women, compared to their male peers, are more likely to achieve status, social mobility and pursue economic gain through the education route.

Despite the progression of some Black females in the British higher education system, there are still serious concerns. Of the White, Black, Asian and mixed ethnicities, it is widely acknowledged that disparities and inequalities abound. In the sphere of university retention or dropout rates at undergraduate level, Black students are almost one-and-a-half times more likely to drop out than White or Asian students (Keohane and Petrie, 2017). In the research by Keohane and Petrie, they explain that

> the literature tends to identify two concepts that help explain the propensity of students to drop out from university. These are a student's sense of belonging (the idea that their aims and identity are in consonance with their experience of the institution); and their level of engagement the extent to which students actively engage with all dimensions of the university experience. (p. 14)

The authors explain that a sense of belonging reflects the degree to which students believe they are integrated into the university space and influenced by personal relationships both in the university and at home. University life can play a significant role in developing a sense of belonging. Engagement, which is the amount of time and effort students are willing to participate in activities, is connected to the institution's endeavours to encourage students to engage in activities. The decreased retention rates for Black females, many of whom entered education as mature students, have been cited by Connor et al. (2004). They also point out that older students tend to take time out of studies for employment and economic reasons. A study carried out at the University of Wolverhampton, for instance, revealed inadequate knowledge of the needs of non-tradition or mature students and student support systems (Pinnock, 2008). For Black students, there is the added component of institutional racism and implicit discrimination (Connor et al., 2004). There are several plausible factors for some Black females entering higher education as mature students leading to decreased retention rates, which in many ways have historical precedence. We will discuss Black Caribbean and Black African women separately to explore the reasons for the decline in retention.

As the daughters of the Caribbean Windrush migrants, many had childcare duties of younger siblings when they were themselves minors. The widespread practice of preparation for motherhood among working-class Caribbean households in Britain, viewed as 'Mammification' (Bernard-Allen, 2016), undoubtedly affected the academic aspirations of second-generation young females. Also, 'girl children', usually the eldest daughter, tended to have excessive household chores, resulting in insufficient time to study, reflective of Caribbean working-class gender relations and domestic organisation. Another significant factor, sparsely featured in the literature, is the link between the education of Black children and African Caribbean Pentecostal churches included as the largest Black social institution. Byfield (2010) provides evidence for the positive impact of contemporary Pentecostal churches on the education of Black children; however, in the 1970s and 1980s, young women, particularly in the north and the Midlands, were discouraged from studying away from their hometown as older members believed that they would not remain committed to a Christian lifestyle due to secular influences. Moreover, the priority for many 'church women' then was fulfilling traditional Christian roles of marriage and children (Toulis, 1995) rather than pursuing higher education. Coupled with reports of both racism (Rampton, 1981) and sexism (Coote and Gill, 1981), it is not difficult to understand the delayed educational opportunities for these mature women and barriers to accessing higher education.

There are different sets of challenges affecting continued studies for African females in higher education, and we cannot provide an overall picture for such a diverse group. Still, we can focus on West African women in Britain. Historically, research suggests a small African minority have lived in Britain from the Roman period and at least for the past four centuries.

In the nineteenth and early mid-twentieth centuries, many Africans, particularly West Africans, have been visible in British universities studying subjects such as medicine, law and theology. Some of these students became members of a Black British middle class, including West Indians (Olusoga, 2016). In general, fewer women than men were sent to study in Britain, but a Colonial Office report of 1955 allowed women and children to join their menfolk. Buchi Emecheta's semi-autobiographical novel *Second Class Citizen* describes poignantly the difficulties and discrimination Africans experienced. By the mid-twentieth century, most African women in Britain were educated at a British university, in contrast to some of the Caribbean women of the Windrush generation who did not acquire a British education from the United Kingdom.

The pursuit of British qualifications for some African women has often been challenging, not least revolving around immigration status, domestic organisation and the lack of recognition of their academic qualifications garnered from their homeland. Concerning domesticity, childcare tends to be a significant issue for working mothers, even more so for West African mothers accustomed to the extended family system. The traditional extended family, which gave psychosocial support to all its members, affects mothers as primary caregivers. Migrant African communities in Coakley's (2016) study of Ireland, for instance, bemoan the lack of support from the extended family, despite factors such as urbanisation, market economies and diseases affecting the contemporary African extended family (Muhwezi, 2007). According to Nesbit and Lynch (1992), West African mothers with higher education aspirations often have four main options for childcare. The first is to pay for private or government-subsidised childcare provision. The second is to organise collaboratively with the father, whereby one partner is a student or works in a shift pattern; thus, both parents provide childcare. The third option is for children to be fostered by a member of the extended family, especially the grandmother, sometimes involving the child being sent back home. The final choice is a private fostering arrangement which appears to have begun in the mid-1950s at the time of the Colonial Office policy change, and well established in parts of Suffolk, Hampshire, Avon, mid-Kent and Sussex. Nesbit and Lynch (1992) provide ample evidence of the widespread practice of White women fostering West African children being. They estimated that there were between 6,000 and 9,000 privately fostered children in Britain in 1992, the majority being of West African origin, and Traynor (2001) estimated an upper end of 9,000 by 1998. Unfortunately, in a limited number of cases, the children were never returned to their biological parents but legally adopted by White foster mothers deemed superior, following a harrowing court battle in the British legal system. The traumas of the foster care regime (Bailkin, 2009) have meant higher education for some West African women has come at a very high price. As well as childcare issues, the inherited prescription of domesticity typically assigned to females in the absence of 'house girls/boys' or domestic labourers has possibly affected these women's ability to continue with higher education. Contemporarily, West African women such as Nigerians and Ghanaians, together with Zimbabweans, have high levels of qualifications (Mitton and Aspinall, 2011). Moreover, Maphosa (2018) research suggests that many Zimbabwean women already had a degree or some other form of education before coming to Britain, but many of their qualifications from their country of origin were not recognised.

A further challenge exists for Black females in higher education who complete their undergraduate studies. It is worth restating the four broad ethnic categories to set the context as White, Black, Asian and Chinese, subdivided accordingly into, say, White British, Black Caribbean and the Asian group Bangladeshi or Indian. The 'other' category refers to individuals who do not come under any of the four categories. There is substantial inequity in achievement outcomes of attaining a good classified honours degree considered a first or upper second class. The largest gap is between Black and White students, followed by 'other' and then Asian students. A total of 80.9 per cent of Whites received a first or upper second class compared to 57.5 per cent of Blacks, 70.5 of Asian and 76.6 per cent of Chinese. Of interest, female students, on the whole, achieve better degree classifications than men except in the case of attaining a first-class degree where there is no significant difference (Higher Education Funding Council for England, 2014). Disconcertingly, when minorities perform better than Whites in Advanced Level certificates (A levels), a precursor for their university placement, they are still less likely to obtain the higher degree classification (*Black, Asian and Minority Ethnic Student Attainment Gap at University*, 2019). The document surmises that even when background and other variables are known to affect degree classification are accounted for, Black students, including women and other minorities, do less well than Whites. Writing of Black women in America, equally applicable to the British context, Bartman (2016, p. 7) aptly states that

> many of the issues Black women currently face in higher education are related to the significant strides made thus far in outpacing all other marginalised groups in enrolment and degree attainment statistics. However, the success this group of students has achieved overshadow their continued need for effective, evidence based strategies designed to promote their continued growth and success in all aspects of higher education.

Both student retention and attainment affect employment opportunities which will be discussed later. Apart from studying at a higher level, there are additional hurdles if Black women decide to choose a career in education. Black teachers, many of whom are female, comprise 1.8 per cent (7.225) of the teacher workforce of 498,100 (Alexander and Shankley, 2020). The negative experience of these teachers with accounts of covert and overt racism has been well documented (Osler, 1997; Carrington and Tomlin, 2000; Blair and Maylor, 1993; Basit et al., 2007; Cunningham and Hargreaves, 2007; Thompson and Tomlin, 2013). Their employment in higher education is also equally troubling. Nicola Rollock's interview with 20 of the total 25 Black female professors for the University and College Union (UCU) portrayed an assiduous 'culture of bullying, racial stereotyping and microaggression' (*Black, Asian and Minority Ethnic Student Attainment at UK Universities*, 2019, p. 7). Not only are there restrictions for Black females in their academic trajectory and career in education, but they experience obstacles in gaining parity in respect of their children's education. Their children's education and parenting also intertwine with success and are significant areas of concern for some.

CHALLENGES WITH CHILDREN IN EDUCATION

Scholars such as Reay (2006) explain that mothers, in general, tend to have direct responsibilities for the education of their children and 'labour' in supporting their children's education. Black mothers may play an even more significant role in their children's education as many appear to constitute single or lone parenting. A recent survey alludes to approximately 44.4 per cent of African children being in lone parent households and 60 per cent of African Caribbean, the highest reported for all ethnic groups (Department for Education and Skills, 2006). However, a cautionary note needs to be issued as Reynolds (2009) describes the African Caribbean mothers in her study as living in different types of family structures not clearly categorised, reflective of Goulbourne and Chamberlain's (1999) large-scale project on Caribbean life in Britain. While some of the women in Reynolds study were married, or in long-term relationships, others had 'visiting relationships', a term describing a family type mainly among the rural poor in the Caribbean. Coakley's (2016) accounts of African migrants in Ireland indicate that some of the participants in his study had family members scattered across the globe. Hence, we can conclude that these women may not be single in the true sense of the word and there is another story behind the official figures.

The active role of Black mothers in the education of their children has been confirmed in studies by Reay (1999) and Tomlin and Olusola (2012), and both middle- and working-class Black mothers may exhibit ways of negotiating, strategising or lack therein, with schools dependent on their social class. Nonetheless, the education of young Black students in the British education system, especially in secondary schools, has been the perennial 'thorn in the flesh', particularly for many Black Caribbean mothers (Mocombe and Tomlin, 2010). It must be emphasised that the desire for a good education for their children motivated early Caribbean migrants to come to Britain during the post-war period (Tomlinson, 1977) and continues to be the case for Black women in general in the twenty-first century. To contextualise the issue of the education of children of Black women, we need first to highlight Bernard Coard's (1971) polemical work, which brought the issue to national attention by describing the experiences of the disproportionate numbers of West Indian children in schools for the 'educationally sub-normal', as they were known in the 1970s. An underlying theme of his research is how the British education system reproduces inequities and enacts forms of implicit discrimination. The ensuing 50-year span of documented extensive research on Black underachievement (Tomlinson, 1977; Rampton, 1981; Swann, 1985; Gillborn and Gipps, 1996; Gillborn and Mirza, 2000; Department for Education and Skills [DfES], 2006; Strand, 2012; Mocombe and Tomlin, 2014) is marked by an equal number of competing theories. These range from wider inequalities in society practised by teachers who exclude pupils based on their race, class and gender and the intersection of these components (Wright et al., 2000; Majors, 2001; Archer and Francis, 2007). In addition, scholars such as Demie (2015) report on the underachievement of Somalian pupils as a group and confirm the inextricable link between stage of English fluency and educational attainment among other African groups such as Congolese speakers of Lingala.

Black underachievement remains problematic when further research on students of Nigerian origin in the London borough of Lambeth perform better than their Caribbean counterparts, and their attainment is similar to high-attaining Chinese and Indian students (Demie and McLean, 2007). A complex picture further emerges as White working-class boys were identified as the lowest achievers of all ethnic groups (Cassen and Kingdon, 2007). To contextualise academic achievement levels, the General Certificate of Secondary Education (GCSE) in Britain measures the achievement of students aged 16. In 2019/2020, the national average score for 'Attainment 8' was 50.2 per cent, measuring pupils' performance in 8 GCSE-level qualifications. Black Africans, on the whole, do better than their Black Caribbean counterparts, with respectively 50.9 per cent achieving the national average compared to 44.0. Both Black African and Caribbean girls do better than their male counterparts, with Black African girls scoring 54.3 per cent compared to boys with 47.4 and Black Caribbean girls 47.8 per cent and 40.1 per cent for boys. To date, White Gypsy and Roma (23.3 per cent) and Traveller of Irish Heritage pupils (31.8 per cent) had the lowest score (see table 5.1).

Yet, despite these observations, there have been concerns regarding school exclusions for Black Caribbean students, causing tremendous anxieties, particularly for mothers. School exclusion refers to students being removed from schools either permanently or for a fixed period of up to 45 days in a school year. It is estimated that Black boys were six times more likely than Whites to be excluded from school (Department for Education and Skills, 2006). According to recent figures by the Department for Education (2020), many Black Caribbean children are more than three times more likely to be permanently excluded from school than any other group, which has implications for mothers as primary caregivers. Racist attitudes and stereotyping by educators are provided as reasons for exclusion, especially the pathologising of the African Caribbean family structure (Afridi, 2004). Pathologising has

Table 5.1 GCSE 2019/2020 Results Based on Ethnicity and Gender

Ethnicity	Boys Score	Boys Pupils	Girls Score	Girls Pupils
All	47.4	286,588	53.1	275,406
Asian	51.9	31,129	57.1	29,894
Bangladeshi	51.5	5,143	56.3	5,229
Indian	58.2	8,308	63.3	7,821
Pakistani	46.8	12,280	51.9	11,995
Asian other	54.5	5,398	60.5	4,849
Black	45.1	16,436	52.6	16,499
Black African	47.4	10,522	54.3	10,777
Black Caribbean	40.1	3,700	47.8	3,678
Black other	42.7	2,214	52.4	2,044
Chinese	65.4	957	69.7	1,002
Mixed	47.7	14,814	54.0	14,667
Mixed White/Asian	52.5	3,410	59.4	3,244
Mixed White/Black African	47.1	1,831	54.9	1,875
Mixed White/Black Caribbean	41.4	3,906	48.1	4,122
Mixed other	49.4	5,667	54.9	5,426
White	47.0	212,811	52.6	203,693
White British	47.0	195,714	52.5	187,307
White Irish	52.3	837	59.0	811
Gypsy/Roma	21.2	687	25.6	667
Irish Traveller	27.8	75	35.4	85
White other	47.8	15,498	53.7	14,823
Other	47.2	5,445	54.3	5,077
Unknown	39.6	4,996	43.4	4,574

Source: GCSE Results (Attainment 8)
https://www.ethnicity-facts-figures.service.gov.uk/education-skills-and-training/11-to-16-years-old/gcse-results-attainment-8-for-children-aged-14-to-16-key-stage-4/latest#main-facts-and-figures

also extended to 'Black' hairstyles, which can also lead to disciplining and exclusions of Black pupils (Joseph-Salisbury and Connelly, 2018).

While there has been a plethora of writings providing explanations for low academic achievement for Black Caribbean pupils, there is relatively sparse research on high-attaining Black students (see, for instance, Rhamie, 2007; Demie et al., 2006; Demie and McLean, 2007; Wright et al., 2020). One study of high-achieving students found that Black students alluded to the role of their mothers as being a critical factor in their motivation to succeed academically (Tomlin and Olusola, 2006). The significance of Black mothers in the education of their high-achieving offspring has been underscored in research by Reynolds (2001), Cork (2005) and Rollock et al. (2015). Black women are seen by writers such as Mirza and Reay (2000) as agents for the community who transform the hegemonic discourse of race through the vehicle of education. Black women's agency in education is evidenced in the supplementary school movement (Maylor et al., 2013). In discussing parental involvement in schools, we also focus on the mother-figure as she tends to be the primary caregiver.

Developing effective parental partnership has increasingly become central to policy documents and is considered the most crucial factor influencing levels of achievement. A total of five areas of parental involvement has been identified by Georgiou (2007, p. 60), including 'parenting, helping with homework, communicating with the school, volunteering at school, and participating in school decision-making'. It has been argued that parents who lack the type of 'cultural capital', predominantly associated with school practices and activities, would inevitably experience barriers where there is a disconnect between parental participation and the cultural capital required to make gains in the education system. According to Georgiou (2007, p. 60), such barriers are, therefore, 'related to the socio-economic status and the educational level of the particular parent'. Any attempt at removing the barriers to parents' involvement in children's education cannot be achieved without the strategies required for positive parental involvement.

Unfortunately, a lack of parental involvement is often interpreted as a lack of interest and Black Caribbean parents (mothers) are often perceived by schools as lacking interest in their children's education (Afridi, 2004). It is often wrongly assumed that generally Caribbean people in Britain are not interested in education, a view, which can be contested with historical analysis. The Caribbean group who came to Britain to rebuild the country during the post-war period had extremely high expectations and aspirations for their children (Tomlinson, 1977). Several first-generation Caribbean people came from rural, post-slavery and colonial societies and were not highly educated. Those from either a middle- or upper-class background were subsumed into the socio-economic lower-class White British community and denied access to key areas of life such as housing and employment. Consequently, some families returned to the Caribbean or migrated to North America who provided opportunities for Blacks in the 1970s due to gains in the Civil Rights Movement (Mocombe and Tomlin, 2013). Many Caribbean individuals did not possess the professional mores, translated as cultural capital due to the reproduction of social class and low-caste status based on their ethnicity, to pass on to the second generation. The negative school experience of parents, themselves as school students, is possibly a contributory factor for their negative attitudes towards teachers (Mocombe and Tomlin, 2010). Conversely, as previously alluded to, many West Africans pursued higher education, sometimes unhindered by undue childcare concerns, especially as children were either fostered or sent back home. This point is critical because the well-established culture of education among West Africans in Britain laid the foundation subsequently for many West African parents to serve as role models, armed with a better understanding of the workings of the British education system. Thus, many contemporary West African pupils, particularly girls, have inherited educational capital. It is possibly a causal effect for the high-achieving students of West African origin in Demie and Lewis's research (2007). It can be argued that teachers may converse more positively with West African mothers, as they tend to be highly educated compared with other Black groups such as Somalis and Congolese, for whom there may be an additional language barrier.

Regarding socio-economic status, research by Rollock et al. (2015) highlighted the strategies employed by Black middle-class parents, many of whom were mothers, who used a wide range of strategies to furnish their children's education. A range of extracurricular activities designed to enhance the abilities and skills of their children were utilised in a concerted way. Lareau (2003) coined the phrase 'concerted cultivation' to describe both Black and White middle-class parents in America who place equal importance on extracurricular activities for creating high-status cultural knowledge, skills in a range of areas, and several interpersonal and personal attributes, such as the ability to collaboratively work with others and self-discipline, and so on. Moreover, in the Rollock et al. (2015) study, parents engaged in a range of out-of-school activities, such as membership in the Junior Windsor fellowship, 100 Black men, participation in musical activities and so on. Despite Black mothers' strategies to advance their children's education, Rollock et al. (2015) reported that these women experienced 'caricatures' and 'racist assumptions' that they were ignorant, inarticulate and uncomposed. One mother, a director of a training company, stated that 'sometimes people categorise you, they expect you to be whatever stereotypical kind of screeching, not able to articulate, Black female' (p. 147). The American context echoes similar findings. For example, Cooper (2007, p. 492) records the interactions of African American mothers and educators who are often assumed to be lone parents, emotional, threatening and aggressive. In addition, many mothers are disillusioned with the types of advice given about their children and feel patronised (Blair, 2001). Many of the difficulties caused between Black parents and White teachers can also be located to the communicative barriers between these two groups who demonstrate different language styles (Tomlin, 1999). This area shall be discussed in depth in chapter 5.

Equally troubling is that even when Black mothers or parents are middle class, they are sometimes positioned as working class. The complexities of Black middle-class parents are often overlooked. Some African Caribbean people born in Britain are ambivalent about occupying a dual identity that is both middle class and Black and seek ways to distance themselves from the negative aspects of White middle-classness such as pretence, snobbery and so on (Archer, 2011). There is significant number of middle-class Africans in Britain. Yet, Musoke's (2016) study of middle-class Ugandan British parents, for instance, were ascribed a working-class status due to their occupation in the United Kingdom and immigration status. Several middle-class Ugandan parents, including mothers, are thrust into skilled manual work, often due to their legal and caste-like minority status ensuing double-class identities. In adopting the concept of Yosso's (2005) community and cultural wealth, Musoke argues that Ugandans from middle-class backgrounds embrace various forms of capital, diverging from traditional Western views of cultural capital, which are often unrecognised by schools. These forms of capital to focus on a few are aspirational: the ability to maintain hopes and dreams for the future despite barriers; the cognitive and social skills attained through communication gained through the acquisition of one or more language/style; social capital which are networks of people and community resources that provide sources of guidance and emotional support to navigate key institutions in the society; and resistant capital refers to those pieces of knowledge and skills garnered through oppositional behaviour that challenges inequality which is grounded in resistance to oppression displayed by communities of colour (Yosso, 2005). These forms of capital contrast with the deficit discourse surrounding Black immigrants, many of whom have cultural capital, but viewed as the wrong currency. Again, the narrative of racism in Musoke's study is a significant factor impacting negatively on the Ugandan British educational experiences and, as we can conclude, has implications particularly for the success of mothers.

PARENTAL CHALLENGES

The adverse experiences of many Black children in the British education system have several dire consequences for women. Cork (2005) emphasises the human consequences behind the statistics, focusing on real-life case studies. If Black boys, in particular, are systematically more likely to be excluded than any other group as portrayed in research (Hamilton, 2017), it affects their employment opportunities or lack thereof (Berthoud, 2009). Consequently, a sense of hopelessness ensues, leading to the attraction of petty and even serious crime, which negatively impacts Black mothers. Black children are overrepresented in Youth Offender Institutions, and the latest figure for Black young people in Youth Offender Institutions is 25 per cent. In other words, a quarter of the youth custody population, according to the Youth Justice Board (2018), is from a Black background. This is a staggering figure when the Black population in Britain is only 3.6 per cent. A significant part of the issue surrounds the criminalisation of Black youth and the racialised discourses of the term 'gang' and its relationship to 'Blackness' which has a long history (see Shankley and Williams, 2020). According to Williams and Clark

(2018), policymakers and politicians have refocused on the 'gang' after the social unrest in England during the summer of 2011. By labelling the social disturbances as a product of a pervasive gang problem in the country, 'the media, politicians, think tanks and academics were quick to evoke the already established view of the gang problem' (p.7) despite the racialised overtones acknowledged by the government. In Williams and Clarke's (2016) study of policing in Manchester, for instance, most young White men, 76 per cent of the sample, committed the most significant proportion of serious youth violence. Paradoxically, young Black men were more likely to be identified as being involved in gang activity, with 89 per cent of those registered as gang nominal. Furthermore, there has been no clear research evidence establishing the link between gangs and violent crimes (Katz and Jackson-Jacobs, 2002). The implications of racialised notions of gangs on Black mothers cannot be overstated. As mothers, they are required to spend an excessive amount of time, on behalf of their children, dealing with the criminal justice system and various agencies, for example, social services. Hence, the lives of these mothers are often impaired, whether or not they are partnered, mitigating the development of their own successes. There persists a high level of anxiety for some Black mothers, whether or not their children are caught in the web of miseducation, the racialised gang culture or the iniquitous criminal justice system. Navigating racialised Western systems for their children is no easy feat for many Black women, which often detracts from their progress in other areas such as education.

Parental fears for their children, including a lack of academic achievement, discrimination and criminality, influence the decision of some African mothers to send their children back to their homeland. The widespread practice of West African parents in Europe and America, sending children back home is evidenced in a study by Bledsoe and Sow (2011). They state that 'almost without exception, every adult of recent West African origin living in Europe and the United States knows about the practice of sending children back to Africa; many know a family who has done so' (p.749). These authors posit that a major reason for this practice is the concern about laxed discipline. Africans see Western methods of child-rearing as spoiling children, which restrict the discipline that parents may deem necessary for developing wellmannered and orderly children, which positively affects learning and career success; a primary factor for migration in the first place is parental ambition for their children's success. Coakley (2016) verifies the differences between the parenting patterns prevalent among Africans in Ireland and the host community. Good manners and respect for elders are instilled in children and seen as demonstration of effective parenting, a similar view mirrored among the African Caribbean community (Callender, 1997). The parenting style found in many Black communities is in opposition to those found in the West, and have been at times a major source of conflict with the authorities. As Bledsoe and Sow (2011, p. 747) perceptively surmise that

> West African immigrants fearing the consequences of their children's indiscipline in the West, where racism and hostility can endanger the entire family, may send unruly children back to the home country. In doing so, we believe, they build on long-standing African disciplinary efforts in hopes of toughening their children's resilience to the challenges in the new place and wait for the risk to dissipate.

The designation of parenting and its effects on employability is another area that impinges on the successes of some Black women. Parenting mainly tends to be conferred to mothers, and the degree of mothering and employment are often interconnected. Duncan et al. (2003, p. 312) point to worker status as somewhat in conflict with good mothering within White British culture. In contrast to African Caribbean mothers, there is little ambivalence about effective parenting and working for several hours outside of the home. Even accounting for the class difference of Black mothers, they saw 'a greater possibility of seeing substantial hours in employment as a built-in component of good mothering' (Duncan et al., 2003, p. 312). One of the authors, [Author B], was bemused with the concept of 'working mothers' because in her experience as a child of the 1960s, most mothers worked and a good many full time. It is generally accepted that women, in general, face several barriers in employment and we shall now see how these are compounded for women of colour. Though the interrelationship between good mothering and work may be negligible, it can be argued that these women fulfil two roles, one at home, which is constant, and the other in the workplace, which depending on the type of work, can be very demanding.

PARTICIPATION IN THE LABOUR MARKET

An analysis of Black women's participation in the labour market has to consider their race, gender and class status. It is also pivotal to briefly mention that there has been a transformation in the British labour market due to interconnected national and international developments. Deindustrialisation and the move to a service economy have informed the labour market landscape driven by globalisation and technological innovations. This, in turn, has contributed to rising wage inequality and the polarisation of employment. Women's ever-increasing participation in the labour market and issues such as workplace diversity have become central concerns. The workplace is no longer a male province. Employment rates for women in the United Kingdom were 53 per cent in 1971 compared to 71 per cent in 2018, although there are variations across ethnic groups. The shifts to more egalitarian social attitudes and the growth of the service industry have increased female labour force participation. As Goos and Manning (2007) observe, this relates to the increasing educational achievement of women.

An examination of Black women's status in the British labour market reveals their continued experience of discrimination and disadvantage in their places of work (Kamasak et al., 2019). They are often viewed in negative stereotypes in the workplace compared with other females, irrespective of their ethnicity. For instance, Brescoll (2016) tentatively explores professional female leaders in the United States across ethnicities and concludes that there is a perception of the 'angry Black woman'. Even a show of a mild form of anger by Black women is often interpreted as her being angrier than displayed. Much of the literature focuses on the gap or 'penalty' between each ethnic group and the British White majority ethnic population (Cheung, 2014). We focus on the gap pertaining to Black women and the challenges presented in three key areas of the labour market, including participation, unemployment and occupational status linked to progression and earnings. We will explore each one in terms of the challenges in the labour market that this group encounters.

The participation rates of Black women have to be set against the national picture of women's employment according to ethnicity. In terms of the participation rates of Black women aged 16–64 in the labour force, it would appear that the rates for Black women are relatively high with 68 per cent (Office for National Statistics, 2020). This compares to the lower rates reported for Pakistani and Bangladeshi women with 40 and 37.4 per cent, respectively. However, Black women's participation rate is below White women employed at 75 per cent and Indian women with 70 per cent. Historically, Black women tend to have higher employment rates than women of other ethnic groups such as Pakistani or Bangladeshi. However, it appears that religious affiliation partially explains the employment penalty (Cheung, 2014) for the latter groups. However, religion alone is not the only additional factor for the 'penalty' experienced by Somalian women. Studies such as Mitton and Aspinall (2011) report on the low levels of employment among Somali women, 14 per cent, in contrast to the relatively high levels of employment among Nigerians and Zimbabweans with 60 and 69 per cent, respectively; figures from the latest Office for National Statistics (2020) suggest that all Black female groups were behind White British women who had 72 per cent. According to Cheung (2014, p. 157), second-generation ethno-religious minorities in Britain continue to suffer substantial employment penalties in the labour market, and visible minorities, including Caribbean, African and Muslim women, suffer the most considerable penalties.

The seemingly high participation in the labour market for some Black women, such as those from a Caribbean background, is not without challenge. Buckner et al. (2007) provide regional variations for Black women's employment based on the African Caribbean female population. Reynolds (2011) posits that their collective status as 'workers', a direct consequence of the combined effects of slavery and colonialism meant that Black women were positioned as a source of inexpensive and flexible labour. She also argues that the collective struggle of Black women in the British labour market is also revealed in the ways that these women continue to collectively mobilise themselves locally and nationally to challenge their shared experience of discrimination in their places of employment.

Despite the active participation of some Black women in the labour market, there are issues of unemployment. For instance, Buckner et al. (2007) find evidence of Black Caribbean women being twice as likely to be unemployed compared to White British women. Similarly, Somali women have high levels of unemployment and economic inactivity, according to Mitton and Aspinall (2011). A total of 12 per cent compared to 4 per cent of White British women in their study were unemployed. As they write,

> The Black African migrant group with the highest unemployment rates was Somalis. Somali women had high levels of economic inactivity. A logistic regression analysis showed that unlike other Black Africans, an 'ethnic penalty' existed for Somalis even after other factors affecting employment such as language competency, health, age, work experience, religion and marital status had been taken into account. (pp. 4–5)

As a backdrop, there has been a marked increase in unemployment in Britain over the past century, particularly in areas of older heavy industries in town and cities in the north of England, Scotland and Wales. The prevailing images of the male and working-class, abandoning derelict and deserted factories, have informed the discourses of unemployment and the unemployed. Showunmi's (2012) enlightening work vividly portrays the social characteristics of unemployment in contemporary Britain by referencing Black and other minority women in various localities in England, including the prosperous south of and the London conurbation. Using 'authentic' voices, she recounts the harrowing experiences these women encounter in finding employment.

OCCUPATIONAL STATUS AND PROGRESSION

Even though many Caribbean people arrived in Britain with skills and qualifications, these were customarily identified as unacceptable in the United

Kingdom, leading many to take the least desirable jobs, which inevitably impacted on their income. Dodgson (1986, p. 64) captures the infelicitous experience of the Windrush women from the Caribbean who migrated to Britain in the late 1940s and 1950s:

> Life was much harder for women than it was for men
> I used to have to take the two children to the child-minder
> and go to work in the factory – I had to catch the bus at
> half-past five . . . I come back and use the coal fire.
> They rent you a room but you can't do anything . . . sometimes
> you had to hide the iron . . . You think it is little hardness
> we suffer in this country.

Black women historically had fewer options in the labour market despite the Sex Discrimination Act of 1975, banning discrimination based on sex or marital status, including employment. Professionally, some White women moved upwards economically, undoubtedly due to the Women's Liberation movement of the 1960s and 1970s influencing public opinion of women's rights. Yet, the needs of Black women have never fully been addressed. Bryan et al. (1985) recount some of the difficulties of migrant women drawn to the 'mother land' in the middle of the twentieth century. Among other aspects of life, the authors illustrate the unmet career aspirations of the second generation. Some of the continued challenges these women experience in their career choices can also be seen in the twenty-first century.

A significant issue for these women is that the labour market segregation is horizontal in that individuals are restricted to specific occupations and vertical, restricting individuals to the lower levels of an organisation. It has been argued that young Black women, like other minorities, view their employment trajectory in very traditional ways. Their educational experiences provide few opportunities for challenging stereotypical ideas of male and female occupations (Beck et al., 2006). Many young women, in general, are still confined to hairdressing, retail, early years and the social care and health professions. Young Black women choose careers that are both 'safe' and feminised options and rely on traditional official routes rather than family and friends, unlike some of their White counterparts (Miller et al., 2004). Some young African Caribbean women are confined to the health and social care sectors, following in the footsteps of the Windrush women. Historically, Caribbean women worked in significant numbers for the National Health Service (NHS). According to the McGregor-Smith Review (2017), occupations requiring intermediate skills, such as nursing assistants, attract more individuals from an African background. Mitton and Aspinall (2011) confirm that health and social care are the main occupations of Zimbabweans. However, significant numbers of African women follow their career trajectory independently to fulfil their own economic needs, unlike in the 1950s when they came primarily to join their husbands. Professional women, including nurses, doctors and lawyers from Nigeria, Zimbabwe and Ghana, now engage in international migration to take advantage of the better pay packages in Britain, often leaving their spouses at home to care for children (Forson, 2007)

It is well established that education is the key to upward social mobility and economic well-being (Erzsébet and Goldthorpe, 2018) and financial viability are often determined by occupational status and is seen as one of the most critical factors in addressing inequalities in the labour market (Heath et al., 2000). As previously indicated the academic achievement of certain Black African groups, such as West Africans and Zimbabweans, are equal to those of Indians. However, Africans do not attain the equivalent employment status as Indians (Berthoud, 2000). Education in the United Kingdom does not necessarily reduce racial segregation in the labour market (King, 1996). Despite many women having high academic aspirations, there are barriers in the labour market. It has been argued that the high numbers of female-headed Caribbean households with dependants can hinder career progression (Peach, 1996). As a counterpoint, it would appear that Black women are increasingly becoming self-employed to combine childcare with work (Duncan et al., 2003)

Research surmises that the educational levels of Black women do not always correspond to their occupational profile in the labour market. According to the McGregor-Smith Review (2017, p. 50), over 40 per cent of all Black African employees with A-level and graduate-level qualifications are overqualified for their current jobs. Mitton and Aspinall (2011) also identify that though levels of unemployment were relatively low for Nigerian females, they face obstacles in translating educational achievement into managerial and professional occupations. They also explain that fewer Black Africans in general than White British workers with degrees had a job matching their qualifications at that level. Their data suggest that Nigerian migrants were overeducated for their respective occupations. A disturbing trend in the Mitton and Aspinall (2011) study is that 'whilst a good proportion of the second generation were accessing professional and managerial occupations, the data suggested polarisation, with many working in low-paying sectors or over-qualified for the jobs they were in' (p.2). Therefore, it can be postulated that if Blacks, especially non-British born, are working in industries below their educational levels, then their income does not reflect their educational status, and there is a pay gap compared to their White counterparts on this basis alone. Further, data from the Office for National Statistics (2018, p. 15) reveals that 'UK born employees in the Black African, Caribbean or Black British group estimated to earn 7.7% less than their UK-born White British counterparts' (p. 15). Significantly, in higher professions such as academia, the pay gap was even more substantial and there are both ethnic and gender penalties. In response to the BBC's Freedom of Information (FOI), Black and Arab academics received an average pay difference of 26 per cent compared with their fellow White colleagues. The penalties for females were increased, taking the disparities in gender pay into account (Croxford, 2018). The Runnymede Trust Report (2015), *Aiming Higher*, outlined the complicated interrelationship of race in the academy, from inequalities in pay and promotion to the challenges of implementing diversity policies as standard practice. In addition, their high levels of self-employment may have been the outcome of facing racial discrimination in the primary labour market.

Women in general often face insurmountable hurdles professionally. In a recent study by Jones (2019), the greatest hindrance for women in employment continues to be centred on work patterns with a culture of long hours, high demands of availability, a lack of progression in part-time occupation and the conflict of these caring responsibilities. The other main barrier to women's advancement, in general, comes from organisational norms and processes that allow gender bias to influence decision-making. When there is a lack of clarity around the standards for recruitment, promotion or pay negotiation, decisions are more likely to be made in ways that disadvantage women, whether because people in power seek those who are like them or because individuals you know is more important than your knowledge or even education. Black women are therefore in a double bind being both Black and female, and for some, there is a triple factor if they are working class. In any event, the binary or trinary position of being both Black and female can be pernicious in professional White spaces. The Sophisticated racism and sexism often come to the fore if they happen to cross the finishing line by securing an interview. Even when Black women are successful by the interview stage, there are challenges so poignantly exemplified in Showunmi's (2016) work. As one woman stated in her research: 'it's the stares that get to me, when you go for an interview and they did not expect your skin colour turning up for the job' (preface). Unfortunately, there is no Affirmative Action in the United Kingdom.

The lack of Affirmative Action as a policy strategy or rigour in providing equal opportunities in the labour market has possibly resulted in some degree of inertia for many leading companies. As we have already discussed, it is often difficult to provide concrete analyses of the attainment for Black women solely as they are sometimes configured within minority ethnic groups as a whole and not gender-specific. Nevertheless, the lack of minorities, including Black females at senior levels, has prompted another Parker Review (2020). The earlier Parker Review of 2017 recognised that the ethnocultural make-up of board membership in many companies needed to change from being all White by 2021. It does not appear that the situation will change any time soon. Of the FTSE (Financial Times Stock Exchange) 100 companies listed on the London Stock Exchange with the highest market capitalisation, the Parker Review revealed that 31 out of 83, a third, still lack any representation of minorities. There are just six directors from a minority ethnic background in the position of chair or chief executive officer in the FTSE 100 and nine in the FTSE 250. At the same time, over a third of FTSE 100 companies do not have any minorities as board members. Unfortunately, women of colour in Britain have been unable to break through the so-called 'glass ceiling' of major companies.

Some of the challenges for some African women are similar to their Caribbean counterparts. African women, such as Ghanaians, Nigerians and Zimbabweans, tend to be well educated, unlike Somalian women, but experience considerable challenges in climbing the career ladder. The main obstacles to their professional success are that Britain is still a racialised, gendered and class-based society. If you are a female from a poor or working-class and Black background there are insurmountable external disadvantages. Black middle-class females who are relatively in a better position in the labour market than their working-class counterparts still face 'ethnic penalties' compared to their White middle-class peers. In other words, they are penalised for their racial and gendered identity, and as we have indicated in chapter 1 their racial identity is the most prominent feature.

Chapter 6

Suffering in Silence
Black British Young Women and Their Well-Being

Jenny Douglas (2013) said, 'Racism is not the only oppression a Black woman faces. She is also oppressed in class terms, as part of the working class and in gender terms because she is a woman.' Douglas's statement reflects the theme of this chapter. The pressure experienced by Black young women in and outside institutions is rarely discussed; instead, more research has focused on the failure of Black boys and Black men. Over the last few years the lack of discussion concerning Black young women has caused concern. Moreover, although much has been said about Black young women and their endless drive towards being strong and resilient (Mizra, 1992), recent information and evidence indicate the opposite. It is noticeable that many Black girls and Black young women are starting to crumble because they are unable to release the internalised stress that arises from the pressure of living with such stereotypes. Much of the evidence has come from anecdotal sources, and provides a starting point for this research. Though according to the Racial Disparities in Mental Health Review (p. 16),

> There is a huge body of evidence that Black African and African Caribbean women are more like to have a common mental health disorder than their White counterparts (DHSC, 2018). Despite this, there is a lower engagement with services despite an urgent need for more access to mental care for Black women in NHS.

This suggests that the mental well-being of Black females sometimes appears at a young age without the necessary intervention.

Through the use of narrative, this chapter will attempt to uncover what is actually going on with Black young women while in education and/or the workforce.

BACKGROUND

While I was attending a conference which took place at Queen Mary University, London, during 2012, a brief discussion took place with an employee from MIND (a national organisation that campaigns on behalf of people with mental health problems) on the need to understand why there appeared to be vast numbers of young women suffering from anxiety or depression and on medication. The employee was there to give a presentation on the work that MIND was doing at both the national and the local level. Much of the evidence which was presented drew on the experiences of people from a wide range of communities who used the services of MIND. However, I noticed a gap and we became embroiled in a brief discussion on the need for data highlighting the experience of Black women, especially young Black women who were in or just leaving higher education. After the conference we exchanged cards and agreed to keep in contact.

It was not until ten months later and through my continued persistence that we were able to meet and continue our discussion on why it appeared that very little was being done in the area of young Black women, or Black women in general, and mental health.

Further discussions revealed that MIND had insufficient information on Black women and their ill health. MIND did, however, have studies that had been collected on Black men. In addition to this I wanted to seek answers to a number of questions: Are Black young women really doing so well? If they are, what is the cost? Are they indeed suffering in silence? Had I started to open up a difficult dialogue – have no connections ever been made between the achievements of Black young women and their lack of self-confidence?

When I was conducting research with Black young women, I had just finished collecting the data for a research project that focused on Black minority ethnic (BME) female leaders. What was both interesting and worrying was that there were similarities between the stories in the two research projects. It was my attempt to seek answers to these questions that inspired me to embark on the current research project.

PURPOSE OF RESEARCH

The purpose of the research is to find out whether Black young women who are confident on the surface are suffering in silence with mental health issues. However, as the writing of this particular chapter progressed, a personal reason emerged for wanting to know more about young Black women and their well-being. A family member suddenly developed major issues that led to a diagnosis of mental illness. It was unexpected, and, initially, we did not know how to handle such an illness, as finding answers to all the questions we wanted to ask got in the way of obtaining the correct support so that the person concerned could move on with their life. Unlike a broken bone or other kinds of illness, when it is the person's mind that is affected, no one understands, or if they do their response is to walk away, find someone to blame and look for a quick solution. Of course, this does not help the situation.

The research is particularly timely, given that it seeks to promote and enhance the concerns voiced by Prime Minister David Cameron on the issue of individual and national well-being. In 2010, the prime minister stated that there was a need to 'take practical steps to make sure government is properly focused on our quality of life as well as economic growth'. In response to this call to action, the Office for National Statistics (ONS) launched a programme of work on measuring national well-being, which Cameron (2010) urged would 'lead to government policy that is more focused not just on the bottom line, but on all those things that make life worthwhile'.

According to the *National Statistician's Reflections on the National Debate on Measuring National Well-being* (July 2011), there is a growing demand from the public for the development of wider measures of well-being, so that government policies can be better tailored to address individual and national priorities, and the long-term implications of our current activities can be better understood.

This proposal is advancing an issue that over the next few years is likely to become fully embedded in government policy. Cabinet Secretary and Head of the UK Home Civil Service Sir Gus O'Donnell confirmed the need for constantly 'developing new and better ways to understand how policy and public services affect well-being', thus indicating a clear commitment from Whitehall to enact real policy change (ONS, 2011).

LITERATURE REVIEW

Black Women and Health

Much has been written in the area of women and health issues (Oakley, 1992; Roberts, 2013); however, much of the early work was based on a biomedical model, which assumed that there were biological differences between 'races' and that these differences led in turn to variations in patterns of health and illness between different ethnic groups (Douglas, 1992). According to Bignall et al.'s (2019) *Review of Mental Health in Britain*,

> There has been recent concern in the growth in women, particularly young women under thirty experiencing mental illness. There is a huge body of

evidence that Black African and African Caribbean women are more like to have a common mental health disorder than their White counterparts. (p. 16)

Various studies (Pachter, 2013; Keith and Lincoln, 2009) have explored the links between perceived racial discrimination and various mental health issues in the lives of Black teenagers and Black adults. The findings are worrying. Keith and Lincoln's work revealed that 'personal encounters with biased treatments are implicated in African American women's lives'. A study conducted by Brown et al. (2003) reported that 82 per cent of African American women reported at least one lifetime episode of everyday discrimination, such as being treated discourteously or called 'derogatory names'. Further studies found that Black women were significantly more likely to report discrimination than White women, and that changes in discrimination were associated with changes in depressive symptoms over time for African American women (Schulz et al., 2006).

A more recent study led by Pachter (2013), carried out with a group of Black teenagers in Philadelphia, reported that 85 per cent of adolescents experienced racial discrimination. During their lifetime, 6 per cent experienced major depression, 17 per cent suffered from anxiety and 13 per cent had social phobia.

BLACK WOMEN IN EDUCATION

As mentioned in previous chapters, the experiences of African American Black women in White colleges have been documented since as far back as the early 1900s. W. E. B. Du Bois (1903, 2003; cited in Winkle-Wagner, 2009) coined the term 'double consciousness' to describe a sense of the multiple identities experienced by Black women in White colleges in relation to the way they negotiate White norms as well as being Black. This sense of multiple identities puts pressure on Black women in general and challenges the notion of self, creating dissonance.

The identity of Black young women is also intertwined with the discussion of intelligence which arises from the work of Jensen in Britain and Eysenck in America. Although this unfortunate episode in academic research happened a long time ago, and its findings have been widely rejected, it has left a lasting impression on the debate on race and education. As a result, the success of Black girls is not openly celebrated; instead, it is seen as perpetuating the matriarchy which has banished Black males from active participation in the family, and which is seen as the main problem of today's Black families which are led by single mothers (Winkle-Wagner, 2009).

Dei et al. (1997) speak of race, class and gender as a set of multiple identities that Black students bring into the classroom. These multiple identities intersect and influence how Black students perceive and respond to the education system, and can determine the success and failure of the individual. The authors observe that race, class and gender influence how teachers respond to Black students. Black students, for example, are more likely to be singled out, stereotyped and labelled as troublemakers than their White counterparts and are also more likely to be excluded from school.

IDENTITY AND 'SHIFTING'

Black girls learn to 'shift' from an early age. To 'shift' is to work overtime when you are exhausted to prove that you are not lazy. Shifting is often internal and invisible. It is the chipping away at oneself, at feelings of wholeness and centeredness – often a consequence of living amid racial and gender bias (Jones and Shorter-Gooden, 2003, p. 7). It is learning how to ignore a comment you believe is racist or to address it in such a way that the person who said it doesn't label you as threatening or aggressive. The pressure of not wanting to fit the profile of being a 'Black' girl or woman is hard. At school, Black girls are often profiled as being loud, over-confident, aggressive and difficult (Weekes, 2002).

As Black girls move into womanhood they have to deal with being told that they are acting 'too Black' or 'not Black enough'. Jones and Shorter-Gooden (2003) state:

> Black women are relentlessly pushed to serve and satisfy others and made to hide their true selves to placate White colleagues, Black men, and other segments of the community.

Black young women learn shifting as a way to accommodate differences in class as well as gender and ethnicity. As Black young women are labelled according to what society believes a Black young woman should be, they constantly change their outward behaviour, attitude, or tone, shifting to 'White', then shifting to 'Black' again, then shifting to 'cool'. It does not stop here, as this shifting behaviour moves into the workplace, where the questioning on what it is to be a Black young woman continues. It becomes an integral part of a Black woman's behaviour. Initially, understanding what is taking place is difficult, as the many rules that are operating are entangled in the notions of Whiteness. The women experience a Whiteness that is different to what they experienced as a child or teenager as it is more sophisticated and complicated. Many Black young women become misunderstood and then struggle to find an identity that embraces their true self. The struggle is internal as they are required to be somebody different to fit into society. While Black women respond to racism and sexism in various arenas, it is in the workplace that they encounter it most (Jones and Shorter-Gooden, 2003). There are indeed many questions that emerge from shifting, although the question that stands out the most is that of impact: What is the long-term effect on one's well-being?

PERCEPTIONS AND EXPECTATIONS

Tsolidis (1990) posits that young Black women have been socially positioned as carrying certain traits and behaviours in society. His view is that society expects Black women to have particular values and to show particular behaviours. They are expected to be 'loud' and 'smart mouthed'. They are also expected, by their school and community and outside their communities, to be poor and sexually promiscuous and to be thieves; these expectations reflect assumed values and ways of being in society. In America, 'Black woman' conjures up a lot of meanings in people's minds (Luke and Luke, 1999), which generally serve to marginalise Black girls. These racial stereotypes produce what Delgado and Stefancic (2001, p. 58) call 'double minorities', an experience which arises from being a working-class woman or an ethnic minority woman, and one which is based on gender and is 'twice removed from the experiences of mainstream America'. In summary, such studies imply that many Black women suffer emotionally because they are unable to view themselves as efficacious and competent actors when treated with suspicion and confronted with dehumanizing interactions (Keith and Lincoln, 2009).

Another area which is contentious yet of interest in the study is the discussion on the beauty of Black girls. Black girls' beauty is never valued and is constantly compared to Eurocentric values of beauty, and the girls are constantly exposed to issues of colourism (Crenshaw, 1995; Etter-Lewis, 1991; Milloy and O'Rourke, 1991). Black women are prone to stereotyping (Jones and Shorter-Gooden, 2003), and this has a huge knock-on effect that can extend to other people's expectations and daily interactions with them. The historical notion of colourism has its roots in Jezebel, an overtly sexualised image of African American women, and in slavery, where 'Mulatto' women who were light-skinned and long-haired were seen as sexually desirable (Collins, 1998). Jezebel's image was contrasted with that of her asexual Mammy, who was seen as big and obese, and was often seen working, serving her masters as a maid (Mitchell and Herring, 1998; West, 1995). Another image that Black girls cannot escape is that of Sapphire, an image created in the 1940s and 1950s to caricature a Black woman radio presenter who was seen as taking pleasure in attacking men. 'Sapphire was seen as loud, crude, argumentative and full of verbal assaults' (Mitchell and Herring, 1998; West, 1995, p. 274).

These behavioural expectations place Black young women in an awkward position; for example, if we go back to the socially constructed perspective that sees Black women as thieves (Luke and Luke, 1999; Delgado and Stefancic, 2001), it has been observed that Black women in general cannot escape this stereotype. When they go shopping they are constantly under surveillance and are followed everywhere as they go about their business because they are seen as thieves. They cannot shake off this shared collective identity or myth which has been imposed on them. They have to cope with the effects of these racial and gendered stereotypes, including bias and mistreatment. These biases can limit access to education and employment opportunities and go further to shape Black girls' identities.

BLACK WOMEN AND MENTAL HEALTH

In summary, it is important to understand and to acknowledge that women from BME groups in the United Kingdom may experience the dual impact of gender inequality within their family or community setting and alienation from mental health services. Specific groups of BME women are heavily represented in psychiatric diagnoses and service use; Pakistani and Bangladeshi women have higher rates of depression than their male counterparts and White British women. However, there are higher rates of diagnosis of psychosis, including bipolar disorder and schizophrenia, among Black Caribbean women than among women from other groups. One could argue that this is partly because racism within society is reflected by racial stereotyping within mental health services.

RESEARCH DESIGN

The research methodology stems from a qualitative approach and includes the use of interactive focus groups and interviews. It was felt that focus groups along with semi-structured interviews were the best research tools to ensure that the Black young women would speak together as a group. The use of focus groups enabled the researcher to get 'upfront and personal' with the chosen participants and to persuade them to share their stories, especially if there was any hint of hesitation. The focus groups provided a safer environment so that the Black young women were able to speak to the researcher.

In addition, the intention of the focus group was to provide an informal atmosphere that encouraged the participants to connect with and support each other during and after the telling of each of their stories.

There were five different but connected focus groups that took place during a 12-month period. Three of the focus groups were held in Nottingham and the other two in London. The focus groups attracted 35 Black young women.

Many of the women had heard about the research project through two key contacts that sent the information around either on social media or through their own personal contacts. The Nottingham contact was the owner of a business that focused on community engagement and hearing the 'real' voice of the community, and was excited about getting involved with the project. The business owner had links to a community radio station that was also pleased to offer some air time. The London contact came through the NUS. I had been invited (at the last minute) to speak at a Black young women's conference, which I agreed to do. The NUS officer heard about my research and wanted to help. The interest just snowballed after this.

The focus groups took place in two venues: a local community setting and a university. Both of the venues were good as the women that agreed to participate in the research were familiar with such settings. The important criteria were that they were both confidential and safe. As a researcher I was there to hear their stories and not to judge or condemn their experiences. All the focus group sessions lasted between two and three hours, which on the surface appeared to be a long time. However, as an experienced researcher working in the area of gender, race and identity, I knew that it was important to allow the participants' time to speak and share their experiences. The focus group sessions were scheduled for either early afternoon or evening. The timing of the sessions was important as many of the women were at college or university, or were seeking or in employment. All of the women were offered their travel money and light refreshments while attending the focus group.

SEMI-STRUCTURED INTERVIEWS

The Black young women that attended the focus groups were given the option of having an interview with the researcher. Five interviews were conducted in the timeframe of the project. Three were with Black young women in Nottingham and the others were with women based or with roots in London.

ETHICAL ISSUES

The research procedures of UCL Institute of Education (UCL IOE) are consistent with the highest standards of research practice, as well as the principles of good practice set out in the Data Protection Act (1998). All research was conducted in line with these standards, with the standards of good ethical and research practice published by the professional societies of the researchers (BSA, BERA), and with the principles of ethical research included in the ESRC Research Ethics Framework (ESRC REF).

All participants were informed about the research study and were informed that their involvement was voluntary. The participants were given the option to opt out of the research at any time during the research study.

THE SAMPLE

The sample was drawn from young Black women who lived in or had connections with either Nottingham or London. The briefing for the agreed contacts was that I wanted young Black women who were interested in the well-being of Black women. I was overwhelmed by the response. A total of 35 women took part in this research project. The majority of the women that took part were from African and African Caribbean backgrounds. However, because of the way in which the women defined themselves, the project also attracted some South Asian young women. The Black young women's ages ranged between 18 and 30 years. There were no set criteria for participation in the project except that the women needed to have an interest in the well-being of Black young women and to be willing to share their experiences. Most of the women either were in education or had just finished and were pursuing lines of employment. The majority of the women had attended compulsory education in the United Kingdom, although some had been educated outside the United Kingdom and had then continued with higher education in England.

FINDINGS

During the focus group discussion, the Black young women were asked questions that related to (1) demographic profile, (2) identity and (3) their well-being. As previously mentioned, the girls were selected through contacts in Nottingham and London. The following section will explore the way in which Black young women challenge and attempt to make sense of the impact of everyday sexism and racism on their daily lives.

> I think that guys have it a lot easier . . . with girls, like, obviously like White girls they do different things with their hair and they have to do certain things like the products they use and stuff, which works for them, but when it comes to the texture of their hair or even our skin colour, or our facial features, they

will be really confused and say racist things without realising. (Black girl from Nottingham)

The preceding comment suggests that the young women interviewed believe that young Black men have things easier when it comes to appearance. The young Black women stressed that perceptions of beauty and appearance forced many young Black women to adhere to the European way of looking. This would mean relaxing their hair, Whitening their skin, changing their body shape and even wanting to be seen as White even though they were physically not White. Miller et al. (2000) suggest that women and girls in Western society experience strong social pressures to achieve a cultural ideal of thinness and perfection in appearance. Miller et al. continue by stating that since the early 1970s women and girls have experienced higher levels of discontent with their bodies than have boys and men. Further evidence (Mintz and Betz, 1986; Parker et al., 1995; Rand and Kuldau, 1990) also suggests that 'body dissatisfaction is viewed as a serious concern because it has been found to be a precursor to serious psychological problems such as depression, social anxiety, poor overall self-esteem, and disordered eating' (Jefferson and Stake, 2009). Despite the high levels of body dissatisfaction, Black women appear to be more satisfied with their body shapes, tend to diet less and report fewer symptoms of disordered eating than White women. Is this because they may be suffering in silence? If so, who will notice that they are suffering?

DESPAIR AND DISCONNECTION WHILE SEEKING WORK

The Black young women were asked the following question: While seeking paid work, have you ever experienced bouts of the following: (1) depression, (2) helplessness, (3) anxiety or (4) lack of motivation?

Dina: The first three definitely.
Ava: All of them.
Mina: Probably all of them except for the anxiety.

Some of the Black young women that were interviewed felt that their well-being was challenged after endless months looking for work. Most of the women had been to university and two had attended Russell Group universities. Others had attended their local further education college. However, it was noticeable that this did not matter as they spent the first few years after leaving university in a continuous search for work, any kind of work.

> I am at the point where with that [looking for work] and other things I got diagnosed with depression and put into therapy to help me with the insecurities that not getting a job and being in that situation have caused. (Young Black woman from Nottingham)

> I can just recall that when I was in college, when I was actually looking for employment, I could not get anything. I went for interviews in places like Primark, but could not get it. Then I decided to go for work experience in McDonalds and that is how I got the job. I used to apply [for jobs] all the time but would be rejected all of the time. (Young Black woman in Nottingham)

As the Black young women retold their stories the room was filled with silence then frustration and bouts of anger. For some it was the first time that they had voiced their experiences on gender, race and identity with other Black young women, and it was difficult as the emotions surrounding the experiences were still very raw. Interestingly, some of the women were making connections as they heard and listened to each of their individual stories, especially when they were asked about their well-being while seeking work.

> I graduated from university in 2011 and have been looking for a full-time job for about a year and a half, two years, but doing part-time work, so, casual at a football club, working in bars, and I have got nothing. I had two interviews on the same day, one was for a part-time job at a place called Workspace (name changed) . . . I was actively seeking jobs, doing application after application, going into places handing out my CV, doing voluntary work, doing course after course to try and help and stop myself from being bored and feeling depressed because of not getting a job and having to go in the Job Centre every two weeks to be treated like you are a piece of meat. (Young Black woman in Nottingham)

Trying constantly to get a job had an impact on the young women's well-being. Even though they were doing their best to keep busy the young women were blaming themselves and trying even harder to secure a position. As one of the young women states:

> It took me a long time to get a job and it affected me.

Psychological well-being is a wide-ranging concept since it concerns individual feelings about daily activities. Theodossiou (1998, p. 86) suggests that 'such feelings range from negative psychological states (dissatisfaction, unhappiness, low self-esteem and so on) through a more positive outlook which extends beyond the absence of dissatisfaction to so-called positive psychological states'. There is much evidence (Showunmi, 2012) to indicate that unemployment has a significant impact on the individual, since it is associated with a rise in anxiety, an inability to face problems, a loss of confidence and a reduction in self-esteem, the ability to enjoy day-to-day activities and the level of general happiness. The following quotation highlights this:

> Seeking employment was horrible. It was not good, like it was not good. I just couldn't understand why I couldn't get a job, like I really couldn't get a job for so long. And I had my A levels and I had done so much voluntary stuff and I was – I felt like when I was going to the few interviews that I did get, I felt they were going so well . . . I just could not get a job and it was really getting me down. (Young Black woman from London)

GRAPPLING WITH THE TERRAIN OF WHITENESS

Worryingly, this decline in self-esteem and confidence in some young women started when they were at university. However, because of the stigma attached to issues around mental health, it was never spoken about, and instead the women suffered in silence. The following extract highlights this:

> I felt like an alien, I felt like an interloper on this course, because everyone around me was White and they are about 18–19 years old and I'm a 30-year-old on the course. . . . Then I thought I don't speak the language, you know, the academic language . . . I started to feel unintelligent. I went to my tutor and I was like, you know, crying, like 'I can't do this any more', 'I need to take some time out', and first I was going to take a year off, you know. (Young Black woman from London)

She continued with her story through sobs, uncontrollable tears and bouts of apologies.

> It got to the stage where I couldn't actually get out of bed anymore. So my bed became a shadow of me. It was terrible, you know. And then I am going to my lectures and I'm crying all the time. I would go to the head of department and I'm crying, which is not me. I'm like 'Oh my gosh', this is just not me, you know. I had to go and see a counsellor, you know, which you know, then I decided – I just thought I'm going to go mad if I don't stop, I'm going mad.

Eventually this young woman sought medical advice and was given medication to ease the bouts of depression. Another issue that the young women had to grapple with is that it was not *culturally* acceptable to talk about mental illness that was for 'White kids': 'depression was not something our people went through'. This led to further distress as the young women had to come to terms with and acknowledge their mental illness on their own.

MISREPRESENTATION

The focus groups attracted women who had young Black daughters, and they either brought them along or spoke about the struggle that their daughters were having. One of the participants said that until she heard about this work she thought it was just her own daughter being very difficult and not wanting to connect with other people.

> From what I observe and the things that she says I think she feels like she has to work a lot harder to be recognised. And I think now that she is older she is finding it more of a challenge because in primary school, I don't know, there appears to be more of an understanding and wanting to develop confidence. When she went to secondary school her confidence along with her self-esteem dropped. (Black woman with a daughter)

Another woman in the group spoke about how Black women wore masks to conceal the struggles that they faced every day. This participant believed that the struggles she referred to arose from politics and from the issues raised by the civil rights movement. One participant who was in work expressed her experience of being a Black woman in society:

> I think that you are automatically looked down on. When I say that I work at the school the first question is, 'Oh so you work as a TA then?' 'No, I teach.' 'Oh, really.' It is like almost a shock that I was able to get a degree and in this day and age it should not be shocking . . . we are able to achieve . . . I don't feel on a par with a White woman. I don't feel that I am treated equally. (Young Black participant in work)

Despite the years of equality Black women appear to be doing badly, yet in the tabloids Black women are portrayed as being strong and resilient and are expected to have unbelievable coping strategies. In contrast, their White counterparts are perceived to be needier and are seen as requiring protection. Many of the women in the study stated that it did not matter how hard they worked as Black women; if a White woman was working at a similar level or maybe slightly lower, they would be noticed before the Black woman.

BRITISHNESS AND IDENTITY

Many of the women that took part in the study spoke about the conflicting issues surrounding their identity during school and university. As the young women started to give their accounts and share what they meant by conflicting issues, the group gave them the opportunity to speak about their lived experience as Black and/or Asian young women. The focus group was being led and shaped by the young women's experiences, which is how such groups should be conducted. Although the length of time scheduled for the focus group was one-and-a-half hours, I brought the focus group to a close after three hours. Much of the discussion focused on what it is to be British and Black; they spoke about their struggles and how these were contributing to their present mental ill-health. Many of their shared experiences were traced back to their early school experiences, which they initially identified as something that was wrong with them as individuals. Listening to the other women in the group (for the first time for some of them) helped them to think critically about their experiences (Bluck et al., 2011). The young women spoke about the curriculum, being 'othered' in the class, loss of confidence and how the system unravelled their whole being.

The following comments illustrate the general points raised when they were asked about being British:

> I don't know, I used to think I knew what British was but I think: how can you define Britishness when the country's national dish is a curry? The football team's main strikers are Ghanaian and African and Jamaican, I think. I don't know, you can't define it. But you find politicians trying to define it. They tell you that you are not British and you don't have British values. (Young Black woman)

[Laughter from the women]

> When I was leaving the sixth form there was this like sense of empowerment of claiming Britishness [amongst BME students] and then I slowly realised that I don't even want it, they can keep it, whatever the hell it means. (Young Black woman)

SUMMARY

As previously mentioned, there is little research that has been conducted on the identities of young Black girls in the British education system. Much of the literature focuses on young Black girls in relation to academic achievement.

This research provides an opportunity to open up a conversation about the well-being of Black young women. As previously stated, the interest from Black young women in this particular research has been overwhelming and there is a genuine desire from the wider community as well as Black young women to do much more.

Throughout the development of this chapter there has been a constant flow of Black young women contacting me because they are in a difficult place: they are finding life very challenging as they are not where they believe they should be after leaving university. Some of these women are in work, but the work is either low-level administration or other types of work that does not reflect their experience and skills. Many of the Black young women that are in casual jobs are still looking for a permanent job, as they believe that they will be able to live a 'normal life' only when they are able to secure a full-time permanent job. This constant search for a job that reflects their needs is exhausting, demoralising and soul-destroying. The Black young women that have shared their experiences in this study are finding challenges not only in the path to work but also in the 'shifting' they are required to do in order to 'fit' or to be accepted into the workplace. How can the Black young women achieve this when the fit is based on implied stereotypical views fuelled through inherent prejudice and bias? Since the research was completed there has been a welcome dialogue on the concerns of young people's well-being. Something that must be considered as a matter of urgency is to conduct further research which has a focus on Black young women and their well-being. Society must recognize that the relentless surge of negativity that is put out through the media is having an impact on the minds of many Black young people. Growing up in an environment that gives out a message that you are not wanted is damaging and in many cases the damage is irreparable.

It has been widely noted that women's issues play a major role in the health of the nation and should be a key consideration for policymakers as they review and/or develop existing services. There is a need for education specialists and mental health practitioners to work together to identify what is really going on with Black young women. Is the shield of confidence that many display actually something to do with their lack of self-esteem? Is there a way that Black young women can be Black and English/British without the need for assimilation? Instead of talking at young people policy makers need to be talking with them about mental health and creating a new discourse which works to destroy existing stereotypes. If one looks at the way in which Black young people with mental health issues or illnesses are portrayed in the media in comparison to White young people, the outcomes are concerning. When reporting on Black young people who are experiencing mental health problems, the media create a somewhat demonic image which incites fear and rage, in contrast to the White person who is usually portrayed as 'suffering' with a mental illness and is then presented as needing care.

Chapter 7

Black Women Reflecting on Being Black in the Academy

Uvanney Maylor and Victoria Showunmi

INTRODUCTION

Collins (2009) encourages Black women to develop new insights about their multiple and varied experiences and identities. In the United Kingdom it is not unusual for Black women academics to share their experiences of working in higher education (e.g. Wright et al., 2007, 2018; Matias, 2012; Rollock, 2012; Bhopal, 2014; Gabriel and Tate, 2017; Rollock, 2019). However, diverse/ oppositional Black academic perspectives in relation to race have been given less public scrutiny and are therefore under-theorised. This chapter illuminates the exploration of identity and career progression through an open dialogue undertaken by two Black (namely African and African Caribbean) female academics in UK higher education. We believe that disseminating our critical reflection of this dialogue will contribute to a deeper understanding of the complexities of Black female identities in the UK academy.

The idea of writing a joint chapter emerged during an initial conversation we had in 2010 where we foregrounded critical incidents which we considered had had a powerful impact on our journey from junior to senior academics in UK universities. According to Tripp (1994):

> The vast majority of critical incidents . . . are not all dramatic or obvious. They're mostly straightforward accounts of very commonplace events that occur in routine professional practice which are critical in the rather different sense that they are indicative of underlying trends, motives and structures. (pp. 24–25).

Interestingly, from this perspective, 'a critical incident is an interpretation of the significance of an event' (Tripp, 1994, p. 8) and the meaning given to the incident by the individual or group concerned. However, an incident designated as 'critical' may not be perceived as critical by an outsider (Cunningham, 2008). Importantly, the critical incidents discussed in this chapter were chosen because of the personal hurt we each felt when we experienced them and the subsequent challenges they posed to us in progressing our academic careers. The chapter reveals how we made sense of the critical incidents in our academic journeys, and how through dialoguing with each other we sought to achieve a shared understanding of each other's lived experiences in academia. This is salient as early on in our discussions, it became clear that our Black identity constructs and notions of Blackness were very different, and consequently influenced the ways in which we interpreted our 'Black' higher education experiences. In part, the Black identity differences we identified were a reflection of how one of us had grown up in a White upper middle-class family (discussed further), and the other, in a Black household, with diverse cultures. A key aspect of the chapter is how we both interpreted the racial micro-aggressions,[1] we encountered in UK universities and how as part of our interpretations, we not only used different theoretical frameworks to analyse our academic experiences (see method) but also dis/connected with each other's perception/understanding of Blackness/Black identities and the critical incidents/academic experiences we shared.

Before outlining our experiences, it is crucial to comprehend the UK higher education context within which our academic experiences are situated.

UK HIGHER EDUCATION

The master narrative in UK higher education is one where White staff predominate academic and senior academic positions (ECU, 2011, 2014; HESA, 2014, 2020; Advance HE, 2020). Black and Minority Ethnic[2] (BME) staff combined account for 10.4% of the higher education population, and those on academic contracts are underrepresented among managers, directors and senior managers (Advance HE, 2020; HESA, 2021). Specifically, Black staff have a 2 per cent representation (HESA, 2021) and those in academic and support positions are less likely to be employed in elite universities (ECU, 2009, 2011; Shepherd, 2011; Zimdars, 2016). There is a gender employment differential between Black women and Black men as Black women are more likely to be employed in UK academia than Black men (ECU, 2014; Advance HE, 2020). Despite this, only one university is led by a Black woman.[3] Research further suggests that the higher education experience for Black staff is one where their leadership abilities are questioned, they experience a lack of career development and promotion (Hey et al., 2011; ECU, 2014; Singh and Kwhali, 2015; UCU, 2016; Advance HE, 2020) and Black cultural capital is undervalued (Yosso, 2005) resulting in a Black professoriate of 0.6 per cent compared with 7 per cent of Asian and 90.9 per cent of White professors in 2019–2020 (HESA, 2021). Interestingly, between 2014 and 2015 to 2019 and 2020 there was an increase of just 50 Black professors from 105 to 155 (HESA, 2021). That is 155 out of a total professorial population of 23,000. Figures such as this support earlier research by the University College Union (UCU) which revealed that White applicants were three times as likely as Black applicants to be appointed as professors (UCU, 2013). Just as there is racial inequality at the professorial level, gender inequality also persists as of the 155 Black professors, only 35 are Black women compared to 12, 860 White male professors and a female professoriate of 6,300 (HESA, 2021; see also Advance HE, 2020), which emphasises the extent to which Black women's leadership qualities are undervalued in UK higher education. A consequence of such undervaluing is Black academic staff seeking employment outside of the United Kingdom (Bhopal, 2014, 2016, 2017, 2018). Notwithstanding, Black academic under-representation is not peculiar to UK higher education. Similar disparities are found in American and Canadian higher education (NCES, 2018; Cukier et al., 2020). Moreover, Collins (2009) views Black women's under-representation in senior positions in US higher education as a form of academic control. Given this, we seek to illuminate how UK higher education spaces, influenced as they are by Whiteness discourses (discussed below), are part of the university norm, and as such, they play a central role in the experiences we disclose in this chapter.

Next, we provide an overview of the data collection process in this research.

METHOD

Data Gathering

We gathered the data by interviewing each other several times during 2010–2015. The semi-structured interviews were conducted face-to-face and lasted between 30 and 60 minutes. The aim was to identify critical incidents which we saw as affecting our academic progression. To elucidate our experiences, we sought to understand how Whiteness is the norm in universities, and how Black people are positioned vis-à-vis that norm. Crucially, we were concerned to explore how Whiteness, with its invisible race privilege (Picower, 2009; Bhopal, 2018; DiAngelo, 2018), has the power to frame Black female academic experiences.

The interviews in turn informed follow-up conversations about the critical incidents identified/shared. Sometimes the follow-up conversations were face-to-face, over the telephone or via email. The conversations lasted from one to three hours, with each conversation taking us a step nearer to deciding which critical incidents we wanted to explore further and/or put in the public domain. The interviews and subsequent dialogic conversations were audiotaped and transcribed verbatim.

Researcher reflexivity is considered salient in trying to make sense of sensitive (Band-Winterstein et al., 2014) and race-related research (Matias, 2012). Thus, we engaged in a process of self-scrutiny to better understand our researcher subjective positions and the impact of such positioning on the data collection and analysis (Denzin and Lincoln, 2002; Denzin and Giardina, 2010). We reflected on and in-depth interrogated/discussed how our differing discourses about being Black either connected or jarred as we grappled with telling our stories about being Black women academics in UK higher education. This reflexive approach was also central to the writing of this chapter, whereby we shared our reflective experiences with critical friends and further reflected on our individual and joint analyses.

Theorising the Data

Each author took a different approach to theorising the critical incidents identified. Author 1[4] utilised critical race theory (CRT) which developed from legal studies in the United States (Delgado, 1995; Tate, 1997) and while more commonly applied within educational analyses in the United States (e.g. Ladson-Billings, 2004; Dixson and Rousseau, 2005) is evident in UK analyses (e.g. Gillborn, 2008, Rollock, 2012, Preston, 2013; Warmington, 2020). In both the United Kingdom and the United States, higher education is considered a self-replicating system of White male power and privilege reinforcing gender and cultural inequity (Mirza, 2013; Hughes and Giles, 2010) which in the view of Hughes and Giles (2010, p. 42) 'promotes many norms and values worth questioning under the lens of CRT'. In this endeavour, two tenets from CRT were particularly useful:

> The intercentricity of race and racism: CRT stems from the premise that race and racism are endemic and permanent in US society . . . and asserts that racism intersects with forms of subordination, based on gender, class, sexuality, language, culture, immigrant status, phenotype, accent and surname.
>
> The centrality of experiential knowledge: CRT recognises that the experiential knowledge of people of color is legitimate, appropriate and critical to understanding analysing and teaching about racial subordination. (Smith et al., 2006, p. 301)

The empowering aspect of CRT for marginalised communities/voices (Castro-Salazar and Bagley, 2010) also struck a chord with Author 1.

[CRT tends] . . . toward a very personal expression that allows our experiences and lessons, learned as people of color, to convey the knowledge we possess in a way that is empowering to us. (Calmore, 1995, p. 321).

In CRT personal narratives/stories are considered appropriate forms to provide evidence and challenge the 'number only' approach to the documentation of inequity or discrimination that tends to support and evidence discrimination from a quantitative rather than a qualitative perspective (Parker and Lynn, 2002). Importantly, CRT seeks to provide counter-stories so as to challenge 'majoritarian [White] stories [that] are not often questioned because people do not see them as stories but as "natural" parts of everyday life' (Solórzano and Yosso, 2002, p. 28; Ladson-Billings and Donnor, 2005; Milner and Howard, 2013). In presenting counter-stories composite characters are considered effective in enabling the reader to comprehend the majority stories/perspectives and racism in education that need to be challenged (e.g., Rollock, 2012). Notwithstanding, in telling her story here Author 1 does not employ this storytelling device. It is not believed, however, that not utilising a composite character detracts from the overarching CRT framework which informs Author 1's theorisation of her data. The theoretical framework itself allowed Author 1 to explore racism in her academic experiences (Ladson-Billings and Tate, 1995), as well as critique dominant White ideologies/privileges ('a system of opportunities and benefits conferred upon people simply because they are White', Solórzano and Yosso, 2002, p. 27). The theoretical framework also enabled Author 1 to assert the validity of her Black knowledge (Delgado Bernal, 2002).

Author 2 drew on Whiteness theory and intersectionality in her data analysis. When discussing *Whiteness theory.* Dyer (1997, p. 65) argues that 'Whiteness is an invisible perspective, a dominant and normative space against which difference is measured'. Interestingly, McIntosh (1988, pp. 147–160) supports Dyer's definition and takes it to an even deeper level, contending that 'Whiteness is the capacity that Whiteness brings for passing unnoticed, un-harassed, "unbothered" through public space'. According to Leonardo (2004, p. 137) 'Whiteness' brings with it 'racial privilege [which] is the notion that White subjects accrue advantages by virtue of being constructed as Whites. Usually, this occurs through the valuation of White skin colour, although this is not the only criterion for racial distinction'. Hunter indicates that 'hair texture, nose shapes, culture, and language also multiply the privileges of Whites or those who approximate them' (Hunter 2002, p. 171). Garner (2006, p. 257) argues that the notion of

> Whiteness is most effectively conceptualised as both a resource and a contingent hierarchy, and its utility is that it enables collective identities to be examined in

a more nuanced way than is allowed for by the hegemonic Black/White, or more accurately, White/non-White paradigms.

Importantly, White privilege is like any social phenomenon:

> It is complex and in a White-supremacist society, all White people [regardless of class background] have some sort of privilege in some settings. There are general patterns, but such privilege plays out differently depending on context and other aspects of one's identity. (Jensen, 2005, p. 8)

Garner (2006) provides a historical timeline which implies that Whiteness follows a pattern that originated in the cultural path of Black America that has since been hijacked by radical elements within the dominant 'White' culture. Such thinking can be traced back through the works of Du Bois (1935, 1977), Hughes (1947), Wright (1992), Ellison (1952), Baldwin (1955) and Fanon (1967). Fanon's work (1967) deals with (Black) desires to inhabit Whiteness, while Harris (1993) has explored Black contentions of 'passing as White' and Twine's (1999) study of Brazil indicates that people of color 'Whiten' up in the census to satisfy personal (yet collectively refuted) desires for (White) privilege. Such desires can, however, be juxtaposed with a survey conducted by Roediger (1999) on Black perspectives which enables one to focus on the genealogy of, and vernacular setting for the expression of Whiteness as 'fear' identified by Morrison (1987, 1993) and hooks (1997).

Discussions about Whiteness and White identity privilege, desires and fears cannot be separated from Black identity discourses. In this respect, it is important to acknowledge Du Bois's autobiographical work *The Souls of Black Folk* in which his 'double consciousness' racialised identity construct was formulated as a social reality (West, 1994). For Du Bois (1995 [1903]) 'double consciousness' is,

> A world which yields him [the Black man] no true self-consciousness, but only lets him see himself through the revelation of the other world. It is a peculiar sensation, this double-consciousness, this sense of always looking at one's self through the eyes of others, of measuring one's soul by the tape of a world that looks on in amused contempt and pity. One ever feels his twoness, – an American, a Negro; two souls, two thoughts, two unreconciled strivings; two warring ideals in one dark body, whose dogged strength alone keeps it from being torn asunder.

Understanding the notion of Whiteness is integral to this chapter because Author 2, while visibly Black, has had the experience of being socialised as White with consequent exposure to White privilege, as part of being raised in a White German Jewish upper-middle-class family. The experiences discussed in this chapter by Author 2 are partly informed by this background and her 'double consciousness' (as articulated by Du Bois) as being Black and White privileged. Though not preoccupied with questions about Black identity and nationality, Author 2 questions her Black self-identity, and in particular, why Black and White academics find it difficult to accept that it is possible for a Black person to have a Black identity with a reference point that is informed by White privilege and without that person desiring to be White and therefore not seen as rejecting an essential aspect of their identity (see later discussion). But wanting instead to be accepted as Black and to be understood as having diverse Black experiences 'without being cursed . . . by [one's] fellows' (Du Bois, 1995 [1903], p. 47).

In the context of complex impactful backgrounds which interact, there are many interwoven factors which shape the experience of the Black woman. The term 'intersectionality' is useful here. It is mostly identified with CRT scholar Crenshaw (1989) who, along with other scholars (e.g., Collins, 2009), contributed to and advocated thinking critically about the multidimensional aspect of women's oppression along race, class and gender lines. According to Delgado Bernal (2002, p. 116) focusing on the intersection of oppression is vital because 'one's identity is not based on the social construction of race but rather is multidimensional and intersects with various experiences'. Many argue that scholars using the 'intersectional approach' will socially locate individuals in the context of their 'real lives' (Weber and Fore, 2007, p. 123). Intersectional discussions examine how both the formal and informal systems of power are deployed, maintained and reinforced in social structures, policies and practices through notions of race, class and gender (Collins, 1998; Weber and Fore, 2007) and sexuality (Strayhorn, 2013).

In providing an overview of each theoretical perspective separately, we recognise that aspects of each overlap, and in some ways are informed by each other, such that, for example, Whiteness and intersectionality are theorised within CRT. This is exemplified particularly by Crenshaw (1989) who advocates intersectionality, while at the same time she is a key proponent of CRT.

THE STOCK STORY: RACIAL IDENTITY CONSTRUCTION

Before examining our individual critical incidents/counter-narratives it is important to understand the stock story from which we juxtapose our higher education experiences. The stock story in this chapter concerns the complexity of racial/cultural identity construction. Here we utilise the perspective of

Goffman (1968) who considers an individual's identity as comprising social, personal and ego identities. Social identity is defined as the category and attributes (e.g., age, gender and class) that a person is deemed by society to possess in relation to others. While personal identity concerns a person's biography, which contains characteristics that are unique to a person and makes him or her an individual in society. Such characteristics also mark out an individual as different:

> Personal identity, I have in mind . . . positive marks or identity pegs, and the unique combination of life history items that comes to be attached to the individual with the help of these pegs for his [sic] identity. (Goffman, 1968, p. 74)

Ego identity describes a person's subjective sense of who they are and how they exist in the world. It also relates to how s/he feels about him or herself. Goffman's notion of identity construction and performance informs our understandings of our identities as Black female academics and lead us to conclude that at the level of personal and ego identity our higher education employment experiences are differently marked by 'race' and class. It is this identity difference and enactment which underlines the ways in which our interpretations of our higher education experiences diverge. Additionally, the Privilege Identity Model (PIE) (Carter et al., 2007) which aims to explore and understand privilege enables us to reflect further on our academic experiences and understanding of Whiteness.

CRITICAL INCIDENTS

In writing this chapter initially we selected four critical incidents for analysis. However, owing to space constraints we only reveal two incidents.

Author 1: Critical Incident – Progressing in Academia

My critical incident is one where a White university colleague and I with the same job title applied to have our university posts re-graded as we both believed that we were working at a higher level than stipulated in our job description. Both of us had the same White line manager. The White staff member was encouraged by the line manager to apply for promotion (rather than re-grading) and their application was formally supported by the White line manager, while I was informed that there is a promotion process when I enquired about the progress of my re-grading application. Subsequently, the White employee was promoted and when I questioned my own lack of promotion my line manager said: 'I didn't think you wanted to apply. I thought you wanted to wait.' 'Wait, for what?' was my reply.

Using CRT as an explanatory framework I interpreted the lack of promotion support I received as one of racism, with the White line manager's non-action influenced by the slavery master servant narrative which views Black people as born to serve rather than lead. The line manager's response reflected 'problematic racialised interpretations' (Nzegwu, 2003, p. 105) about Black people's ability which were compounded by a negation of my aspirational capital (Yosso, 2005) and willingness to take on extra responsibility. Moreover, I was already working above the level of my pay grade and consistently showed that I fulfilled the higher-grade role criteria (as stipulated by the university). Yet there was no formal approach or quiet word with the university hierarchy on my behalf. Why? Because my White colleague was viewed as having 'leadership potential' (comment by the line manager) and I was not. That is, despite me having a similar workload with numerous management responsibilities, which also required me to demonstrate leadership skills, which needless to say I consistently did, and this was verified in my annual appraisals.

CRT encourages individuals to challenge their negative experiences. Byrd (2009, p. 598) suggests that Black staff should 'seek to change the situation' they find themselves in. Zamudio et al. (2009, p. 461) similarly emphasise the need for developing 'a tactical strategy for . . . change'. Therefore, I endeavoured to change my employment position by applying for my post to be re-graded. But again I encountered another (White) stumbling block, this time in the form of my university deputy vice chancellor (DVC). Sometime following re-submission of my re-grading application, I raised the subject of promotions at an academic staff meeting led by the DVC, but he did not answer the question I posed. Immediately following the meeting simultaneously a White colleague and I approached the DVC. I was still in search of an answer to the question I had asked about promotions, but instead of responding to my repeated question, the DVC asked my colleague which academic department she was in, and then he turned to me and said, 'And you, you must be admin?' It was the condescending way in which he said 'admin' as if I was some inferior being in the room which stunned me into silence. Furious, I just stared at him while my colleague told him that we were both in the same academic department. I then walked off wondering how the DVC of a university with an ethnically diverse academic staff body, and with an equal opportunities and race equality policies, could say what he said. How could he assume that I was an administrator when I had asked him a question relating to academic staff promotion in an academic staff meeting attended only by academic staff? But more than that, why did I not openly challenge the racism of the DVC? Why did I allow myself to be marginalised and devalued in a public forum? In that moment why did I not see that challenging racism head-on is a strategy of resistance and survival (Kohli, 2009) and a way of achieving social justice? These are questions I still ask myself today.

Despite the university employing ethnically diverse staff, for the DVC, I did not embody the right kind of academic diversity for his university (Carbado and Gulati, 2004; Ahmed, 2009). It was clear he preferred White academics. Moreover, my questioning of my lack of promotion highlighted a racism he did not want exposed; hence he dismissed me as 'admin'. Drawing on Ladson-Billings and Donnor (2005, p. 281) leads me to conclude that 'despite [Black people's] academic credentials and experience, [their] racial identity always serves as a mitigating factor for determining [their] authority and legitimacy'. Similarly, Nzgewu (2003, pp. 116–117) suggests 'any issue that challenges the structures prescribed natural order or threatens its legitimacy and hierarchical order, academically appears unnatural and is subsequently "normalised" as pointless'. Given this, my then quest for promotion could be viewed as unnatural and if acceded to would have challenged the institutional status quo. By not acknowledging me as an academic and/or engaging with my question arguably, the DVC maintained the normalisation and entrenchment of White power in academia.

My experiences of racism in UK higher education are not unique (e.g. Wright et al., 2007; ECU, 2011; UCU, 2013; Bhopal, 2014; Morgan, 2014) or confined to the United Kingdom (e.g. Byrd, 2009; Lloyd-Jones, 2009; Matias, 2012; Garrison-Wade et al., 2012). Drawing on Foucault's (1979) notion of disciplinary power, Collins (2009) points out that Black women are now employed in institutions including higher education which they were previously excluded from, and consequently, those institutions/organisations have to find ways of regulating or controlling Black women. As she said, 'If you can no longer keep Black women outside, then how can they best be regulated once they are inside?' (Collins, 2009, p. 268). It would seem that universities try to control Black academics by keeping them in subordinate positions and contending that they do not desire promotion; a factor which would also seem to be supported by the numbers in junior positions in the United Kingdom (ECU, 2014; Advance HE, 2020).

If I was to challenge the university's positioning of me I realised that I needed to change universities. Empowered by my engagement with CRT (Author, 2009) in deciding to leave the university I resolved to focus on the positive; that is I have a lot of experience, knowledge and skills to contribute in a senior role. Findings by Jean-Marie et al. (2009, p. 573) suggest that by focusing on 'the negative [potential Black women leaders] can lose sight of the positive . . . and what is possible', and instead should 'process [negative experiences] in constructive ways'. Wilkinson and Blackmore's (2008, p. 128) study of leadership among non-Anglo-Australian women in Australia indicates that it is possible for non-White women to turn 'their [negative] outsider status into a form of 'power [of resistance] or positive capital' (Wilkinson and Blackmore, 2008, p. 127), and as argued by Yosso (2005) Black people have a lot of resistance capital which has been utilised in education. Importantly as Hall contends, 'When you set the terms in which the debate proceeds, that is an exercise of symbolic power' (Hall, 1988, p. 71, cited by Wilkinson and Blackmore, 2008, p. 131) and resistance.

Smith et al. (2006) draw attention to racial battle fatigue and the emotional, psychological and physical impact of racial micro-aggressions on people of color. This reflects my experiences in White higher education spaces which have been a constant battle fighting against White staff dysconscious racism (King, 1991) as part of trying to get my voice heard and respected, and ultimately attaining a senior position. Battered and bruised, emotionally (Ahmed, 2004) I am worn out from all this fighting.

In the next section Author 2 introduces her identity background followed by a critical incident encountered in higher education.

Author 2: 'Who am I'? And Where Do I Belong in Academia?

As an academic in higher education I have often asked myself the questions, 'Who am I?' And 'do I belong in the academy?' Black skinned, I was adopted by White German Jewish upper-middle-class parents as a baby and brought up in rural middle-class England. The complexity is that as a Black person I am perceived by some (White and Black people) in the United Kingdom as having the same shared experiences as all other Black people, and yet by others, because of being socialised White, as set apart from most Black people. There is a notable absence of literature addressing notions of Whiteness through the lens of a 'Black' skinned person who is socialised in a White world. Consequently, I draw on Shelby Steele's (1988) early work where he dares to interrupt the thinking that middle-class Black Americans are 'somehow expected to celebrate the Black underclass as the "purest" representation of African American identity'. Interestingly, Steele maintained that he had more in common with middle-class Americans than underclass Blacks. There are indeed some parallels with my own experiences in the United Kingdom in the story that he shares about the discussion he has with a friend about being Black middle class. The following extract captures the essence of Steele's conversation:

> Not long ago, a friend of mine, Black like myself, said to me that the term 'Black middle class' was actually a contradiction in terms. Race, he insisted, blurred class distinctions among Blacks. If you were Black, you were just Black and that was that. When I argued, he let his eyes roll at my naïveté. Then he

went on. For us, as Black professionals, it was an exercise in self-flattery, a pathetic pretension, to give meaning to such a distinction. Worse, the very idea of class threatened the unity that was vital to the Black community as a whole. After all, since when had White America taken note of anything but color when it came to Blacks? He then reminded me of an old Malcolm X line that had been popular in the sixties. 'Question: What is a Black man with a Ph.D.? Answer: A nigger.' (Steele, 1988, pp. 680–681)

The critical incident discussed next illustrates how 'Whiteness' and the concept of 'White privilege' have influenced my experiences of cultural dissonance as a Black middle-class female in higher education. The incident forms an integral part of my multiple identities.

Author 2: Critical Incident – Cultural Dissonance

I started working in academia when asked to consider a position as part of a national initiative to increase the number of BME students entering teacher training programmes within English universities. The project involved both quantitative and qualitative research to identify the support needs that BME students may have. What was apparent was that they were looking for a Black researcher – not any Black researcher, but one with the qualities they believed would 'fit' in the academy. These are the attributes that are not written into the role specification but communicated through non-verbal agreement prior to or during the interview: the hidden questions, 'Will they fit with the team?' and 'How do they look and present themselves?' The questions have both class and 'race' undertones. The notion of bringing difference to the team could be seen as desirable – encouraging inclusion or creating a greater understanding in the workforce. In this instance it may have been tokenism. I fully accept that my socialised White upbringing will have perhaps made it easier for me to display the attributes that they desired for the post but there was certainly no 'acting White' from me – I was simply being myself. I attended a very informal interview with the Dean of Faculty. I was being employed on the basis of an oral reference from the principal of my college, who happened to be a friend of the person who wished to employ me. This experience contradicts that of many Black intellectuals who often do not have the networks or social contacts that my upbringing had afforded me.

The job raised a number of racial and class issues for me – the first from a completely unexpected source. I had started to date a Black male of Jamaican descent whose upbringing and awareness of being Black was very different to mine. He had a master's degree, yet was finding it very difficult to find meaningful employment. He was extremely resentful and upset that I ('some White coconut' – a name he called me because of my privileged 'White' upbringing) should be granted the opportunity to work in the academy without the need to apply formally. At the time I had no idea why he would display such negativity towards me; I thought he would be pleased. However, I enquired with my new boss whether I could bring another person into the project as an adviser. There are many questions that occur from this difficult and challenging situation. Why did I feel the need to entertain his abusive insults and at the same time attempt to accommodate his needs? Was I trying to compensate for my 'Whiteness'?

I did not understand that I was passing over my own opportunity to a frustrated and angry man who wished for the entry into academia that I had been given and perhaps, the experience of White privilege that he purported to detest. Was this an act of sexism or racism or both, or was it his perception of my 'upper-middle-class privilege' that was tearing him apart? Whatever it was, it started me in the process of questioning who I was and whether I was 'Black' enough to work on such a project. I had always been surrounded by a very middle-class White community – and my accent and behaviour were, I suppose, very 'White'. It could be argued that, as a Black person who has been socialised 'White', in theory I have gained 'unearned advantages that Whites, by virtue of their race, have over people of Color' Leonardo (2004, pp. 137–144). Such examples include access to resources, organisational structures, systems and processes which give credit and power to the 'White' voice. This means I constantly have to play down my experience of White privilege and justify my existence because my experience does not mirror the norm for many Black people. It gets even more complex, because even though I have numerous experiences of racism, I find myself minimizing these experiences. I find it difficult to connect with emotions when it comes to racism because I do not feel it is speaking to me or my inner socialised White self. It is only when Black academics hear my story and their emotions have been stirred that I am able to recognise the extent of the racial experience encountered. Research (e.g., Banks, 1992; Phoenix, 2000) suggests that people who have experienced complicated emotional trauma may repress, deny or even develop their own strategies to deal with what others may view as a disconnect of emotions. Are such ways of thinking developed in a conscious or unconscious way?

The opportunity that had arisen at the university would enable me to help BME student teachers. It was a privilege I was happy to share with my Jamaican friend. He, however, believed that the post should have been given to someone like him, someone who was far more Black (Black in the sense of understanding the cultural dimension of Blackness) than I was. Some would connect my behaviour as being dismissive (something I did not understand until later in life), others expressed concern with my disconnect. I was very conscious of the gap in Blackness, but at the same time lacked certain cues which would have come from the lived experience.

When I reflect back, it was one of those bizarre situations that had occurred because of my 'Whiteness' and the need of people like my friend to stop my progress because of the pain that society had placed onto him because of his Blackness. I felt I had entered into a vacuum of guilt about my White-privileged upbringing – this guilt that Jensen (2005) refers to about White people when they express remorse for slavery or about racism more generally. Being socialised White confers on me a burden which could be the same as 'White guilt'. The question I have to contend with is, does it include the same issues that other Whites discuss, such as feeling personal responsibility for slavery, job discrimination, colonialism and other crimes against racial minorities? To which I would say 'no' because as Leonardo (2004, pp. 137–144) suggests this 'kind of guilt can be a paralysing sentiment that helps neither Whites nor People of Color', and I do not intend to be paralysed by guilt.

However, being socialised as White can cause problems, and the incident shared is not an isolated case as there have been more incidents where Black colleagues have fought against my Whiteness. I remember having a discussion with another Black staff member who believed Black people socialised as White were part of the problem, as we may have been seen by other Black people as 'uncle Toms' who were easily accepted in the academy. What this person failed to understand is that 'Blacks' in my position are not acting White to move up the system: they have been socialised White (Showunmi, 2012) which is entirely different. There is also a failure to recognise that just as Black people experience racism from White staff who feel they do not fit in the academy, Black staff who are socialised White may doubly experience rejection from other Black staff who equally feel they do not belong in the academy.

While one understands the difficulty in attempting to conceptualise what is being said, some, including Black colleagues, confuse the notion of being socialised White as the same as 'acting White'. It is completely different. The notion of being socialised White takes place from a time when a baby has been given away by their biological parents to people who are not from the same ethnic origin. The baby is raised into the culture(s), class and lifestyle of the new adopted parents. Is this where cultural dissonance begins? In other words, the notion of Whiteness is central to who I am. It may not be clear to readers how I have benefited from 'White' upper-middle-class privileges (such as access to private education) and the unspoken code of Whiteness (knowing what is required and/or how to behave in certain situations without this being spelt out) which I argue is reflected in my everyday mannerisms/behavioural patterns and deployment of cultural, linguistic and social capital (e.g., being 'prepared' to enter and negotiate schooling/higher education/professional employment) in professional spheres. I also acknowledge that through an invisible knapsack of 'unearned assets' (Leonardo, 2004) I have been able to convert Whiteness as a way of enhancing my higher education progression.

My university appointment in the early twenty-first century represented the first Black staff member appointed to the faculty of education. One of my roles was to investigate the lived experiences of Black student teachers on teacher education programmes. The dean accepted me as a member of academic staff – highly recommended through a very good source. However, I had a different reception from many of the academic staff. They had been in their positions for many years – and were not about to submit themselves to scrutiny by a recent appointment who happened to be 'Black'. In their minds this project had been inflicted onto them without prior consultation – and much of their anger was directed to me, it felt as though they were saying 'Who is she and who invited her to the scholarly table?' It was difficult to know whether the staff were questioning the appointment because of how they felt about Black students not being good enough, or because of their overall perceptions of Black people.

The next academic year two new appointments were made, two Black academics – was the thinking within the department that it was time for a change? Had the first appointment of a Black researcher helped to pave the way for these new appointments? I remember being excited until the welcome I received from one of them was not what I had expected. Had the same recurring question returned: 'Is this the kind of Black we are expected to be?' Yet again I had been misunderstood and hung out to dry while the two 'proper' Black academics established their position within the academy.

REFLECTING ON OUR EXPERIENCE OF WRITING THE CHAPTER

A verbatim transcription of our experience follows.

A1: What in terms of sharing your story were you expecting to get out of [writing] this Chapter?

A2: That's a really good question and for me when I went into this in terms of sharing with yourself as a friend and also as a colleague it initially felt safe to talk about the Whiteness and who I am and not to be chastised by anybody. My experiences are mine and I am a Black female who has experienced a whole range of different issues and ok I might be seen as a *so* called Black *girl* or whatever it is that I used to be called when I first came here [London]. I ask the question, 'so why is it that you can have posh White girls and not so posh White girls?' So why can't you have a mixture of Black people? Why does there have to be one type of Black? Being the right kind of Black is what we as

Black people experience in the academy. I've learnt something from that and this is how I need to tackle it. So that's why I wanted to do it, what about you?
A1: I don't know what I expected, but it has been painful.

Leonardo and Porter (2010, p. 140) contend that 'participating in public race dialogue' can be painful. Writing this chapter has been an emotional rollercoaster for us. Completing the chapter was the first opportunity we both had to intellectualise our constructions of Blackness together. There were many tortuous times during the period of writing when we danced around each other's feelings attempting to gain further insight into how the other was feeling. Burke et al. (2000, p. 306) observe that while naming one's oppressive experiences 'is difficult and emotionally demanding' (see also Holmes, 2010) it 'is a necessary step', especially if Black academics are to 'develop strategies that will assist in the struggle against social, cultural and institutionalised oppression' (ibid., 302). However, one of the key difficulties we really struggled with is that racialised higher education employment experiences Author 1 held onto and regarded as salient, Author 2 dismissed as 'baggage', immaterial to her/the Black academic experience. As 'baggage', the experiences Author 1 recounted such as her lack of promotion vis-à-vis her former White colleague was considered 'burdensome' by Author 2, and needing to be let go of otherwise they would affect her ability to function effectively. In addition to being 'burdensome', they were dismissed as 'insignificant' and as not warranting a comment or the level of critique that Author 1 gave them. As can also be seen from this chapter's discussion the relevance of race and racism in the experiences highlighted or the aptness of CRT in further understanding was not apparent to Author 2.

Interestingly, Author 2 was able to intellectually engage with Author 1's racialised experiences yet was unable to emotionally feel what Author 1 felt about the racist experiences she encountered. This lack of emotion frustrated Author 1, because at times speaking to Author 2 felt as though she was speaking to somebody White and in many respects, she felt Author 2's reaction epitomised White staff perceptions of Black staff having 'chips' on their shoulders (discussed in Maylor, 2009). However, as we broke through the yoke of difficulty, we recognised that we were treading on ground that was unfamiliar to either of us; Author 1 because she gained strength from using CRT as a tool to unravel her racialised experiences, and Author 2 as her work encompassed intersectionality as a theoretical framework along with Whiteness theory. Nonetheless, there were periods throughout the writing process when we talked intensively about the many experiences which would either leave us hungry for more information or frustrated and concerned that the other had been hurt or misunderstood. Despite these difficulties, we contend that the process has been worthwhile as it has helped to forefront the different processes and understandings that individuals struggle with as they work through what it is like to be a 'Black' academic within higher education. It has also pointed to the need for greater scrutiny and theorisation of the term 'Black' and the theoretical tools that can be applied to such analyses.

CONCLUDING THOUGHTS

Throughout the development of this chapter we grappled with trying to understand what Whiteness meant to us as individuals and how it was experienced in UK academia. Our qualitative reflections enabled us to work through the personal nature of 'race', language and White privilege/power, while the PIE model helped us to acknowledge the ways we were both 'victims' and in the case of Author 2, a perpetrator in the systems of 'Whiteness'. Only by exploring and critiquing our own experiences with Whiteness were we able to consciously address conceptions of White privilege and move the conversation forward. Giving our selves the space as Black academics to write and understand the ways in which our intersectional identities and higher education experiences/critical incidents intersected was important. What is perhaps problematic is that such dialogues would not have taken place if we had not been open to challenging our own understanding of Whiteness within the context of who we are as Black female academics. In spite of the moments of silence and the shutting down of difficult dialogues encountered, we were nevertheless able to continue our quest for further knowledge and understanding; an understanding which has helped us to recognise (from the other's perspective) the ways in which White privilege puts Black academics, regardless of background, at a disadvantage.

Crucial to both of the stories discussed in this chapter is the question of fitting in/being out of place in academia and having the right to occupy senior positions. Author 2's story is particularly poignant being raised as White and upper-middle class ultimately she should 'fit in' without question as academia is underpinned by White privilege and White middle-classness. Yet occupying this space has not been easy because it is not just the 'Blackness' that seems to get in the way of acceptance and progression in academia as gender and class are integral to being perceived/accepted as the appropriate fit or not within the academy. The questions posed around her 'Black' identity have also led to Author 2 further questioning who she is and who or what determines who is Black or White.

This chapter has shown that 'Black' recognition (whether by White or Black staff) in academia is qualified and contingent. Moreover, it underlines the complexity of the term Black (Author 1, 2009) and the extent to which intersectionality cannot be ignored in any analysis of Black identities

(Brah and Phoenix, 2004; Phoenix, 2009). On the one hand, the experiences revealed by Author 2 exemplify Gilroy's (2002) view of ethnic absolutism in which

> the absolutist view of Black and White cultures, as fixed, mutually impermeable expressions of racial and national identity, is a ubiquitous theme in racial 'common sense', but it is far from secure. It is constantly under the challenge of Blacks who pass through the cultural and ideological net which is supposed to screen Englishness from them. (Gilroy, 2002, pp. 68–69)

On the other hand, the racialised experiences of Author 1 reinforce Gilroy's (1990, p. 114) perspective that Blackness can be a 'disqualifier from membership of the national [White] community' (of which higher education is representative) and that of Byrd (2009, p. 595) who notes that Black academics have 'to pass the test [amongst Whites] of being knowledgeable or being qualified to perform in the capacity of a leader'. Author 1's story suggests that despite now occupying a senior position she has yet to pass this test; a factor exemplified by the White male governor who stated that her position should be occupied by a White male.

It might be argued that part of the difficulty we encountered in our quest to attain senior posts is that we sought affirmation and recognition of our knowledge and abilities in 'prized' exclusive White spaces. Simply, this is not the case. That UK academia is a White space cannot be denied, and the higher up one goes in search of promotion the Whiter that space becomes. To not engage with the space or to see it as untouchable would be to deny ourselves opportunities to progress and to utilise our cultural capital (Yosso, 2005) and leadership skills/qualities in academic departments. This would also serve to deny students from diverse ethnic opportunities to be taught by Black academics, and in doing so, maintain the status quo whereby only White academics are considered knowledgeable.

Clarke (2008) questions whether individuals choose their identity or is it beyond their control? In other words to what extent is one's identity socially and psychologically constructed by one's self, society and/or others (Berger and Luckmann, 1971)? The differing analyses applied to the critical incidents shared in this chapter make it clear that Black identities cannot be put into neat boxes, and as, there is no one Black experience or homogeneous Black identity, Black identity labels have to be interrogated. This is imperative if universities are to become more inclusive spaces and purveyors/acceptors of difference.

Overall, the chapter exposes contradictions in Black women's academic experiences which are not simply explained away by racism, gender or class background. Our interpretation of our higher education experiences highlights the need for a reimagining of Blackness where it is not considered a space of contradiction (Wright, 2004; Roberts, 2014) or conflict. Our experiences call for further unpacking of diverse Black staff academic experiences. They also beg the question as to what extent the experiences and dilemmas we have spotlighted are more universal than we imagine and experienced by other women of colour. Perhaps this could be future storytelling.

NOTES

1. Smith et al. (2006, p. 300) define racial micro-aggressions as 'subtle, stunning, cumulative, verbal and non-verbal insults layered with racism, sexism, elitism and other forms of subordination'. They contend that

> People of Color are faced with interpreting the subtleties of micro-agressions, deciphering the layers of discrimination included in the insults, and deciding whether or not to respond, and how to respond to each put down. Therefore, the micro-aggressions cause unnecessary stress to People of Color while privileging Whites. (p.300)

2. Black and Minority Ethnic includes Black, Chinese, Asian and mixed ethnic staff (Advance HE, 2020).
3. In 2015 Baroness Valerie Amos became the first Black female head of a UK university. She was director of the School of Oriental and African Studies, University of London, between 2015 and 2020, and in 2020 took up the post of Master of University College, Oxford; another first. Baroness Doreen Lawrence was the second Black female head of a university. She was chancellor of De Montfort University between 2016 and 2020.
4. In telling our stories we use the names Author 1 and Author 2.

Chapter 8

Flip the Script and Change the Narrative

THE EMOTIONAL BURDEN OF RACISM

Racism is an endemic and normal phenomenon in White-dominated societies. The emergence and evolution of racism have morphed into an invisible burden that challenges the social, psychological, emotional and intellectual soul of diverse groups of Black people. Unfortunately, many White people can't, don't or have no desire to acknowledge this invisible burden that fuels much of their privilege and prosperity. In fact, racism is endemic and is primarily a fight that Black people have fought and continue to fight. The manifestation of everyday racism produces burdens that plague and often cripple creativity, ingenuity and communication. First, the emotional burden of sophisticated and everyday racism compels Black women to prove that they are twice as good as White women. This emotional burden can manifest itself in racial stress and unrealistic notions of perfection. Second, the burden of sophisticated and everyday racism can cause internal conflict, insecurities and a desire to be accepted by Whiteness at the expense of Blackness. Sophisticated racism rests on the premise that only traditionally White social cues, language and ways of acting in public, the workplace and school spaces are acceptable. Black people are expected to follow White patterns of behaviour which may not harmonise with their cultural norms.

In this chapter, we describe a range of experiences that depict everyday racism in White-dominated societies. Through biographical narratives, we illuminate the reality of managing everyday racism and upholding cultural integrity. In addition, we will provide a set of strategies that we recommend to 'flip the script and change the narrative' on how Blacks view themselves, their situation and the source of racism. Flipping the script and changing the narrative is a tool of empowerment that enables Black people to expose racist actions and shift the burden onto the racist. The narratives provide insights into various racist situations that burden Black consciousness and reality. 'Flip the script and change the narrative' uses reverse psychology as a technique for managing everyday racism. When Blacks are subjected to sophisticated racism, we suggest reversing patterns of thought, behaviour and response. Flip the script and change the narrative compels Black people to do something unexpected, revolutionary and affirming in the face of duplicitous racist actions.

STRATEGIES FOR MANAGING SOPHISTICATED AND EVERYDAY RACISM

As Black people in a White majority society, we are treated differently from all other races of peoples, especially the White population. We contend that the adverse treatment that Black people endure is the result of White people's desire to protect their privileges and White fear of Black prowess. Thus, the strategies that follow are designed to support the empowerment of Black voices while also shifting the burden onto Whiteness. It is not easy to extricate yourself from an emotional and upsetting incident and adopt a calm approach which puts you back in control. However, these strategies have supported our transition from tattered victim of racism to empowered champion of social justice.

There are Five major strategies we employ to 'flip the script and change the narrative.' Each strategy is supported by nuanced questions and an illustrative narrative. The strategies include questioning, documenting, behaving, advocating and documenting in ways that counter racist discourse and behaviour.

QUESTIONING

Asking critical questions can help illuminate racist discourse, actions and content. Questioning allows us to confront racism with a reasoned response and argument. In addition, asking direct questions requires focused responses that can expose racist actions. To flip the script and change the narrative it is important to reflect on and use effective questions. The following questions can initiate a discussion or silence racist discourse.

1. What compels you to believe what you believe?
2. Why do you believe that my race makes me inferior to you?
3. Can you repeat what you just said? Slowly.
4. Do you hear what you are saying?

5. Do you believe that behaviour promotes integrity and intelligence?
6. What do you hope to achieve from this racist behaviour?

CARING

Self-care is essential to navigating everyday racism. The weight of racial stress is overwhelming and most Black people are not aware of its damaging impact on their emotional and mental health. It is important to find an effective outlet to release anger, guilt, exhaustion and frustration.

1. Keep a journal
2. Discuss how you feel with your partner, friends, counsellor or religious leader
3. Meditate to maintain a calm and measured disposition
4. Join a support group
5. Exercise

BEHAVING (EMPOWERED)

Black people throughout the diaspora must continue to 'take the high road' when confronted with everyday racism. Though racial stress or the taxing reality of being Black in White society is a menacing and omnipresent pressure, we must rise above the depressive nature of Whiteness. Being mindful of how we communicate is crucial. Hence, facial, body and verbal languages require a concerted effort to both teach and empower. Empowered behaviour may require:

1. Ignoring racism is sometimes the best behaviour
2. Responding with dignity through an aloof posture can disarm racist actions
3. Requesting a private conversation
4. Providing resources for learning about racial realities

ADVOCATING

Advocating for professional equity, physical safety and mental health is imperative to support empowered behaviour. When facing everyday racism, Black women must find ways to recharge. They must marginalise Whiteness to diminish its importance. On the micro or personal level advocating for space, time or activities to counteract (with dignity) ignorant Whiteness must be prioritized. In addition, advocating for racial justice on a macro level is equally important. Advocating can be accomplished through:

1. Contacting local politicians
2. Joining grassroots organizations
3. Knowing and promoting policies and procedures in the workplace
4. Reporting (with documentation) racist incidents to authority and support person
5. Networking with others to support mental, social, and physical health (White Ally, other minorities and family)

DOCUMENTING

It is important that Black people learn the art of effective document collection and writing. This is one of the most potent weapons at our disposal. While verbal dexterity and precision must be cultivated, we have found that documenting everyday racism in the form of a report or letter can yield positive outcomes. Providing evidence for your case is both cathartic and empowering. It also enables Black people to offload some of the emotional trauma which arises from negative experiences. Documenting is an invaluable strategy to manage everyday racism. Documentation can be in the following forms:

1. Email, Texts, Instant Messages
2. Social Media Platforms (be sure the information is authentic)
3. Recorded conversations
4. Reports
5. Articles and other scholarship (books, poems, presentations)

If the act of questioning, caring, behaving, advocating and documenting seems like a lot of work, it is! However, practising these strategies is both taxing and liberating in the face of everyday racism. Though there are alternative strategies (protest, marching, sit-ins, litigating) and even physical reactions (fighting, yelling, pushing) for dealing with racism in everyday situations, the strategies presented support behaviours and actions that yield an effective outcome.

FLIP THE SCRIPT AND CHANGE THE NARRATIVE

The following biographical narratives provide a glimpse of the reality of everyday racism. The narratives demonstrate the nuanced reality of how

Black people, and particularly Black women and girls, reveal the association between racist distractions and how it impacts their socio-psychic reality. Each of us interprets racist responses very differently and it's the differences that make everyday racism multifaceted and fluid. 'Flipping' and 'changing the narrative' from the role of victim to empowered individual allows Black women to take control of their own story.

THE BURDEN OF PERFECTION

Melissa was a young Black girl who attended an extremely competitive and private academic school since fourth grade. Going to school in a sociocultural reality that promoted Whiteness as superior was met with social, cultural and emotional challenges. As a Black teenager Melissa had to manage the complexion of her beautiful brown skin against a White and Asian beauty standard, the prowess of being a student who was also a great athlete, and the pressure of being a top academic student. Every day Melissa had to manage racist curriculum content, cultural incompetence from teachers and racist comments about her belonging at the school. Though her parents were financially wealthy, and Melissa had all the social and material trappings of the average teenager at her school, her race meant that she had to contend with subtle, unconscious, intentional and pernicious racism.

On a warm spring afternoon after track practice, Melissa was approached by a White teammate who asked if she was recruited to the school on a track scholarship. Melissa was shocked and disturbed by her question because they had both been at the school for six years. She looked at her teammate and asked, what are you really asking me? What are you trying to say? Her teammate responded, 'umm I just wanted to know if you were getting a scholarship because you're so good'. 'Why would I get a scholarship'? 'Is it because I'm Black or because you think I need the money or both'? Melissa retorted. Her teammate responded, 'I guess I wasn't thinking, I guess I got you mixed up with' and she didn't complete the sentence. At this point Melissa was clearly agitated but instead of further discussion she just walked away frustrated. A week later Melissa and Veronica were in the quad eating lunch when they overheard a group of White and Asian girls discussing how it was impossible for Melissa to be a top student in all her classes. Speaking loudly, one of the students suggested that her good grades might be a result of cheating. After seeing Melissa's distressed demeanour, Veronica, who was White, stood up and chastised the group for being racist and mean. Melissa didn't say anything, she tried to ignore the comments and wanted nothing more than to feel the comfort of her parents. Though she felt she had to be perfect to be accepted, she knew even the illusion of perfection was an unnecessary burden.

The reality of sophisticated and everyday racism creates a level of racial stress that is not conducive to safe learning or healthy identity development. The emotional toll that everyday racism has on Black girls is a heavy burden. Melissa, likely unaware, was able to question, behave and allow an ally to support her through the everyday racism that she faced at her school.

SWIMMING IN OVERT RACISM

The following narrative is based on the daily life of seven-year-old Elsie as she began her journey at a new school. A new swimming club was just opening at the school. Elsie was a fantastic swimmer and had swum since she was four. She attended a local swimming club where she had progressed to the gold level and was able to swim a mile in a week. She was really excited about the swimming club and decided to put herself forward.

Elsie was invited to attend a trial swim in a set timed limit. She came in as one of the fastest swimmers. However, she was not chosen to join the club. Instead, a White child was chosen. Elsie was distraught and could not understand why she was not chosen to join the swimming club. She was visibly upset and confused, and her mom consoled her at the poolside. Before they left the pool Elsie and her mom found out that the child that was chosen was not able to swim. Her mother explained that sometimes things are not fair, and that she was treated unfairly because she was not White.

Elsie's mother could not accept the outcome of the trial for the swimming club. She realised that this was going to be another difficult conversation. She sent a letter to the school swimming club coach copying in the head teacher to ask if there had been a mix up with the names, as the girl they had selected was a non-swimmer. The coach was adamant that the correct girl had been chosen and Elsie was excluded from swimming club. Elsie was relegated to the non-swimmers' class until the next swimming trial took place in three months. Elsie continued to swim and progress with the swimming club outside the school, although her enthusiasm had been adversely affected by her rejection. Nonetheless, Elsie's family encouraged her to continue to work on her swimming.

It is important to support the emotional health of children who experience everyday racism. Elsie's mom quickly and appropriately nurtured her through the disappointing news with a simple but effective conversation. In addition, her mom was able to advocate for her child despite the overt racism that took place at the swim trials and in the comments from the head of school.

PARENTHOOD IN BLACK AND WHITE

Tayla was an average academic student but was taller than average. She didn't find school particularly exciting or useful. As a 13-year-old, she was in the pubescent, social and emotional space as most teens. However, because she was taller than her classmates, teachers often thought she was older than her actual age. To her White teachers, Tayla was not only perceived as older, but she was also seen as aggressive, confrontational and uncooperative. One of her teachers expressed her concern for Tayla's 'attitude' in an email to her parents.

> (3:31 p.m. email)
> Hello Mr. & Mrs. Robinson,
> I am emailing because today Tayla refused to complete the reading assignment in class. She disobeyed a direct request and excused herself from the reading group to sit alone and engage on her iPhone. This behaviour is unacceptable, and she is assigned to in-school suspension for the next 3 days. We have scheduled a conference for tomorrow at 10 a.m. Please let me know your concerns.

> (5:22 p.m. email)
> Hello Mrs. Caster,
> I am surprised to hear that Tayla is assigned detention. She was visibly upset when she arrived home and her father and I had to comfort her distress. She says that the story that was read made her uncomfortable and you wouldn't give her an alternative assignment. We are not happy nor in agreement with your assigning our daughter to detention and will discuss this matter further. While the conference was scheduled without appropriate notification, I will be able to attend. FYI, Tayla will follow her regular schedule tomorrow.

At 10 a.m. the following morning, Mrs Robinson, the principal, counsellor and Mrs Caster met to discuss the incident. Mrs Robinson was hyper-aware that she was the only non-White person in the room. As she listened to Mrs Caster recount her version of the story, she took notes. Mrs Robinson then spoke clearly and directly to the educators. She stated that the book was inappropriate and was banned in many school districts across the country because of racist language. In addition, she expressed that to use it in class, the teacher must be aware of personal biases and the social and cultural reality of her students. Mrs Robinson looked at Mrs Caster and stated,

> My daughter was emotionally distressed during the reading of that book because of negative racial language, and she told you. Tayla's behaviour was in direct response to your disrespectful behaviour towards her emotional and cultural needs and I think she handled the situation appropriately.

Mrs Caster was not happy with Mrs Robinson's response and was very negative about Tayla's behaviour. Mrs Robinson asked if any other Black or White students were uncomfortable with the book. The exchange went back and forth until the principal stepped in, reassured that Tayla would not be in school suspension and that an alternative assignment would be provided. Mrs Robinson thanked the principal and asked to transfer Tayla to another class. She also requested that the school remove the book from the curriculum.

Some of the most racially contentious encounters can happen between a Black family and a whitewashed curriculum. Often White teachers are unaware how racialized realities impact the school curriculum. In this case, the curriculum was not even discussed as a problem in the scenario. While there are differing perspectives on Tayla's behaviour, there must also be an examination of the teacher's behaviour and the curriculum offerings. It is imperative that human behaviour and the curriculum undergo a clear and comprehensive assessment before any action is taken. Unfortunately, the emotional and mental health of Tayla was not a factor from the teacher's perspective. It is good that Tayla was able to support self-care as she expressed her feelings to her parents.

A HOSTILE RECEPTION

Dolly arrived at her breast screening appointment in a rush. The screening took place in a mobile unit where parking was problematic. Dolly quickly parked her car and raced to the entrance of the mobile unit to inform the receptionist that she needed to purchase a parking ticket. The receptionist looked surprised when she arrived and asked 'So who are you? Do you have an appointment?' Dolly was taken aback by the hostile reception she experienced, and replied, 'Good afternoon. I was trying to explain . . .'

Dolly was interrupted with a dismissal hand wave and the interaction quickly went downhill. Dolly tried to keep focused and headed to the parking machine to purchase the ticket, returning in under a minute. The receptionist again asked if she had an appointment. Dolly replied, 'Yes, of course, the appointment is for 3:30 p.m.' Feeling put off, Dolly asked the receptionist if she was always equally hostile to other Black women or all women coming for an important screening test. The receptionist was stunned by the direct question and blamed her snappy behaviour on the fact that it was her first day back after quarantine and that she was worried about catching COVID-19. Dolly replied that how she greeted her was not good and that she should perhaps consider finding a job which didn't involve interacting with the public, especially when women were already feeling anxious about a mammogram.

The receptionist stared at Dolly in defiance and a deadly silence followed, as Dolly waited to be seen.

Her appointment time arrived and unfortunately the person doing the screening turned out to be the radiologist/receptionist who had displayed the hostile behaviour. Dolly entered the room and the deadly silence continued. Dolly noticed her heart had started to beat faster, and the radiologist asked if she was OK with her doing the screening. Initially, Dolly replied yes, then she asked what the screening involved and decided to ask for another person. The radiologist/receptionist left swiftly, and the other radiologist took over. Dolly was very relieved and asked the other radiologist if the receptionist had been offered any cultural competence training.

This everyday experience is important because some people do not even realise they are being racist. The radiologist/receptionist had not maintained the professional standard of behaviour expected in a healthcare environment. Her vitriol attitude, lame excuse and defiant behaviour is indicative of someone who is defending the exposure of their racism. Dolly could have responded in a more aggressive manner but chose to ask questions and respond to the situation with dignity.

CONCLUSION

This chapter offers strategies to enable Black people the power to 'Flip the script' on sophisticated and everyday racism. The goal of the strategies is to change the outcome of racist behaviours directed against Black people, and Black women and girls. Though the narratives encapsulate the lived experiences of everyday reality for many Black women and girls, these experiences are relatable to other racially minoritized people. Given the narratives that have been shared in this chapter, it is natural that each will trigger a different thought process, experience memory and strategy for handling everyday racism. The aim has been to illustrate how difficult dialogues, situations, experiences and behaviours can be tackled, then managed. The pressures and racial stress that Black women are subjected to can be insurmountable. The ultimate survival disposition, however, is to be resilient and strong, while hiding vulnerability and emotions. This reality has its roots in the violent exploitation of women in slavery (see chapter 2). Enslaved women retained their resilience in the face of unspeakable treatment. Giving in to emotion was condemned and thus controlling emotive expression was a survival skill. This tradition of emotional toughness is an illusion. It is based on disassociation, where you are so traumatized that you emotionally, physically or mentally disconnect from the incident, experience or dialogue.

Disassociation enables victims to survive on a daily basis and without it racial trauma would become overwhelming. Unfortunately, disassociation from racial trauma does not last and there is a time when racist incidents, experiences, conversations and behaviours must be handled. The strategies provided in this chapter support a healthy way to handle sophisticated and everyday racism.

Chapter 9

Conclusion

In the course of this book, we have attempted to provide a detailed analysis of everyday racism experienced by Black women, comprising African and African Caribbean, within the British context. At the very beginning we sourced the discussion through our own portraits which aimed to capture in a microcosmic way some of the complexities and maze of racial identity. In chapter 1 notions of 'race', racisms, institutional, structural and anti-Black racism were important starting points as bases for the discussion on everyday racism. Ideas of Whiteness in relation to Blackness were discussed. Conceptually, race is an unsustainable category but constitutes a social reality which we aimed to encapsulate throughout this book. Although racism is established as the central feature of Black women's lives, we, nonetheless, explored the experiences of Black women through an intersectional prism of race, class and gender. Fortuitously, we were able to critique some of the findings of the highly controversial CRED or Sewell Report (2021). The Report found no evidence for the continued use of the term 'institutional racism' contemporarily, suggesting that institutional racism was a thing of the past. We demonstrated that institutional racism is indeed alive and well and manifested in everyday practices, and there is no dearth of research regarding the negative impact of racism in major areas of life such as income, health and education.

Racism has been discussed in the earlier chapters of this book. It has been identified as complex and giving rise to an ever-evolving set of challenging behaviours towards Black and minority groups. Decades have passed as we have tried to understand and recommend ways in which communities are able to address approaches to tackling everyday racism. There have been many different initiatives based on the need for change. Generation after generation of young people have reinvented the wheel without recognising that much has already been said and done.

New epithets are used for the same solutions to racism. Similar ideas have been around for decades but may appear innovative because they are labelled differently. One example is the International Day for the Elimination of Racial Discrimination (established by the UN in 1966 and marked on 21 March 2021). 'Juneteenth' became a federal holiday on 18 June 2021, celebrating the end of slavery in the United States. We have yet to reap the benefits of this type of initiative.

The terms used to denote Black people have also changed over time. One example is the change from the term 'Negro' in the early twentieth century, which developed into the 'N' word, then 'coloured people' and now 'Black', as discussed in chapter 1. There is an urgent need for a national and international debate on appropriate terminologies for populations of African descent. If not now, when? The manner of describing the population under consideration is of paramount importance.

Research on race, ethnicity and society, including health, is growing in Western Europe, following a much longer tradition in North America. The terms and concepts of ethnicity need to be explicitly defined to permit a better understanding of research across diverse research communities and to facilitate regional and international comparisons. Despite the ongoing debate, terms such as Negro, Black, Black African, African Caribbean and African American are still entrenched in scientific writings and may be both offensive and inaccurate. There is a recognition that both race and ethnicity are difficult concepts, and while there is a conceptual distinction between race and ethnicity, these terms are often used interchangeably or as synonyms.

The traditional concept of race refers to biological homogeneity as defined by a few phenotypical features. The term was first introduced in 1749, when it served as a convenient label; it was not based on scientific evidence. The current consensus is that race as a term has very little value. The genes responsible for different physical characteristics (such as skin colour and facial features) continue to create our identities although they account for a very small proportion of our genome. Scientists continue to unravel the mysteries of DNA, but it is clear that the multiple unique combinations of characteristics which make up an individual are not dictated by the colour of a person's skin. The unstable concept of 'race' nevertheless continues to underpin much of the discourse in social science.

Martin Luther King's famous 'I have a dream' speech, made on the steps of the Lincoln Memorial in Washington on 28 August 1963, is relevant here:

> I have a dream that little children will one day live in a nation where they will not be judged by the color of their skin but by the content of their character.

Conclusion

Agyemany et al. (2005) argue that ethnicity is a multidimensional concept which is neither simple nor consistent as it comprises one or more of the following: shared geographical origins or social background, a common language or religious tradition and a shared culture or traditions that are distinctive and maintained between generations, which leads to a sense of group identity. The characteristics that define ethnicity are not fixed and have changed and will continue to change over time, which make the use of the term difficult, especially in research. In some parts of Europe, the term 'race' is being abandoned in place of ethnicity, whereas in the United States, both ethnicity and race are being used interchangeably. In the United States race has been used as a proxy indicator for socio-economic deprivation, which then negates, for example, the existence of economically advantaged African Americans.

Although socio-economic status is crucial in exploring ethnic disparity in societal issues, it is inadequate when seeking to understand ethnic differences. The notion of self-definition is therefore gathering pace.

The drawback to this approach is that people change their perception of their own identity over time depending on context, although this fluidity also has its strengths. Terms such as Black, Black African and African American (include AFRICAN Caribbean) hide the extensive heterogeneity within the groups of African descent populations in the United States and the United Kingdom. Using these broad terms does not harmonise with the self-definition of ethnicity. Lack of sensitivity to nuances of identity weakens the value of ethnic categorisation, for instance, as a means of providing culturally appropriate professional services.

The complexity of 'Black' as an ethnic marker and identity as a tangled web were discussed in chapter 2. Very often nomenclatures for people of colour including women exist without their consultation, and Whiteness is normalised. Much of this goes back to the plantocracy system embedded in chattel slavery critical to our understanding of the subsequent colour-coded system that developed and its interplay in the lives of Black women. The 'Big House' was used as a metaphor for the interactions of Black people in White spaces and we coined the term 'White woman syndrome' (WWS) to describe the ambivalent and at times aversion that some White women exhibited towards Black women. We argued that much of this antipathy is based on historical memory retention. The issue of a Black identity was interrogated, and the multi-layered dimensions of identity were explored to delineate the identity of Black women from Africa compared to those from the Caribbean. Carol Dweck (2006) discusses the role of mindsets which she describes as powerful beliefs that are in one's mind. She sees it as expanding or developing the self to learn something new. It can be argued that a shift or change in mindsets is key to unlocking the potential of agency in responding strategically to everyday racism.

Chapter 3 defines and elaborates on the concept of sophisticated and everyday racism. A framework for understandings of sophisticated and everyday racism is provided. Manifestations of the diverse forms of racism experienced by Black people in a range of contexts are detailed. These elucidate the strong negative impact on the well-being of minorities and underline the privilege enjoyed by White people. The phenomenon of White supremacy is also mentioned.

Language is an important aspect of identity for any group and research on Black women in Britain is often investigated within the broader context of institutional and systemic racism, without regards to its expressions through communicative interactions. In chapter 4 it was identified that Black women in Britain speak a number of different languages and dialects and many tend to be multilingual. We first explored some of the languages spoken by Black females in this chapter. The African world view reflecting the African community system (ACS) and ethnography of speech underpinned the discussion on language style of Black women in the diaspora, including Britain. The presentation of self with an in-depth discussion on ideas of 'loudness', among some Black females in education and its polar opposite silence as a strategic tool utilised by some females were featured in this chapter. It also explored non-verbal interactions and paralinguistic facets of speech, and the denotations of these components encoded in the communication of Black women, particularly in Britain. Importantly, attention was drawn to the implications of the language style in domains of education and the professional environment.

We moved from the background and theoretical context to the overarching theme of managing sophisticated and everyday racism. The challenges to the success of some Black women were rigorously investigated in chapter 5 centred on four key areas: the education of Black females; the education of their children; parenting; and their participation in the labour market. The discussion first revolved around the notion of success. The chapter outlined the inhibitors to the success of African and African Caribbean women. It reviewed literature confirming that Black female students have high participation rates in higher education, reported on both sides of the Atlantic. As demonstrated in this chapter, high educational achievement among Black women does not guarantee success in the labour market. Not only have these women experienced obstacles in acquiring their own education; some of these women, particularly African Caribbean mothers, face difficulties in accessing quality education for their offspring. For some African women the pursuit of education, especially in the past, entailed their children being fostered by White families. Parenting as an important element in the lives of many females was also discussed in this chapter. The racialised discourse of the gang culture for some young Black men has significantly affected the lives of some mothers, especially when their offspring are embroiled in the criminal justice system where they are overrepresented. Some African parents have sent their children back to their homeland as a remedial strategy for bringing recalcitrant young people in line and this too has not been an easy option which has ramifications for both mothers and children. The challenges for Black women in the labour market are an area of concern and experience ethnic penalties. For West African women in particular, many of whom are highly educated, their academic background is often incompatible with their professional profile, with many being confined to the care industry. The income levels of Black women lag behind their White female counterparts. In organisations in the United Kingdom, White women have to break the proverbial glass ceiling, but for Black women there is a concrete ceiling to smash.

The focus for chapter 6 was on research into the mental and emotional state of some young Black women. We explored through narratives how some were suffering silently and their well-being was compromised as a result of racism. The young women and girls in these narratives have been subjected to the sophisticated and everyday racism detailed in chapter 3. The internal oppression they have suffered has frequently done irreparable damage to their mental health.

The remaining chapters of the book dealt with managing sophisticated and everyday racism. Chapter 7 featured the dislocation of Whiteness by the presence of Black bodies in the academy. The experiences of Black women in the academy are documented and analysed in this chapter. The literature on Black academics in the United Kingdom is emerging although their numbers are relatively small. The positionality of both White and Black educators is critical to locating issues of race, class and gender or its intersectionality.

Chapter 8 is pivotal in that it examines how Black women can adopt strategies to manage sophisticated and everyday racism. We use the term 'flip the script' and change the narrative as reference points for these strategic approaches. Black people can potentially use the suggestions in this chapter to counter the sophisticated and everyday racism they are subjected to.

It is evident that Britain is not yet a post-racial society which has completed the long journey to equality of opportunity. We know that prejudice and discrimination can still cast an ominous shadow over our lives. Outright racism still exists in Britain, whether it surfaces as graffiti on someone's business, violence in the street or prejudice in the labour market. It can cause a unique and indelible pain for the individual affected and has no place in any civilised society, but the fact remains it is alive and well.

The more insidious form of racism, sophisticated racism, remains uncharted territory and is the central theme of the book alongside strategic tools for managing diverse and complex forms of racism. We hope this book has offered a fresh approach to discourses on race by examining how Black women can employ their own agency in areas such as education and employment and live productive and fulfilling lives.

White people, particularly men, continue to be in a position of dominance because of power structures, which are enacted and re-enacted in relationships in a number of domains, for example, in the workplace, gender relationships and everyday social encounters. Black women in societies such as Britain are an oppressed group, subordinated by both their gender and racial caste status in the power pyramid. As Harris (2015) puts it, 'Our authentic collective and individual selves are usually hidden by racist and sexist stereotypes that we can't seem to shake – or rather, images that other folks won't let us shake' (xii). Irrespective of class we are faced with racism in our daily encounters.

We hope that this book has provided a light in the dark shadows by equipping Black women and the wider community of colour with some strategies to manage sophisticated and everyday racism.

References

Ackah, William, Dodson, Jualynne, and Smith, Drew R. (eds) (2017) *Religion, Culture Spirituality in Africa and the African Diaspora.* New York/Abingdon, Oxon: Routledge, pp. 115–128.

Adams, M., Bell, L. A., and Griffin, P. (eds) (1997) *Teaching for Diversity and Social Justice: A Sourcebook.* New York: Routledge.

Advance, H. E. (2020) *Equality + Higher Education Staff Statistical Report.* London: Advance HE.

Afridi, A. (2004) *System or Stereotype: What Can We Do to Mainstream Anti Discriminatory Practice and Effective Teaching and Learning in Birmingham Schools* (Research Report). Birmingham: Birmingham Race Action Partnership.

Aguirre, A. (2000) *Women and Minority Faculty in the Academic Workplace: Recruitment, Retention and Academic Culture.* San Francisco: Jossey-Bass.

Agyemang, C., Bhopal, R., & Bruijnzeels, M. (2005). Negro, Black, Black African, African Caribbean, African American or what? Labelling African origin populations in the health arena in the 21st century. *Journal of Epidemiology & Community Health,* 59 (12), 1014–1018.

Ahmed, S. (2004) *The Cultural Politics of Emotion.* New York: Routledge.

Ahmed, S. (2009) Embodying Diversity: Problems and Paradoxes for Black Feminists? *Race Ethnicity and Education,* 12 (1): 41–52.

Ahmed, S. (2012) *On Being Included: Racism and Diversity in Institutional Life.* Durham, NC: Duke University Press.

Aldred, J., and Ogbo, K. (eds) (2010) *The Black Church in the 21st Century.* London: Darton, Longman and Todd.

Alexander, C., and Shankley, W. (2020) Ethnic Inequalities in the State Education System in England. In B. Bryne, C. Alexander, O. Khan, J. Nazroo, and W. Shankley (eds) *Inequality in the State of the Nation.* Bristol: University of Bristol, Policy Press.

Altink, H. (2005) Deviant and Dangerous: Pro-Slavery Representations of Jamaican Slave Women's Sexuality, c. 1780–1834. *Slavery and Abolition,* 26 (2): 271–288.

Anderson, C. (2016) *White Rage: The Unspoken Truth of Our Racial Divide*. New York: Bloomsbury.

Anim-Addo, Joan (2014) Activist-Mothers Maybe, Sisters Surely? Black British Feminism, Absence and Transformation. *Feminist Review*, 108: 44–60.

Anzaldúa, G. (1987) *Borderlands/La Frontera: The New Mestiza*. San Francisco, CA: Aunt Lute Books.

Appiah, Kwame Anthony (2018) *The Lies That Bind: Rethinking Identity–Creed, Country, Colour, Class, Culture*. New York: Liveright.

Archer, L. (2008) The New Neoliberal Subjects? Young/er Academics' Constructions of Professional Identity. *Journal of Education Policy*, 23 (3): 265–285.

Archer, L., and Francis, B. (2007) *Understanding Minority Ethnic Achievement: Race, Gender, Class and 'Success.'* London: Routledge.

Archer, L., Hollingsworth, S., and Halsall, A. (2007) 'University's not for Me – I'm a Nike Person': Urban, Working-Class Young People's Negotiations of 'Style', Identity and Educational Engagement. *Sociology*, 41 (2): 219–237.

Arday, J., and Mirza, H. S. (eds) (2018) *Dismantling Race in Higher Education: Racism, Whiteness and Decolonising the Academy*. London: Palgrave Macmillan.

Arthur, J. (2008) *The African Diaspora in the United States and Europe: The Ghanaian Experience*. Aldershot: Ashgate Publishing Group.

Avent Harris, J. R. (2021). The Black Superwoman in spiritual bypass: Black women's use of religious coping and implications for mental health professionals. *Journal of Spirituality in Mental Health*, 23(2), 180–196.

Bakare-Yusef, B. (1997) Raregrooves and Raregroovers: A Matter of Taste, Difference and Identity 81 Bibi Bakare-Yusuf. In H. Mirza (ed.) *Black British Feminism: A Reader*. London: Routledge, pp. 81–96.

Bailkin, J. (2009, March) The Postcolonial Family? West African Children, Private Fostering, and the British State. *The Journal of Modern History*, 81: 87–121.

Baldwin, J. (1955) *Notes on a Native Son*. Boston, MA: Beacon Books.

Barone, C. (2006) Cultural Capital, Ambition and the Explanation of Inequalities in Learning Outcomes: A Comparative Analysis. *Sociology*, 40 (6): 1039–1058.

Bartman, C. (2015) African American Women in Higher Education: Issues and Support Strategies. *College Students Affairs Leadership*, 2 (2), Article 5: 1–9.

Basit, T. N., Mcnamara, O., Roberts, L., Carrington, B., Maguire, M., and Woodrow, D. (2007) The Bar is Slightly Higher: The Perception of Racism in Teacher Education. *Cambridge Journal of Education*, 37 (2): 279–298.

Basit, T. N., Roberts, L., McNamara, O., Carrington, B., Maguire, M., and Woodrow, D. (2006) Did they Jump or Were They Pushed? Reasons Why Minority Ethnic Trainees Withdraw From Initial Teacher Training Courses. *British Educational Research Journal*, 32 (3): 387–410.

BBC Two – Black and British: A Forgotten History (Television Programmes Black and British: A Forgotten History).

Beck, V., Fuller, A., and Unwin, L. (2006) Safety in Stereotypes? The Impact of Gender and 'Race' on Young People's Perceptions of Their Post-Compulsory Education and Labour Market Opportunities. *British Educational Research Journal*, 32 (5): 667–686.

Bell, E., and Golombisky, K. (2004) Voices and Silences in Our Classrooms: Strategies for Mapping Trails Among Sex/Gender, Race, and Class. *Women's Studies in Communication*, 27 (3): 294–329.

Berger, P., and Luckmann, T. (1971) *The Social Construction of Reality: A Treatise in the Sociology of Knowledge*. London: Penguin.

Bernard-Allen, V. (2016) *It is Not Good to Be Alone; Singleness and the Black Seventh-Day Adventist Woman*. London: Institute of Education, UCL.

Bernstein, B. A., & Pachter, L. M. (2003). Cultural considerations in children's pain. *Pain in Infants, Children, and Adolescents*. Philadelphia: Lippincott, Williams and Wilkins, 142–156.

Berthoud (2009) Patterns of Non-Employment, and of Disadvantage, in a Recession. Working Paper No. 2009–23, Institute for Social and Economic Research, University of Essex. https://www.ippr.org/news-and-media/press-releases/recession-leaves-almost-half-young-Black-people-unemployed-finds-ippr (Accessed 30 May 2020).

Bhavnani, R., Mirza, H. S., and Meetoo, V. (2005) *Tackling the Roots of Racism: Lessons for Success*. Bristol: The Polity Press, University of Bristol.

Bhopal, K. (2014) *The Experience of BME Academics in Higher Education: Aspirations in the Face of Inequality*. London: The Leadership Foundation.

Bhopal, K. (2018) *White Privilege: The Myth of a Post-Racial Society*. Bristol: Policy Press.

Bhopal, K. (2020) Gender, Ethnicity and Career Progression in UK Higher Education: A Case Study Analysis. *Research Papers in Education*, 35 (6): 706–721.

Bignall, T., Jeraj, S., Helsby, E., and Butt J. (2019) *Racial Disparities in Mental Health: Literature and Evidence Review*. Health and Wellbeing Alliance and Race Equality Foundation. https://raceequalityfoundation.org.uk/wp-content/uploads/2020/03/mental-health-report-v5-2.pdf (Accessed 15 April 2021).

Bivens, D. (2005). What is internalized racism. *Flipping the script: White privilege and community building*, 43–51.

Black, Asian and Minority Ethnic Student Attainment Gap at University: Closing the Gap (2019a) Universities & National Union of Students. https://www.universities.ac./policy-and-analysis/reports/Pages/bame-student-attainment--universities-closing-the-gap.aspx (Accessed 30 May 2020).

Black, Asian and Minority Ethnic Student Attainment at Universities: Closing the Gap (2019b, May) https://www.universities.ac./policy-and-analysis/reports/Documents/2019/bame-student-attainment--universities-closing-the-gap.pdf.

Blair, M., and Maylor, U. (1993) Issues and Concerns for Black Women Teachers in Training. In I. Siraj-Blatchford (ed.) *'Race', Gender and the Education of Teachers*. Buckingham: Open University Press, pp. 55–73.

Bledsoe, Caroline H., and Sow, Papa (2011, August) Back to Africa: Second Chances for the Children of West African Immigrants. *Journal of Marriage and Family*, 73: 747–762.

Bodi, Erzsébet, and Goldthorpe, John H. (2018) *Social Mobility and Education in Britain: Research, Politics and Policy*. Cambridge: Cambridge University Press.

Bostock, Jo (2014) *Meaning of Success: Insights From Women at Cambridge.* Cambridge: Cambridge University Press.

Bourdieu, P. (1986) The Forms of Capital. In J. Richardson (ed.) *Handbook of Theory and Research for the Sociology of Education.* New York: Greenwood, pp. 241–258.

Bourdieu, P. (1992) *Language and Symbolic Power.* Cambridge: Polity Press.

Bourdieu, P., and Passeron, J. C. (1977) *Reproduction in Education, Society and Culture.* Beverly Hills, CA: Sage.

Brah, A., and Phoenix, A. (2004) Ain't I a Woman? Revisiting Intersectionality. *Journal of International Women Studies*, 5 (3): 75–86.

Brescoll, V. (2016) Leading With Their Hearts? How Gender Stereotypes of Emotion Lead to Biased Evaluations of Female Leaders. *The Leadership Quarterly*, 27: 415–428.

Brodkin, K. (1999) *How Jews Became White Folk and What That Says About Race Relations in America.* New Brunswick, NJ: Rutgers University Press.

Brooks, R. (2009) *Racial Justice in the Age of Obama.* Princeton, NJ: Princeton University Press.

Brown, K. D. (2014) Teaching in Color: A Critical Race Theory in Education Analysis of the Literature on Pre-Service Teachers of Color and Teacher Education in the US. *Race, Ethnicity and Education*, 17 (3): 326–345.

Bryan, B. Dadzie, and Scafe, S. (1985) *Heart of the Race: Black Women's Lives in Britain.* London: Virago.

Bryne, B., Alexander, C., Khan, O., Nazroo, J., and Shankley, W. (eds) (2020) *Ethnic, Race and Inequality in the UK: State of the Nation.* Bristol: University of Bristol, Policy Press.

Buckner, L., Yeandle, S., & Botcherby, S. (2007). Ethnic minority women and local labour markets. *Manchester: Equal Opportunities Commission*, 772.

Bukodi, Erzsébet, and Goldthorpe, John H. (2018) *Social Mobility and Education in Britain: Research, Politics and Policy.* Cambridge: Cambridge University Press.

Burke, B., Cropper, A., and Harrison, P. (2000) Real or Imagined – Black Women's Experiences in the Academy. *Community, Work and Family*, 3 (3): 297–310.

Butler, A. S. (2007) *Women in the Church of God in Christ: Making a Sanctified World.* Chapel Hill: University of North Carolina Press.

Byfield, C. (2010) Education and the Black Church. In J. Aldred and K. Ogbo (eds) *The Black Church in the 21st Century.* London: Darton, Longman and Todd, pp. 148–163.

Byrd, M. (2009) Telling Our Stories of Leadership: If We Don't Tell Them They Won't Be Told. *Advances in Developing Human Resources*, 11 (5): 582–605.

Caldwell, L. D., and Bledsoe, K. L. (2019) Can Social Justice Live in a House of Structural Racism? A Question for the Field of Evaluation. *American Journal of Evaluation*, 40 (1): 6–18.

Callender, C. (1997) *Education for Empowerment: the Practice and Philosophies of Black Teacher.* Stoke-on-Trent: Trentham Books.

Callender, C., Robinson, Y., and Robertson, A. (2006) *The Impact of Ethnic Monitoring on the Achievement of Black and Minority Ethnic Students in ITE*. London: Report for Multiverse.

Calmore, J. (1995) Racialized Space and the Culture of Segregation: "Hewing a Stone of Hope From a Mountain of Despair." *University of Pennsylvania Law Review*, 143 (5): 1233–1273.

Caraballo, L. (2019) Being "Loud": Identities-in-Practice in a Figured World of Achievement. *American Educational Research Journal*, 56 (4): 1281–1317.

Carbado, D., and Gulati, M. (2004) Race to the Top of the Corporate Ladder: What Minorities Do When They Get There. *Washington and Lee Law Review*, 61: 1645–1694.

Carrington, B., and Tomlin, T. (2000) Towards a More Inclusive Profession: Teacher Recruitment and Ethnicity. *European Journal of Teacher Education*, 23 (2): 139–157.

Carter, J., Fenton, S., and Modood, T. (1999) *Ethnicity and Employment in Higher Education*. London: Policy Studies Institute.

Castro-Salazar, R., and Bagley, C. (2010) 'Ni de aqui ni from there'. Navigating Between Contexts: Counter-Narratives of Undocumented Mexican Students in the United States. *Race Ethnicity and Education*, 13 (1): 23–40.

Chakelian, Anoosh (2020, 15 June) The 375 Government Recommendations Boris Johnson Could Use Instead of Launching Yet Another Commission on Inequality. *New Statesman Online*. https://www.newstatesman.com/2020/06/375-government-recommendations-boris-johnson-could-use-instead-launching-yet-another (Accessed 9 April 2021).

Channer, Y. (1995) *I Am a Promise: The School Achievement of British African Caribbeans*. Trentham: Stoke-on-Trent.

Chase, S. (2010) Narrative Inquiry: Multiple Lenses, Approaches, Voices. In W. Luttrell (ed.) *Qualitative Educational Research: Readings in Reflexive Methodology and Transformative Practice*. New York and London: Routledge, pp. 208–236.

Cheung, S. Y. (2014). Ethno-religious minorities and labour market integration: generational advancement or decline?. *Ethnic and Racial Studies*, 37(1), 140–160.

Childs, E. C. (2005) Looking Behind the Stereotypes of the "Angry Black Woman:" An Exploration of Black Women's Responses to Interracial Relationships. *Gender and Society*, 19 (4): 544–561.

Christie, P. (2003) *Language in Jamaica*. Kingston: Jamaica Arawak.

Church of England (2021, April) From Lament to Action. The Report of the Archbishops' Taskforce. https://www.churchofengland.org/sites/default/files/2021-04/FromLamentToAction-report.pdf (Accessed 22 April 2021).

Clarke, S. (2008) Culture and Identity. In T. Bennett and J. Frow (eds) *The Sage Handbook of Cultural Analysis*. London: Sage Publications, pp. 510–529.

Coakley, L. (2016) African Migrants in Ireland: The Negotiation of Belonging and Family Life. In Mary Gilmartin and Allen White (eds) *Migrations: Ireland in a Global World*. Manchester: Manchester University Press.

Coleman, Coard B. (1971) *How the West Indian Child is Made Educationally Sub-Normal in the British School System.* London: New Beacon Books.

Collins, P. H. (1998) *Race, Class, and Gender: An Anthology.* Belmont, CA: Wadsworth Publishing, Minnesota Press.

Collins, P. H. (2004) *Black Sexual Politics: African Americans, Gender, and the New Racism.* New York: Routledge.

Collins, P. H. (2009) *Black Feminist Thought: Knowledge, Consciousness and the Politics of Empowerment*, 3rd edition. London and New York: Routledge.

Commission on Race and Ethnic Disparities (2021, March) The Report. https://assets.publishing.service.gov.uk/government/uploads/system/uploads/attachment_data/file/974507/20210331_-_CRED_Report_-_FINAL_-_Web_Accessible.pdf (Accessed 7 April 2021).

Commission on Race and Ethnic Disparities: The Report (Updated/Amended April 2021). https://www.gov.uk/government/publications/the-report-of-the-commission-on-race-and-ethnic-disparities/foreword-introduction-and-full-recommendations#fn:1.

Connolly, P. (1998) *Racism, Gender Identities and Young Children: Social Relations in a Multi-Ethnic Inner-City Primary School.* London: Routledge.

Connor, H., Tyers, C., Modood, T., and Hillage, J. (2004a) *Why the Difference? A Closer Look at Higher Education Minority Ethnic Students and Graduates* (Research Report No. 552). London: Department for Education and Skills.

Connor, H., Tyers, C., Modood, T., and Hillage, J. (2004b) *Why the Difference? A Closer Look at Higher Education Minority Ethnic Students and Graduates. Department for Education and Skills Research Report 552.* London: Department for Education and Skills. http:wwwdfes.gov.uk/research/data/uploadfiles.

Cooper, C. (2007) School Choice as "Motherwork": Valuing African-American Women's Educational Advocacy and Resistance. *International Journal of Qualitative Studies in Education*, 20 (5): 491–512.

Coote A., and Gill, T. (1981) *Women's Rights: A Practical Guide*, 3rd edition. Harmondsworth: Penguin.

Cork, L. (2005) *Supporting Black Pupils and Parents: Understanding and Improving Home School Relations.* Abingdon, Oxon: Routledge.

Cose, E. (1993) *The Rage of a Privileged Class.* New York: Harper Collins.

Cousins, S. (2019) *Overcoming Everyday Racism.* London: Jessica Kingsley Publishers.

Crenshaw, K. (1989) *Demarginalizing the Intersection of Race and Sex: A Black Feminist Critique of Antidiscrimination Doctrine, Feminist Theory, and Antiracist Politics.* University of Chicago Legal Forum, pp. 139–167.

Croxford, R. (2018) Ethnic Minority Academics Earn Less Than White Colleagues. *The BBC* [Online]. https://www.bbc.co./news/education-46473269 (Accessed 10 May 2020).

Crozier, G., and Davies, J. (2007) Hard to Reach Parents or Hard to Reach Schools? A Discussion of Home-School Relations, With Particular Reference to Bangladeshi and Pakistani Parents. *British Educational Research Journal*, 33 (3): 295–313.

Cunningham, M., and Hargreaves, L. (2007) *Minority Ethnic Teachers' Professional Experiences: Evidence From the Teacher Status Project.* DfES Research Report RR853.

Davis, A. (1981) Reflections on the Black Woman's Role in the Community of Slaves. *Black Scholar,* 12 (6): 2–15.

Davis, S. M. (2018) Taking Back the Power: An Analysis of Black Women's Communicative Resistance. *Review of Communication,* 18 (4): 301–318.

DeGruy, J. (2005) *Post Traumatic Slave Syndrome: America's Legacy of Enduring Injury and Healing.* Milwaukie, Oregon: Uptone Press.

Delgado, R. (ed.) (1995) *Critical Race Theory: The Cutting Edge.* Philadelphia, PA: Temple University Press.

Delgado, R., and Stefancic, J. (eds) (1997) *Critical White Studies: Looking Behind the Mirror.* Philadelphia: Temple University Press.

Delgado, R., and Stefancic, J. (eds) (2005) *The Derrick Bell Reader.* New York: New York University Press.

Delgado Bernal, D. (2002) Critical Race Theory, Latino Critical Theory, and Critical Raced-Gendered Epistemologies: Recognizing Students of Color as Holders and Creators of Knowledge. *Qualitative Inquiry,* 8 (1): 105–126.

Demie, F., and Lewis, K. (2010) White Working-Class Achievement: An Ethnographic Study of Barriers to Learning in Schools. *Educational Studies,* 37 (11): 245–264.

Demie, F., and McLean, C. (2007) Raising the Achievement of African Heritage Pupils: A Case Study of Good Practice in British Schools. *Educational Studies,* 33 (4): 415–434.

Demie, F., Tong, R., Taplin, A., and Hutter, C. (2006) *The Achievement of African Heritage Pupils: Good Practice for Lambeth.* Research and Statistics Unit, London Borough of Lambeth, March.

Department for Education (2020) On Absence and Exclusion. https://www.ethnicity-facts-figures.service.gov./education-skills-and-training/absence-and-exclusions/pupil-exclusions/latest#permanent-exclusions-by-ethnicity.

Department for Education and Skills (2006) *Ethnicity and Education: The Evidence on Minority Ethnic Pupils Aged 15–16.* Research Topic Papers. London: Department for Education and Skills.

DfE (Department for Education) (2014) *Statistical First Release GCSE and Equivalent Attainment by Pupil Characteristics in England, 2012/13, SFR 05/2014.* London: DfE.

Diangelo, R. (2018a) *White Fragility.* London: Beacon Press.

Diangelo, R. (2018b) *White Fragility: Why It's So Hard for White People to Talk About Racism.* Boston, MA: Beacon Press.

Dixson, A. D., and Rousseau, C. K. (2005) And We Are Still Not Saved: Critical Race Theory Ten Years Later. *Race Ethnicity and Education,* 8 (1): 7–27.

Dodgson, E. (1986) *Motherland: West Indian Women to Britain in 1950s.* London: Heinemann Educational Books.

Drew (Forthcoming) *Racialization and Black Health: Transatlantic Social and Religious Perspectives.*

Du Bois, W. E. B. (1903 [1995]) *The Souls of Black Folk*. New York: Penguin Putnam.
Du Bois, W. E. B. (1970 [1939]) *Black Folk, Then and Now: An Essay in the History and Sociology of the Negro Race*. New York: Octagon Books.
Du Bois, W. E. B. (1971a [1897]) The Conservation of Races. In Julius Lester (ed.) *The Seventh Son: The Thought and Writings of W.E.B. Du Bois*. New York: Random House, Vol. I, pp. 176–187.
Du Bois, W. E. B. (1971b [1935]) A Negro Nation Within the Nation. In Julius Lester (ed.) *The Seventh Son: The Thought and Writings of W.E.B. Du Bois*. New York: Random House, Vol. II, pp. 399–407.
Du Bois, W. E. B. (1977 [1935]) *Black Reconstruction in the United States, 1860–1880*. New York: Kraus International.
Duncan, S., Edwards, R., Reynolds, T., and Alldred, P. (2003) Motherhood, Paid Work and Partnering: Values and Theories: *Work, Employment and Society*, 17 (2): 309–330.
Duveen, G. (1993) The Development of Social Representations of Gender. *Papers on Social Representations*, 2 (3): 171–177. http://www.psr.jku.at/PSR1993/2_1993Duvee.pdf (Accessed 7 January 2020).
Duveen, G., and Lloyd, B. (1986) The Significance of Social Identities. *British Journal of Social Psychology*, 25: 219–230.
Dyer, R. (1997) *White*. London: Routledge.
Eddo-Lodge (2018) *Why I'm No Longer Talking to White People About Race*. London: Bloomsbury.
EHRC (Equality Human Rights Commission) (2010) *How Fair is Britain? The First Triennial Review*. London: Equality and Human Rights Commission.
Ellison, R. (1952) *Invisible Man*. New York: Random House.
Emecheta, Buchi (1983) *Second Class Citizen*. London: George Braziller.
Ellis, C., and Bochner, A. P. (2000) Auth-Oethnography, Personal Narrative, Reflexivity: Researcher as Subject. In N. Denzin and Y. S. Lincoln (eds) *The Handbook of Qualitative Research*, 2nd edition. Thousand Oak, CA: Sage, pp. 733–768.
Equality Challenge Unit (ECU) (2011) *The Experience of Black and Minority Ethnic Staff in Higher Education in England*. London: ECU.
Erickson, F. (1984) Rhetoric, Anecdote and Rhapsody: Coherence Strategies in a Conversation Among Black American Adolescents. In D. Tannen (ed.) *Coherence in Spoken and Written Discourse*. Norwood, NJ: Ablex, pp. 81–154.
Essed, P. (1991) *Understanding Everyday Racism: An Interdisciplinary Theory*. Newbury Park, CA: Sage.
Evans, G. (1988) Those Loud Black Girls. In D. Spender and E. Sarah (eds) *Learning to Lose: Sexism and Education*. London: The Women's Press, pp. 183–190.
Evans-Winters, V. E., and Esposito, J. (2010) Other People's Daughters: Critical Race Feminism and Black Girls' Education. *Educational Foundations*, 24 (Winter/Spring): 11–24.
Fanon, F. (1967) *Black Skin, White Mask*. New York: Grove Press.
Fordham, S. (1993) "Those Loud Black Girls": (Black) Women, Silence, and Gender "Passing" in the Academy. *Anthropology and Education Quarterly*, 24 (1): 3–32.

Forson, C. (2007) *Social Embeddedness, "Choices" and Constraints in Small Business Start-Up: Black Women in Business*. PhD Thesis, Queen Mary University of London.

Foster, M. (1989) It's Cookin' Now: A Performance Analysis of the Speech Events of a Black Teacher in an Urban Community College. *Language in Society*, 18 (1): 1–29.

Foster, M. (1991) Constancy, Connectedness and Constraints in the Lives of African American Teachers. *NWSA Journal*, 3 (2): 233–261.

Foucault, M. (1979) *Discipline and Punish: The Birth of the Prison*. New York: Scocken.

Freire, J. L. (2016) Whitening, Mixing, Darkening, and Developing: Everything But Indigenous. *Latin American Research Review*, 51 (3): 142–160.

Garner, S. (2006) The Uses of Whiteness: What Sociologists Working on Europe Can Draw From US Research on Whiteness. *Sociology*, 40 (2): 257–275. GCSE Results (Attainment 8). www.GOV.UK https://www.ethnicity-facts-figures.service.gov.uk/education-skills-and-training/11-to-16-years-old/gcse-results-attainment-8-for-children-aged-14-to-16-key-stage-4/latest#main-facts-and-figures (Accessed 15 April 2021).

Georgiou, S. N. (2007) Parental Involvement: Beyond Demographics. *International Journal About Parents in Education*, 1: 59–62.

Gillborn, D. (1990) *Race, Ethnicity and Education*. London: Unwin Hyman.

Gillborn, D. (2008) *Racism and Education: Coincidence or Conspiracy*. London: Routledge Falmer.

Gillborn, D., and Gipps, C. (1996) *Recent Research into the Achievements of Ethnic Minority Pupils*. London: Ofsted.

Gillborn, D., and Mirza, H. S. (2000) *Educational Inequality: Mapping Race, Class and Gender*. London: Ofsted.

Gilroy, P. (1987) The Myth of Black Criminality. In P. Scraton (ed.) *Law, Order, and the Authoritarian State*. Milton Keynes: Open University Press.

Gilroy, P. (1990) Nationalism, History and Ethnic Absolutism. *History Workshop Journal*, 30 (1): 114–120.

Gilroy, P. (2002) *There Ain't No Black in the Union Jack*, Routledge Classics edition. London and New York: Routledge.

Giroux, H. (1997) *Channel Surfing: Racism, the Media, and the Destruction of Today's Youth*. New York: St Martin's Press.

Glynn, M. (2013) *Black Men, Invisibility and Crime: Towards a Critical Race Theory of Desistance*. London: Routledge.

Goffman, E. (1968) *Stigma: Notes on the Management of Spoiled Identity*. London: Pelican.

Gordon and Yowell (1999) Cultural Dissonance as a Risk Factor in the Development of Students. In Robert J. Rossi and Samuel C. Stringfield (eds) *Education Reform and Students at Risk: Studies of Education Reform*. DIANE Publishing.

Goulbourne, H., and Chamberlain, M. (1999) Living Arrangements, Family Structure and Social Change of Caribbeans in Britain. In *ESRC Population and Household Change for Research*. Swindon: Economic Social Research Council.

Goulbourne, H., and Chamberlain, M. (2001) *Caribbean Families in a Trans-Atlantic Context*. London: Macmillan.

Goulbourne, H., Reynolds, T., Solomos, J., and Zontini, E. (2010) *Transnational Families, Ethnicities, Identities and Social Capital*. London: Routledge.

Green, E. (2016, December 5) Are Jews White? Trump's Election Has Reopened Questions That Have Long Seemed Settled in America—Including the Acceptability of Open Discrimination Against Minority Groups. *The Atlantic*. https://www.theatlantic.com/politics/archive/2016/12/are-jews-white/509453/ (Accessed 26 April 2021).

Griffin, C. (1996) Experiencing Power: Dimensions of Gender, Race and Class. In Nickie Charles and Felicia Hughes-Freeland (eds) *Practising Feminisms: Identity, Difference, Power*. London: Routledge, pp. 180–201.

Griffin, R. A. (2012) In the Salon: Black Female Faculty 'Talking Back' to the Academy. *Women and Language*, 35 (2): 75–79.

Hairston, K., and Strikland, M. (2011) Growing …But Constrained: An Exploration of Teachers' and Researchers' Interactions With Culture and Diversity Through Personal Narratives. *The Qualitative Report*, 16 (2): 341–357.

Hall, S. (1989) Cultural Identity and Cinematic Representation. *Framework: The Journal of Cinema and Media*, 36: 68–81.

Hall, S. (2000) Old and New Identities, Old and New Ethnicities. In L. Back and J. Solomon (eds) *Theories of Race and Racism: A Reader*. London: Routledge, pp. 144–153.

Hall, S., and du Gay, P. (eds) (2011) *Questions of Cultural Identity*. London: Sage Publications Ltd.

Hamilton, D. G. (2017) Too Hot to Handle: African Caribbean Pupils and Students as Toxic Consumers and Commodities in the Educational Market. *Race, Ethnicity and Education*, 21 (5): 573–792.

Hargreave, L., and Cunningham M. (2007) *Minority Ethnic Teachers' Professional Experiences: Evidence From the Teacher Status Project*. Research Report RR853: Dfes.

Harris, C. (1995) Whiteness as Property. In K. Crenshaw, N. Gotanda, G. Peller, and K. Thomas (eds) *Critical Race Theory: The Key Writings That Formed the Movement*. New York: The New Press, pp. 276–291.

Harris, Cheryl I. (1993) Whiteness as Property. *Harvard Law Review*, pp. 1707–1791.

Heath, S. (1983) *Ways With Words: Ethnography of Communication in Communities and Classrooms*. Cambridge: Cambridge University Press.

Henry, V. (2015) *Mind the Gap: Academically Successful African Caribbean Heritage Students, Learning Identities and the Cultural Assets Mediating Learning by Veronica Henry*. PhD Thesis. Manchester: Manchester Metropolitan University.

Herrnstein, R., and Murray, C. (1994) *The Bell Curve: Intelligence and Class Structure in American Life*. New York: Free Press.

Hersi, F. (2019) *On Being Somali: Not Black Enough, Not Muslim Enough*. https://www.amaliah.com/post/21386/there-is-no-racism-in-islam-but-there-is-racism-in-the-muslim-community-being-somali (Accessed 7 July 2020).

Hey, V., Dunne, M., Aynsley, S., Kimura, M., Bennion, A., Brennan, J., and Patel, J. (2011) *The Experience of Black and Minority Ethnic Staff in Higher Education*. London: Equality Challenge Unit.

Higher Education Funding Council for England (HEFCE) (2014) *Differences in Degree Outcomes: Key Findings. Issues Report.* March 2014/03. http://www.hefce.ac./media/hefce/content/pubs/2014/201403/HEFCE2014_03.pdf (Accessed 1 June 2020).

Higher Education Statistics Agency (HESA) (2014) Staff at Higher Education Institutions in the United Kingdom. Statistical First Release Online. www.hesa.ac.uk (Accessed September 2014).

Hill Collins, P. (1990) *Black Feminist Thought: Knowledge, Empowerment and the Politics of Consciousness.* London: Unwin Hyman.

Holmes, M. (2010) The Emotionalization of Reflexivity. *Sociology,* 44 (1): 139–154.

hooks, b. (1994) Talking Back; Tongues of Fire: Learning Critical Affirmation. In *Sisters of the Yam: Black Women and Self-Recovery.* Boston: South End Press, pp. 31–40.

hooks, b. (1997) Representing Whiteness in Black Imagination. In R. Frankenberg (ed.) *Displacing Whiteness: Essays in Social and Cultural Criticism.* Durham, NC: Duke University Press, pp. 165–179.

hooks, b. (2000) *Feminist Theory: From Margin to Centre.* New York/Abingdon Oxon: Routledge.

hooks, b. (2015) *Talking Back Thinking Feminist, Thinking Black.* New York/London: Routledge.

Horowitz, Donald L. (1973) Colour Differentiation in the American Systems of Slavery. *The Journal of Interdisciplinary History,* 3 (3): 509–541.

Hou, F., and Myles, J. (2013) Interracial Marriage and Status-Caste Exchange in Canada and the United States. *Ethnic and Racial Studies,* 36 (1): 75–96.

Houston, M. (2000) Multiple Perspectives: African American Women Conceive Their Talk. *Women and Language,* 1 (23): 11–17.

Hughes, L. (1947) *The Ways of White Folks.* New York: Routledge.

Hughes, R., and Giles, M. (2010) CRiT Walking in Higher Education: Activating Critical Race Theory in the Academy. *Race, Ethnicity and Education,* 13 (1): 41–57.

Hull, G. T., Scott, P. B., and Smith, B. (eds) (1982) *All the Women Are White, All the Blacks Are Men, But Some of Us Are Brave: Black Women's Studies.* New York, NY: The Feminist Press.

Hung, D., Lim, S. H., and Jamaludin, A. B. (2010) Social Constructivism, Projective Identity, and Learning: Case Study of Nathan. *Asia Pacific Education Review,* 12 (2): 161–171.

Hunter, M. (2002) 'If You're Light You're Alright': Light Skin Color as Social Capital for Women of Color. *Gender and Society,* 16 (2): 171–189.

Husband, C. (1982) *Race in Britain: Continuity and Change.* London: Hutchinson and Co.

Hymes, D. (1972) Directions in Sociolinguistics: The Ethnography of Communication. In J. Gumperz and D. Hymes (eds) *Models of Interaction of Language and Social Life.* New York: Holt, Rinehart and Winston, pp. 35–37.

Ifejola, F. (2019) *The Only Accurate Part of 'BAME' is the 'And'...* https://folukeafrica.com/the-only-acceptable-part-of-bame-is-the-and/ (Accessed 12 May 2020).

Ignatiev, N. (1995) *How the Irish Became White.* New York/London: Routledge.

Ivy, J. (2010) Choosing Futures: Influence of Ethnic Origin in University Choice. *International Journal of Educational Management,* 24 (5): 391–403.

Jean-Marie, G., Williams, V., and Sherman, S. (2009) Black Women's Leadership Experiences: Examining the Intersectionality of Race and Gender. *Advances in Developing Human Resources*, 11 (5): 562–581.

Jenson, R. (2005) *The Heart of Whiteness: Confronting Race, Racism, and White Privilege*. San Francisco: City Lights.

Johns, C. (2010) *Guided Reflection*. London: Wiley-Blackwell.

Johnson, Joy L., Lorraine Greaves, and Robin Repta (2009) International Journal for Equity in Health. *International Journal for Equity in Health*, 8: 14.

Jones, C. (2006) Falling Between the Cracks: What Diversity Means for Black Women in Higher Education. *Policy Futures in Education*, 4 (2): 145–159.

Jones, C., and Shorter-Gooden, K. (2003) *Shifting: The Double Lives of Black Women in American*. New York, NY: Harper Collins.

Jones, L. (2019, October) *Women's Progression in the Workplace Global Institute for Women's Leadership, Kings College London*. London: Government Equality Office.

Jones-Rogers, S. (2019) *They Were Her Property: White Women as Slave Owners in the American South*. London: Yale University Press.

Joseph-Salisbury, R., and Connelly, L. (2018) If Your Hair Is Relaxed. White People Are Relaxed. If Your Hair Is Nappy, They're Not Happy: Black Hair as a Site of "Post-Racial" Social Control in English Schools. *Social Sciences*, 7 (11): 219. https://www.manchester.ac./discover/news/ethnic-minorities-better-qualified/; http://hummedia.manchester.ac./institutes/code/briefingsupdated/how-are-ethnic-inequalities-in-education-changing.pdf (Accessed 10 June 2020)

Kamasak, R. Mustafa, Ozbilgin, F., Yavuz, M., and Akalin, C. (2019) Race Discrimination at Work in the United Kingdom. In J. Vassilopoulou, O. Kyriakidou, V. Showunmi, and J. Brabet (eds) *Race Discrimination and the Management of Ethnic Diversity at Work: European Countries Perspectives*. United Kingdom: Emerald.

Katz, J., and Jackson-Jacobs, C. (2004) The Criminologists' Gang. In C. Sumner (ed.) *The Blackwell Companion to Criminology*. Oxford: Blackwell, pp. 91–124.

Keith, V. M., Lincoln, K. D., Taylor, R. J., and Jackson, J. S. (2010) Discriminatory Experiences and Depressive Symptoms Among African American Women: Do Skin Tone and Mastery Matter? *Sex Roles*, 62 (1–2): 48–59.

Keohane, Nigel, and Katherine, Petrie (2017) *On Course for Success: Student Retention at University*. London: Social Market Foundation. https://www.smf.co.uk/publications/course-success-student-retention-university/ (Accessed 7 June 2020).

Kerr, Sandra (2018) *Race at Work 2018 Scorecard Review Report. The McGregor-Smith Review One Year On*. London: Department for Business, Energy and Industrial Strategy. https://www.gov.uk/government/publications/race-at-work-2018-mcgregor-smith-review-one-year-on (Accessed 18 June 2020).

Kerswill, P., and Sebba, M. (2011) *From London Jamaican to British Youth Language: The Transformation of a Caribbean Post-Creole Repertoire into New Multicultural London English*. Paper Presented to the Society of Pidgin and Creole Linguists. Accra, Ghana.

King, J. E. (1991) Dysconscious Racism: Ideology, Identity, and the Miseducation of Teachers. *The Journal of Negro Education*, 60 (2): 133–146.

Kochman, T. (1981) *Black and White Styles in Conflict*. Chicago and Illinois: University of Chicago Press.

Kohli, R. (2009) Critical Race Reflections: Valuing the Experiences of Teachers of Color in Teacher Education. *Race Ethnicity and Education*, 12 (2): 235–251.

Koonce, J. B. (2012) "Oh, Those Loud Black Girls!": A Phenomenological Study of Black Girls Talking With an Attitude. *Journal of Language Literacy Education*, 8 (2): 26–46.

Ladson-Billings, G. (2004) What is Critical Race Theory and What's It Doing in a Nice Field Like. In G. Ladson-Billings and D. Gillborn (eds) *The Routledge Falmer Reader in Multicultural Education*. San Francisco: Jossey-Bass Wiley, pp. 49–63.

Ladson-Billings, G., and Donnor, J. (2008) The Moral Activist Role of Critical Race Theory Scholarship. In N. K. Denzin and Y. S. Lincoln (eds) *The Landscape of Qualitative Research*. Los Angeles, CA: Sage Publications, pp. 279–301.

Ladson-Billings, G., and Tate, W. F. (1995) Toward a Critical Race Theory of Education. *Teacher College Record*, 97 (1): 47–68.

Lareau, A. (2003) *Unequal Childhoods: Class, Race, and Family Life*. Berkeley, CA: University of California Press.

Larsen, Nella (1929) Passing. Alfred A. Knopf, New York.

Law, I., Phillips, D., and Turney, L. (eds) (2004) *Institutional Racism in Higher Education*. Stoke on Trent: Trentham Books.

Leath, S., Martinque J., Jerald, M. C., and Perkins, T. R. (2021) An Investigation of Jezebel Stereotype Awareness, Gendered Racial Identity and Sexual Beliefs and Behaviours Among Black Adult Women. *Culture, Health & Sexuality: An International Journal for Research, Intervention and Care*, pp. 2–16.

Leathwood, C., Maylor, U., and Moreau, M.-P. (2009) *The Experiences of Black and Minority Ethnic Staff in Higher Education: Literature Review*. London: Equality Challenge Unit.

Leonardo, Z. (2004) The Color of Supremacy: Beyond the Discourse of 'White Privilege'. *Educational Philosophy and Theory*, 36 (2): 137–144.

Leonardo, Z., and Porter, R. (2010) Pedagogy of Fear: Toward a Fanonian Theory of 'Safety' in Race Dialogue. *Race Ethnicity and Education*, 13 (2): 139–157.

Levine, N. (1977). The myth of the Asiatic Restoration. *The Journal of Asian Studies*, 37(1), 73–85.

Lei, J. L. (2003) (Un)Necessary Toughness?: Those "Loud Black Girls" and Those "Quiet Asian Boys." *Anthropology & Education Quarterly*, 34 (2): 158–181.

Linton, R., and McLean, L. (2017) I'm Not Loud, I'm Outspoken: Narratives of Four Jamaican Girls' Identity and Academic Success. *Girlhood Studies*, 10 (1): 71–88.

Lloyd-Jones, B. (2009) Implications of Race and Gender in Higher Education Administration: An African American Woman's Perspective. *Advances in Developing Human Resources*, 11 (5): 606–618.

Mac an Ghaill, M. (1988) *Young Gifted and Black: Student-Teacher Relations in the Schooling of Black Youth*. Milton Keynes: Open University Press.

Mac an Ghaill, M. (1992) Coming of Age in 1980s England: Reconceptualizing Black Students' Experience. In D. Gill, B. Mayor, and M. Blair (eds) *Racism and Education: Structures and Strategies*. London: Sage Publication in association with Open University.

Mac an Ghaill, M. (1994) *The Making Men, Masculinities, Sexualities and Schooling*. Buckingham: Open University Press.

MacPherson, W. (1999) The Stephen Lawrence Inquiry: Report of an Inquiry. https://assets.publishing.service.gov.uk/government/uploads/system/uploads/attachment_data/file/277111/4262.pdf (Accessed 5 April 2021).

Manchester University and Joseph Rowntree Foundation ESRC Report (2014, March) *Dynamics of Diversity: Evidence From 2011 Census*. Centre on Dynamics of Ethnicity (CoDE).

Maphosa, N. (2018) *What Am I Doing Here? Zimbabwean Learners' Perceptions of Adult Numeracy Courses in England*. PhD Thesis. Bolton: University of Bolton.

Maylor, U., Dalgety, J., and Ross, A. (2003) *Minority Ethnic Teachers in England*. London: GTC.

Maylor, U. (2009) Is It Because I'm Black? A Black Female Research Experience. *Race, Ethnicity and Education* (Special Issue: 'Black Feminisms and Postcolonial Paradigms: Researching Educational Inequalities'), 12 (1): 53–64.

Maylor, U., Rose, A., Minty, S., Ross, A., Issa, T., and Kuyok, K. A. (2013) Exploring the Impact of Supplementary Schools on Black and Minority Ethnic Pupils' Mainstream Attainment. *British Educational Research Journal*, 39 (1): 107–125.

Mbiti, J. (1990) *African Religions and Philosophy*. Portsmouth, NH: Heinemann.

McIntosh, P. (1988). *White privilege and male privilege: A personal account of coming to see correspondences through work in women's studies* (Vol. 189). Wellesley, MA: Wellesley College, Center for Research on Women.

McIntosh, P. (1992) White Privilege and Male Privilege: A Personal Account of Coming to Correspondences Through Work in Women's Studies. In M. Andersen and T. Morrison (eds) *Playing in the Dark: Whiteness in the Literary Imagination*. New York: Vintage.

McIntosh, P. (2009a) 'They Do Not Relate to People Like Us': Black Teachers as Role Models for Black Pupils. *Journal of Education Policy*, 24 (1): 1–21.

McIntosh, P. (2009b) What is the Meaning of Black?: Researching 'Black' Respondents. *Ethnic and Racial Studies*, 32 (2): 369–387.

McIntosh, P. (2010) Notions of Diversity, British Identities and Citizenship Belonging. *Race, Ethnicity and Education*, 13 (2): 233–252.

Miller, K. J., Gleaves, D. H., Hirsch, T. G., Green, B. A., Snow, A. C., & Corbett, C. C. (2000). Comparisons of body image dimensions by race/ethnicity and gender in a university population. *International Journal of Eating Disorders*, 27(3), 310–316. Wiley Online Libdrary.

Millward, J. (2010) "The Relics of Slavery:" Interracial Sex and Manumission in the American South. *Frontiers: A Journal of Women Studies*, 31 (3): 22–30.

Milner, H. R., IV, and Howard, T. C. (2013) Counter-Narrative as Method: Race, Policy and Research for Teacher Education. *Race Ethnicity and Education*, 16 (4): 536–561.

Mirza, H. (1993) *Young, Female and Black*. London: Routledge.Mirza, H. S. (1995) Black Women in Higher Education. In L. Morely and V. Walsh (eds) *Defining a Space/Finding a Place in Feminist Academics: Creative Agents for Changes*. London: Taylor and Francis.

Mirza, H. S. (ed.) (1997) *Black British Feminism: A Reader*. London: Routledge.

Mirza, H. S. (2003) All the Women Are White, All the Blacks Are Men – But Some of Us Are Brave; Mapping the Consequences of Invisibility for Black and Minority

Ethnic Women in Britain. In D. Mason (ed.) *Explaining Ethnic Differences: Changing Patterns of Disadvantage in Britain.* Bristol: Policy Press.

Mirza, H. S. (2006) Transcendence Over Diversity: Black Women in the Academy. *Policy Futures in Education,* 4 (2): 101–113.

Mirza, H. S. (2007) Gendered Choices and Transitions: Part-time Pathways, Full-time Lives. Women in Lifelong Learning Network Conference. Keynote Presentation: The In/visible Journey: Black Women's Lifelong Lessons in Higher Education. May 2007. Birbeck: University of London.

Mirza, H. S. (2009) *Race, Gender and Educational Desire: Why Black Women Succeed and Fail.* Oxon: Routledge.

Mirza, H. S. (2013) The University Professor is Always White. *The Guardian,* 28 January.

Mirza, H. S., and Joseph, C. (2012) *Black and Postcolonial Feminism in New Times.* Abingdon, Oxon: Routledge.

Mirza, H. S., and Reay, D. (2000a) Redefining Citizenship: Women Educators and 'The Third Space.' In M. Arnot and J. Dillabough (eds) *Challenging Democracy: International Perspectives on Gender, Education and Citizenship.* London & New York: Routledgefalmer.

Mirza, H. S., and Reay, D. (2000b) Spaces and Places of Educational Desire: Rethinking Black Supplementary School as a New Social Movement. *British Journal of Sociology,* 34 (3): 521–544.

Mitchell-Kernan, C. (1971) Language Behaviour in a Black Urban Community. *Monographs of the Language-Behaviour Laboratory,* No. 2. Berkley, CA: University of California.

Mitchell-Kernan, C. (1972) Signifying, Loud-Talking and Marking. In T. Kochman (ed.) *Rappin' and Stylin' Out. Communication in Urban Black America.* Urbana, IL: University of Illinois Press, pp. 315–335.

Mitton, L., and Aspinall, P. J (2011) *Black Africans in the UK: Integration or Segregation.* UPTAP Research Findings.

Mocombe, P. C. (2006) The Sociolinguistic Nature of Black Academic Failure in Capitalist Education: A Reevaluation of 'Language in the Inner city' and Its Social Function, 'Acting White'. *Race Ethnicity and Education,* 9 (4): 395–407.

Mocombe, P. C., and Tomlin, C. (2010) *Oppositional Culture Theory.* Lanham, MD: University Press of America.

Mocombe, P. C., and Tomlin, C. (2013) *Language Literacy and Pedagogy in Post Industrial Societies: The Case of Black Academic Underachievement.* New York/ London: Routledge.

Mocombe, P. C., Tomlin, C., and Callender, C. (2017) *The African-Americanisation of the Black Diaspora in Globalisation or the Contemporary Capitalist World System.* Lanham, MD: University Press of America.

Mocombe, P. C., Tomlin, C., and Showunmi, V. (2016) *Jesus and the Streets: The Loci of Causality for the Intra-Racial Gender Academic Achievement Gap in Black Urban America and the United Kingdom.* Lanham, MD: University Press of America.

Mocombe, P. C., Tomlin, C., and Wright, C. (2014) *Race and Class Distinctions Within Black Communities: A Racial Caste-in-Class.* New York/Abingdon, Oxon: Routledge.

Montecinos, C. (1995) Critical Race Methodology: Counter-Storytelling as an Analytical Framework for Education Research. *Qualitative Inquiry*, 8 (1): 23–44.

Morgan, J. (2014) 'Walkout' by Black Members at UCU Event. *Times Educational Supplement*, 19 November.

Morgan, M. (2002) *Language, Discourse and Power in African American Culture*. Cambridge: Cambridge University Press.

Morris, M. W. (2016) *Pushed Out: The Criminalization of Black Girls in School*. New York, NY: The New Press.

Morris, T. D. (1996) *Southern Slavery and the Law, 1619–1860*. Chapel Hill, London: The University of North Carolina Press.

Morrison, T. (1997) *Toni Morrison's World of Fiction*. New York: Whitston Publishing Company.

Morrison, Toni (1988) Beloved. 1987. *New York: Plume*, p. 252.

Muhwezi, W. W., Agren, A., Neema, S., Musisi, S., and Maganda, A. K. (2007) Life Events and Depression in the Context of the Changing African Family: The Case of Uganda. *World Cultural Psychiatry Research Review*, 2007: 10–26.

Musoke, W. N. (2016). *An ethnographic study of Black Ugandan British parents' experiences of supporting their children's learning within their home environments* (Doctoral dissertation, London Metropolitan University).

National Audit Office (NAO) (2002) *Widening Participation in Higher Education in England*. HC 485, Session 2001–2002. London: NAO.

National Church Leaders Forum Press Release Statement (NCLF) (2021, April 6). https://myemail.constantcontact.com/Black-Church-leaders-respond-to-Commission-on-Race-and-Ethnic-Disparities--The-Report.html?soid=1101637163520&aid=fyqS_yCZLno (Accessed 6 April 2021).

Nesbit, A., and Lynch, M. (1992) African Children in Britain. *Archives of Disease in Childhood*, 67: 1402–1405. https://www.ncbi.nlm.nih.gov/pmc/articles/PMC1793778/pdf/archdisch00632-0094.pdf (Accessed 8 June 2020).

Noden, P., Shiner, M., and Modood, T. (2014) *Black and Minority Ethnic Access to Higher Education A Reassessment Philip*. London: London School of Economics and Political Science. https://blogs.lse.ac.uk/equityDiversityInclusion/2014/08/Black-academia-in-britain/ (Accessed 10 June 2020).

Nottinghamshire County Council Education Department (1992) *An Enquiry into Pupils Exclusions From Nottingham Secondary School*. No 15/89 Nottingham: Nottinghamshire County Council Education Department and Advisory and Inspection Service.

Nzegwu, N. (2003) O Africa: Gender Imperialism in Africa. In O. Oyewumi O (ed.) *African Women and Feminism*. New Jersey: Africa World Press, pp. 99–157.

Office of National Statistics: Ethnicity Pay Gaps in Great Britain (2018) https://www.ons.gov.uk/employmentandlabourmarket/peopleinwork/earningsandworkinghours/articles/ethnicitypaygapsingreatbritain/2018 (Accessed 18 June 2020).

Office for National Statistics: Labour Market Status by Ethnic Group. https://www.ons.gov.uk/employmentandlabourmarket/peopleinwork/employmentandemployeetypes/datasets/labourmarketstatusbyethnicgroupa09 (Accessed 18 June 2020).

Office for National Statistics: Population of England and Wales. https://www.ethnicity-facts-figures.service.gov.uk/uk-population-by-ethnicity/national-and

-regional-populations/population-of-england-and-wales/latest (Accessed 3 April 2021).
Office for National Statistics: Updating Ethnic Contrasts in Deaths Involving the Coronavirus (COVID-19), England and Wales: Deaths Occurring 2 March to 28 July 2020. https://www.ons.gov.uk/peoplepopulationandcommunity/birthsd eathsandmarriages/deaths/articles/updatingethniccontrastsindeathsinvolvingthe coronaviruscovid19englandandwales/deathsoccurring2marchto28july2020#main -points (Accessed 3 April 2021).
Office for Students (2020) Equality and Diversity. https://www.officeforstudents.org .uk/data-and-analysis/equality-and-diversity/ (Accessed 30 May 2020).
Okeke, Chinedu, I. (2014) Effective Home-School Partnership: Some Strategies to Help Strengthen Parental Involvement. *South African Journal of Education*, 34 (3): 1–9.
Okpewho, I. (1992) *African Oral Literature*. Bloomington and Indianapolis: Indiana University Press.
Olusoga, D. (2016) *Black and British: A Forgotten History*. London: Macmillan.
Open Letter by British Academics Cited in the Guardian. https://docs.google .com/document/d/1EQwtYRfT6Mxx-30T-FGthcA5eaf8M5YuJSXBNnyN-Ww/ edit; https://www.theguardian.com/world/2021/apr/02/historian-and-hundreds-of -academics-attack-no-10s-race-report?CMP=Share_iOSApp_Other&fbclid=IwA R0CmBG2Ct1JCaLWcPz8yyPOlxzmD3TxakOEvswMY6z2fYvj9FxH_XTyxxE (Accessed 14 April 2021).
Orbe, M. (1998) *Constructing Co-Cultural Theory: An Explication of Culture, Power, and Communication*. Thousand Oaks, CA: Sage.
Osler, A. (1997) *Education and Careers of Black Teachers: Changing Identities, Changing Lives Paperback*. Buckingham: Open University.Palmer, L. A. (2010) *The Politics of Loving Blackness in the UK*. PhD Thesis. University of Birmingham.
Parfitt, T. (2020) *Hybrid Hate: Conflation of Antisemitism and Anti-Black Racism From the Renaissance to the Third Reich*. New York, NY: Oxford University Press.
Parker, L., and Lynn, M. (2002) What's Race to Do With It? Critical Race Theory's Conflicts With and Connections to Qualitative Research Methodology and Epistemology. *Qualitative Inquiry*, 8 (1): 7–22.
Parker, P. S. (2002) Negotiating Identity in Raced and Gendered Workplace Interactions: The Use of Strategic Communication by African American Women Senior Executives Within Dominant Culture Organizations. *Communication Quarterly*, 50 (3–4): 251–268.
Perry, Keisha-Khan Y. (2013) *Black Women Against the Land Grab: The Fight for Racial Justice in Brazil*. Minneapolis, MN: University of Minnesota Press.
Phillips, M., and Phillips, T. (2009) *Windrush: The Irresistible Rise of Multi-Racial Britain:* London: Harper Collins.
Phoenix, A. (2009) Belonging and Unbelonging From an Intersectional Perspective Gender. *Technology and Development*, 13: 21–41.
Picower, B. (2009) The Unexamined Whiteness of Teaching: How White Teachers Maintain and Enact Dominant Racial Ideologies. *Race Ethnicity and Education*, 12 (2): 197–215.

Pinnock, Katherine (2008) *Embedding Equality and Diversity in the Curriculum: Developing and Disseminating Effective Practice.* Wolverhampton: Policy Research Institute, University of Wolverhampton. www2.wlv.ac.uk/equalopps/latee_2_report_FINAL_KT.doc (Accessed: 31 May 2020)

Population of England and Wales: Ethnicity Facts and Figures. https://www.ethnicity-facts-figures.service.gov.uk/uk-population-by-ethnicity/national-and-regional-populations/population-of-england-and-wales/latest (Accessed 1 April 2021).

Preston, J. (2013) *Whiteness in Academia: Counter-Stories of Betrayal and Resistance.* Cambridge: CSP.

Public Health England (2020a, June) *Beyond the Data: Understanding the Impact of COVID-19 on BAME Groups.* London: Public Health England. https://assets.publishing.service.gov.uk/government/uploads/system/uploads/attachment_data/file/892376/COVID_stakeholder_engagement_synthesis_beyond_the_data.pdf (Accessed 14 April 2021).

Public Health England (2020b, August) *Disparities in the Risk and Outcomes of COVID-19.* London: Public Health England. https://assets.publishing.service.gov.uk/government/uploads/system/uploads/attachment_data/file/908434/Disparities_in_the_risk_and_outcomes_of_COVID_August_2020_update.pdf (Accessed 14 April 2021).

Public Health England Report (2020) *Beyond the Data: Understanding the Impact of COVID-19 on BAME Groups.* https://assets.publishing.service.gov.uk/government/uploads/system/uploads/attachment_data/file/892376/COVID_stakeholder_engagement_synthesis_beyond_the_data.pdf (Accessed September 2020).

Pulido, L. (2015) Geographies of Race and Ethnicity 1: White Supremacy Vs White Privilege in Environmental Racism Research. *Progress in Human Geography*, 39 (6): 809–817.

Purwar, N. (2004) Fish in or Out of Water: A Theoretical Framework for Race and the Space of Academia. In I. Law, D. Phillips, and L. Turney (eds) *Institutional Racism in Higher Education.* Stoke-on-Trent: Trentham Books.

Race Disparity Audit, October (2017) Revised March (2018). London: Cabinet Office. https://www.gov.uk/government/publications/race-disparity-audit (Accessed 10 July 2019).

Rampton, A. (1981) *West Indian Children in Our Schools.* Interim Report of the Committee of the Inquiry into the Education of Children from Ethnic Minority Groups. London: HMSO.

Rampton, Ben (2010) Crossing into Class: Language, Ethnicities and Class Sensibility in England. In Carmen Llamas and Dominic Watt (eds) *Language and Identities.* Edinburgh, UK: Edinburgh University Press, pp. 134–143.

Reay, D. (2001) Finding or Losing Yourself?: Working-Class Relationships to Education. *Journal of Education Policy*, 16 (4): 333–346.

Reay, D. (2006) Engendering Social Reproduction: Mothers in the Educational Marketplace. *British Journal of Sociology of Education*, 19 (2): 195–209. https://doi.org/10.1080/0142569980190203.

Reay, D. (2017) *Miseducation: Inequality, Education and the Working Classes.* Bristol: Policy Press.

Reece, R. L. (2021). The gender of colorism: Understanding the intersection of skin tone and gender inequality. *Journal of Economics, Race, and Policy*, 4 (1), 47–55.

Reisman, K. (1970) Cultural and Linguistic Ambiguity in a West Indian Village. In N. Swzed and J. Whitten (eds) *Afro-American Anthropology: Contemporary Perspectives*. New York: Free Press, pp. 129–144.

Reisman, K. (1974) Contrapuntal Conversations in an Antiguan Village. In R. Bauman and J. Sherzer (eds) *Exploration in the Ethnography of Speaking*. Cambridge: Cambridge University Press, pp. 110–124.

Reynolds, T. (2001a) Black Mothering, Paid Work and Identity Tracey. *Ethnic and Racial Studies*, 24 (6): 1046–1064.

Reynolds, T. (2001b) Re-Thinking a Black Feminist Standpoint. *Ethnic and Racial Studies*, 25 (4): 591–606.

Reynolds, T. (2002). Re-thinking a black feminist standpoint. *Ethnic and Racial Studies*, 25 (4), 591–606.

Reynolds, T. (2009a) Exploring the Absent/Present Dilemma: Black Fathers, Family Relationships, and Social Capital in Britain. *Annals of the American Academy of Political and Social Science*, 624: 12–28.

Reynolds, T. (2009b) Transnational Family Networks, Cultural Belonging and Social Capital Among Second-Generation British-Caribbean 'Returning' Migrants. *Ethnic and Racial Studies*, 33 (5): 797–815.

Reynolds, T. (2011). Caribbean second-generation return migration: transnational family relationships with 'left-behind'kin in Britain. *Mobilities*, 6(4), 535–551.

Rhamie, J. (2007) *Eagles Who Soar: How Black Learners Find the Path to Success*. Trentham: Stoke on Trent.

Richardson, H. (2020) Black Pupils Face Trebled Exclusion Rate in Some Areas of England. Education and Social Affair Reporter for the BBC. https://www.bbc.co.uk/news/education-53516009 (Accessed 31 July 2020).

Rickford, J., and Rickford, A. (1976) Cut Eye and Suck Teeth: African Words and Gestures in New World Guise. *Journal of American*, Folklore July September, pp. 294–309.

Rigby, K., & Cox, I. (1996). The contribution of bullying at school and low self-esteem to acts of delinquency among Australian teenagers. *Personality and Individual differences*, 21 (4), 609–612.

Roberts, D. E. (1997) *Killing the Black Body: Race, Reproduction, and the Meaning of Liberty*. New York: Pantheon Book.

Roberts, L. (2014) *Critical Race Theory as a Space of Interdisciplinarity*. Manchester: Manchester Metropolitan University, pp. 1–9.

Roediger, D. (1999) *Black on White Writers on What It Means to Be White*. New York: Schocken.

Rollock, N. (2012) The Invisibility of Race: Intersectional Reflections on the Liminal Space of Alterity. *Race, Ethnicity and Education*, 15 (1): 65–84.

Rollock, N., Gillborn, D., Vincent, C., and Ball, S. J. (2015) *The Colour of Class: The Educational Strategies of the Black Middle Class*. Abingdon, Oxon: Routledge.

Ross, A. (2001) Towards a Representative Profession: Teachers From the Ethnic Minorities. Paper Presented to the Seminar on the Future of the Teaching Profession, December 11. London: Institute for Policy Studies in Education.

Scott, K. D. (2000) Crossing Cultural Borders: "Girl" and "Look" as Markers of Identity in Black Women's Language Use. *Discourse & Society*, 11: 237–248.

Scott, K. D. (2002) Conceiving the Language of Black Women's Everyday Talk. In M. Houston and O. I. Davis (eds) *Centering ourselves: African American Feminist and Womanist Studies of Discourse*. Cresskill, NJ: Hampton Press, pp. 53–73.

Scott, K. D. (2013) Communication Strategies Across Cultural Borders: Dispelling Stereotypes, Performing Competence and Redefining Black Womanhood. *Women's Studies in Communication*, 36: 312–329.

Scott, K. D. (2017) Young, Shifting, and Black: Leaving the Language of Home and Back Again—A Cautionary Tale of Crossing Race and Gender Borders. *Qualitative Inquiry*, 23 (2): 119–129.

Sebba, M. (2007) Caribbean Creole and Black English. In D. Britain (ed.) *Language in the British Isles*. Cambridge: Cambridge University Press, pp. 276–292.

Sefa Dei, G. J. (1997). Race and the production of identity in the schooling experiences of African Canadian youth. Discourse: *Studies in the cultural politics of education*, 18(2), 241–257.

Shankley, W., and Williams, P. (2020) Minority Ethnic Groups, Policing and the Criminal Justice System in Britain. In B. Bryne, C. Alexander, O. Khan, J. Nazroo, and W. Shankley (eds) *Ethnicity, Race and Inequality in the UK: State of the Nation*. Bristol: Policy Press, University of Bristol, pp. 51–72.

Shealey, M. (2006) The Promises and Perils of "Scientifically Based" Research for Urban Schools. *Urban Education*, 4 (1): 5–19.

Sheldon, G. (2016) *Trauma and Race: A Lacanian Study of African American Racial Identity*. Waco, TX: Baylor University Press.

Shepherd, J. (2011) 14,000 British Professors – But Only 50 Are Black. *The Guardian*, 27 May.

Shorter-Gooden, K. (2004) Multiple Resistance Strategies: How African American Women Cope With Racism and Sexism. *Journal of Black Psychology*, 30 (3): 406–425.

Showunmi, V. (2012) *Why British Black Women Have Difficulty Finding Employment*. London: The Edwin Mellen Press.

Smedley, A., and Smedley, B. D. (2005) Race as Biology is Fiction, Racism as a Social Problem is Real: Anthropological and Historical Perspectives on the Social Construction of Race. *American Psychologist*, 60 (1): 16–26.

Smith, D. L. (1993) Let Our People Go. *Black Scholar*, 23 (3/4): 75–56.

Smith, W., Yosso, T., and Solórzano, D. (2006) Challenging Racial Battle Fatigue on Historically White Campuses: A Critical Race Examination of Race-Related Stress. In C. Stanley (ed.) *Faculty of Color: Teaching in Predominantly White Colleges and Universities*. Bolton, Massachusetts: Anker Publishing Company, Inc., pp. 299–327.

Smitherman, G. (1977) *Talkin' and Testifyin:' The Language of Black Experience*. Boston: Houghton Mifflin Co.

Solórzano, D., and Yosso, T. (2002) Critical Race Methodology: Counter-Storytelling as an Analytical Framework for Education Research. *Qualitative Inquiry*, 8 (1): 23–44.

Spears Brown, C., & Bigler, R. S. (2005). Children's perceptions of discrimination: A developmental model. *Child development*, 76 (3), 533–553.

Stanley, C. (2006) Colouring the Academic Landscape: Faculty of Colour Breaking the Silence in Predominantly White Colleges and Universities. *American Educational Research Journal*, 43 (4): 701–736.

Steele, C. (1998) Stereotyping and Its Threat Are Real. *American Psychologist*, 53 (6): 680–681.

Steele, Shelby. (1988) On Being Black and Middle Class. *Commentary*, 1 January 1988. http://www.commentarymagazine.com/viewarticle.cfm/on-being-black-and-middle-class-7372 (Accessed 15 June 2010).

Stepakoff, S. (2020) Hiding in Plain Sight: Judaeophobia in Swift's Portrayal of the Yahoos in Gulliver's Travels. *Swift Studies*, 35: 106–151.

Stillwell, A., and Lowery, B. (2020) Gendered Racial Boundary Maintenance: Social Penalties for White Women in Interracial Relationships. *Journal of Personality and Social Psychology*. Advance Online Publication. https://doi.org/10.1037/pspi0000332.

Strand, S. (2012) The White British-Black Caribbean Achievement Gap. Test, Tiers and Teacher Expectations. *British Educational Research Journal*, 28 (1): 75–101.

Strayhorn, T. (ed.) (2013) *Living at the Intersections*. Charlotte, NC: Information Age Publishing.

Sullivan, K. (2005) Racist Bullying: Creating Understanding and Strategies for Teachers. *Education, Culture, and Values*, 2: 118–135.

Sutcliff, D., and Tomlin, C. (1986) The Black Church. In D. Sutcliffe and A. Wong (eds) *Language of the Black Experience*. Oxford: Blackwell, pp. 15–31.

Sweet, P. (2020, February) 11% of FTSE 100 Board Directors Are BAME. *Accountancy Daily*. https://www.accountancydaily.co/11-ftse-100-board-directors-are-bame#:~:text=The%20latest%20data%20reveals%20that,ethnic%20and%201%25%20other%20ethnic (Accessed 23 June 2020).

Syed, J., and Ali, Faiza (2011) The White Woman's Burden From Colonial Civilisation to Third World Development. *Third World Quarterly*, 32 (2): 349–365.

Taliaferro-Baszile, D. (2006) Rage in the Interests of Black Self: Curriculum Theorizing as Dangerous Knowledge. *Journal of Curriculum Theorizing*, 22 (1): 89–98.

Tannen, D. (1980) Oral Literate Strategies in Discourse. *Linguistic Reporter*, 22 (9): 1–3.

Tate, W. F. (1997) Critical Race Theory and Education: History, Theory, and Implications. *Review of Research in Education*, 22: 195–247.

Taylor, C. (1992) *Multiculturalism and "The Politics of Recognition"*. Princeton: Princeton University Press.

The Members of the Archbishops' Anti-Racism Taskforce (2021) *From Lament to Action: The Report of the Archbishops' Anti-Racism Taskforce*. London: Church of England. https://www.churchofengland.org/sites/default/files/2021-04/FromLamentToAction-report.pdf (Accessed 26 April 2021).

The Time for Talking is Over. Now is the Time to Act: Race in the Workplace. The McGregor-Smith Review (2017) https://assets.publishing.service.gov.uk/government/uploads/system/uploads/attachment_data/file/594336/race-in-workplace-mcgregor-smith-review.pdf (Accessed 25 June 2020).

Theodossiou, I. (1998). The effects of low-pay and unemployment on psychological well-being: a logistic regression approach. *Journal of health economics*, 17(1), 85–104. ELSEVIER.

Thompson, D., and Tomlin, C. (2013) Recruiting Minority Ethnic Students on to Initial Teacher Training Courses. *Widening Participation and Lifelong Learning*, 15 (3): 47–65.

Tomlin, C. (1999) *Black Language Style in Sacred and Secular Contexts*. Brooklyn, New York: Medgars Evers College (CUNY), Caribbean Diaspora Press.

Tomlin, C. (2006, June) Training for Wolverhampton Ethnic Minority Achievement Service on: 'The Educational Implications of African Heritage Language Style.'

Tomlin, C. (2019) *Preach It! Understanding African Caribbean Preaching*. London: SCM Press.

Tomlin, C., and Bryan, B. (2009) The Writing Performance in English of African Heritage Students in Two Urban Environments: Birmingham, England and Kingston, Jamaica. *Journal of Education and Development in the Caribbean*, 10 (1): 1–32.

Tomlin, C., and Olusola, M. (2012) *Schools and Marginalized Youth: An International Perspective* (ed. W. T. Pink). Cresskill, NJ: Hampton Press.

Tomlinson, S. (1977) *Education of Ethnic Minority Children*. London: Commission for Racial Equality.

Tomlinson, S. (2013) My University Life as a Woman Professor. *The Guardian*, 31 January.

Toulis, N. R. (1997) *Believing Identity: Pentecostalism and the Mediation of Jamaican Ethnicity and Gender in England*. Oxford: Berg.

Traynor, Joanna (2001) Losing Touch: The West African Families Who Choose to Send Their Children to Private White Foster Mothers. *The Guardian Online*. https://www.theguardian.com/society/2001/jul/25/adoptionandfostering.guardiansocietysupplement (Accessed 8 June 2020).

Tripp, D. (1994). Teachers' lives, critical incidents, and professional practice. *Qualitative Studies in education*, 7(1), 65–76. International Journal of Qualitative Studies in Education.

Trudgill, P. (1990) *Sociolinguistics: An Introduction*. Harmondsworth: Penguin.

Tsolidis, G. (1990). Ethnic minority girls and self-esteem. *Hearts and Minds: self-esteem and the schooling of girls*, 53–9. The Falmer Press. London.

Twine, F. W. (1999) Bearing Blackness in Britain: The Meaning of Racial Difference for White Birth Mothers of African-Descent Children. *Social Identities: Journal of Race, Nation and Culture*, 5 (2): 185–210.

Twine, F. W. (2010) White Like Who? The Value of Whiteness in British Interracial Families. *Ethnicities*, 10 (3): 292–312.

UCU (University College Union) (2013) *The Position of Women and BME Staff in Professorial Roles in UK HEIs*. London: UCU.

Umolu, A. O. (2014) Gender and Race in UK Organisations: Case Study of Nigerian and Indian Women. *Gender Behaviour*, 12: 6045–6058.

UN Experts Condemn UK Commission on Race and Ethnic Disparities Report. Statement is Issued by Independent Experts* of the Special Procedures of the United Nations Human Rights Council. https://www.ohchr.org/EN/NewsEvents/Pages/DisplayNews.aspx?NewsID=27004&LangID=E (Accessed 4 May 2021).

Van Dijk, T. A. (2000) *New(s) Racism: A Discourse Analytical Approach.* Unpublished Chapter. http://www.discourses.org/OldArticles/New(s)%20racism%20-%20A%20discourse%20analytical%20approach.pdf (Accessed 29 April 2021).

Van Dijk, T. A. (2012) The Role of the Press in the Reproduction of Racism. *Migrations: Interdisciplinary Perspectives*, 15–29.

Wade, L. (2011, January 28) Irish Apes: Tactics of Dehumanisation. *Sociological Images.* https://thesocietypages.org/socimages/2011/01/28/irish-apes-tactics-of-de-humanization/ (Accessed 23 April 2021).

Wallace, M. (1978/2015) *Black Macho and the Myth of the Superwoman.* New York: The Dial Press.

Walker, A. (1983) *In Search of Our Mothers' Gardens: Womanist Prose.* San Diego, New York, London: Harcourt Brace Jovanovich.

Walker, A. (2005) *The Complete Stories.* London: Phoenix.

Ward, L. M., Seabrook, R., Grower, R. P., Giaccardi, S., and Lippman, J. (2018) Sexual Object or Sexual Subject? Media Use, Self-Sexualization, and Sexual Agency Among Undergraduate Women. *Psychology of Women Quarterly*, 42 (1): 29–43.

Warmington, P. (2014) *Black British Intellectuals and Education: Multiculturalism's Hidden History.* London: Routledge.

Warmington, Paul (2020) Critical Race Theory in England: Impact and Opposition. *Identities Global Studies in Culture and Power*, 27 (1): 20–37.

Weber, L., and Fore, E. (2007) Race, Ethnicity, and Health: An Intersectional Approach. In *Handbook of the Sociology of Racial and Ethnic Relations.* Boston: Springer, pp. 191–218.

West, C. (1993) *Race Matters.* Boston: Beacon Press.

West, C. (1994) The Dilemma of the Black Intellectual. *The Journal of Blacks in Higher Education*, 2: 56–67.

White Paper (2004) *The Future of Higher Education.* Race Impact Assessment. White Paper and the Higher Education Act (2004) (CM5735).

Wilkinson, J., and Blackmore, J. (2008) Re-Presenting Women and Leadership: A Methodological Journey. *International Journal of Qualitative Studies in Education*, 21 (2): 123–136.

Williams, P., and Clarke, B. (2016) *Dangerous Associations: Joint Enterprise, Gangs and Racism.* Centre for Crime and Justice Studies. www.crimeandjustice.org.uk/publications/ dangerous-associations-joint-enterprise-gangs-and-racism (Accessed 7 July November 2019).

Williams, P., and Clarke, B. (2018) The Black Criminal Other as an Object of Social Control. *Social Sciences*, 7 (11): 234–248.

Wilson, M. (1999) Who Has the Right to Say? Charles W. Chesnutt, Whiteness and the Public Space. *College Literature*, 26 (2): 18–34.

Winfrey Harris, T. *The Sisters Are Alright: Changing the Broken Narrative of Black Women in America.* Oakland, CA: Berrett-Koehler Publisher.

Woodson, C. G. (1990, 1933). *The Mis-Education of the Negro.* Trenton, NJ: Africa World Press.

Woolmore, T. (2016) *Keep on Moving: Black Responses to Racism and Government Policy in Chapeltown During the 1980s.* BA Dissertation. Queen's University in Belfast.

Wright, C. (1992) Early Education: Multiracial Primary School Classrooms. In D. Gill, B. Mayor, and M. Blair (eds) *Racism and Education: Structures and Strategies.* London: Sage.

Wright, C., Maylor, V., and Pickup, T. (2020) *Young British African and Caribbean Men Achieving Educational Success: Disrupting Deficit Discourses About Black Male Achievement.* London: Routledge.

Wright, C., Maylor, U., and Watson, V. (2018) Black Women Academics and Senior Managers Resisting Gendered Racism in British Higher Education Institutions. In O. N. Perlow, D. I. Wheeler, S. L. Bethea, and B. M. Scott (eds) *Black Women's Liberatory Pedagogies.* Cham, Switzerland: Palgrave Macmillan, Springer Nature, pp. 65–84.

Wright, C., Thompson, S., and Channer, Y. (2007) 'Out of Place'-Black Women in British Universities. *Women's History Review,* 16 (2): 127–144.

Wright, C., Weeks, D., McGlaughlin, A., and Webb, D. (eds) (2000) *Race, Class and Gender in Exclusion from School.* London and New York: Falmer Press.

Wright, M. M. (2004) *Becoming Black: Creating Identity in the African Diaspora.* Durham and London: Duke University Press.

Wright, R. (1992 [1945]) *Black Boy.* New York: Harper Collins.

Yosso, T. (2005) Whose Culture Has Capital? A Critical Race Theory Discussion of Community Cultural Wealth. *Race, Ethnicity and Education,* 8 (1): 69–91.

Young, I. (2005) Inheriting the Criminalized Black Body: Race, Gender, and Slavery in "Eva's Man." *African American Review,* 39 (3): 377–393.

Youth Justice Board (2018) Youth Justice Statistics, 2017/18. https://assets.publishing.service.gov.uk/government/uploads/system/uploads/attachment_data/file/887644/assessing-needs-of-sentenced-children-youth-justice-system.pdf (Accessed 7 July 2019).

Zamudio, M., Bridgeman, J., Russell, C., and Rios, F. (2009) Developing a Critical Consciousness: Positionality, Pedagogy and Problems. *Race, Ethnicity and Education,* 12 (4): 455–472.

Zeleza, P. T. (2006) The Inventions of African Identities and Languages: The Discursive and Developmental Implications. In Olaoba F. Arasanyin and Michael A. Pemberton (eds) *Selected Proceedings of the 36th Annual Conference on African Linguistics.* Somerville, MA: Cascadilla Proceedings Project, pp. 14–26.

Index

academia: author experiences of, xxi, xxii; career progression in, 114–15, 120–23; challenges for Black women in, 81–82; employment overview, 114–15; pay gap in, 94; reflections on. *See* Black female reflections on academia; sophisticated racism in, 48–52, 54
Ackah, William, 3
ACS. *See* African communication system
'acting White', 56–57, 126
activist behaviour, 20–24
Adams, M., 14
advocacy, 135–36
Affirmative Action, 28, 44, 94
African American students, 77, 78
African background: and class, 38; and educational achievement, 83, 85–86; and family structure, 82; and higher education participation, 79–80; and identities, 36–37; and occupational status/progression, 92–93, 95; and 'sending children back', 88, 89; terminology relating to, 1–2
African Caribbean background: and family structure, 82; terminology relating to, 1–2
African Caribbean students, 77

African communication system (ACS), 62
African students, 77
African world view, 62
Agyemany, C., 145
Ahmed, Sara, 46, 49, 52, 58
Ali, Faiza, 9
Amos, Baroness Valerie, 131n3
Anderson, C., 35
anti-Black racism, 13–15
anti-racism, as sophisticated racism, 43–44
appearance, 102, 105–6
Archer, L., 39
Aspinall, P., 91, 93
aspirational capital, 87
Avent Harris, J. R., 148
avoidance strategy, 71–72

Baartman, Saarti (Sarah), xix
Bakare-Yusuf, B., 36
Bartman, C., 81
BBT. *See* Black British talk
beauty, 102, 105–6
Bell, E., 68
belonging, in higher education, 78, 123–24, 129
Bernstein, B. A., 100
Bhavnani, R., 10

'Big House' metaphor, 18–19; Black and White women in, 24–25, 27–28; and colourism, 19–20; and interracial relationships, 19, 25–26; and language, 61; myth of seductive temptress, 26–27; strategic behaviours, 20–24

Bignall, T. (Mental Health Review), 97, 99–100

Black and minority ethnic (BAME), use of term, 2–3

Black British talk (BBT), 63–64, 72

Black culture, 30–31

Black female reflections on academia: background, 113–15; career progression, 120–23; cultural dissonance, 124–27; experience of reflecting, 127–29; final insights, 129–31; method, 115–19; racial identity construction, 119–20

Black girls' presentation of self, 65–69

Black identity: authors' experiences of, xvi–xxii, 119, 123–27; and British identity, xx–xxii, 37, 110; concept of, 35–38, 130

Black Lives Matter (BLM) movement, xv

Black males: educational achievement of, 83; and gangs, 87–88; slavery and sexual exploitation of, 26, 27

Blackmore, J., 122–23

Blackness: and class, xviii–xix, 38–39, 123–25; and colourism, 19–20, 33–34, 102; and shadism, 45; understandings of, 13–15

Black staff in higher education, 114–15

Black students in higher education, 77–82

Black women: agency of. *See* strategic response to racism; employed in higher education, 114–15; and feminism, 3, 15, 29–30; gender as secondary to Blackness, 49–50; higher education participation of, 77–82; involvement in children's education, 82, 84–87, 139–40; labour market participation of, 89–91; languages of. *See* language(s); literature/discourses on, 1, 3, 4, 15; loudness/silence of, 65–68; occupational status/progression of, 91–95, 114–15, 120–23; parental challenges for, 88, 89, 93; stereotypes of, 27, 55–57, 102–3; terminology relating to, 1–3; as threat in workplace, 27–28, 49–50; in UK context, 1–2; understanding experiences of, 3–5, 15; wellbeing. *See* mental health and wellbeing of Black Women; and White women in plantocracy, 25, 27–28. *See also* Black female reflections on academia

Black youths, 87–88

Bledsoe, Caroline H., 88, 89

Bledsoe, K. L., 12

BLM. *See* Black Lives Matter movement

body language, 69–70

Bonsu-Liburd, Esther, 64

Bostock, Jo, 76

breast screening narrative, 140–41

Brescoll, V., 90

British identity, xx

Britishness and identity, xx, 37, 110

Brodkin, K., 10

Bryan, B., 64, 92

Buckner, L., 91

bullying, xvii–xviii

Burke, B., 128

Butler, A. S., 73

Byfield, C., 79

Caldwell, L. D., 12

Calmore, J., 117

capital, 85, 87, 123

Caraballo, L., 66–67

career status and progression, 28–29, 91–95, 114–15, 120–23

Caribbean background: and class, 38–39; and educational achievement,

83, 85; and family structure, 82; and higher education participation, 79; and identities, 35–37; and language, 72; and occupational status/progression, 91–92; and racism, 58–59; terminology relating to, 1–2
Caribbean creole, 61, 64–65. *See also* Jamaican Creole (JC)
caring, 135
casual racism, 51
Cheung, S. Y., 90
childcare, 80, 93
children: educational achievement/underachievement, 82–87, 93; and parental challenges, 87–89. *See also* school context
churches, xx, xxi, 67, 79
Clarke, B., 87–88
Clarke, S., 130
class: and Blackness, xviii–xix, 38–39, 123–25; intersection with race and gender, 11, 13; and parental involvement in education, 85–87
Coakley, L., 82, 88
Coard, Bernard, 82–83
co-cultural theory, 71
code-switching, 64, 72–74
Collins, P. H., 122
colonisation, 2
colourism, 19–20, 33–34, 102
Commission on Race and Ethnic Disparities: The Report (2021) (CRED), 11–13, 53–54, 143
communication: in education, 65–70; loudness, 65–68; non-verbal and paralinguistic, 69–70, 73; in workplace, 70–74. *See also* language(s); speech
community nomination, 4
complicit behaviour, 20–24
Connor, H., 77, 78
Cooper, C., 86
COVID-19 pandemic, 12–13
CRED. *See Commission on Race and Ethnic Disparities: The Report*

Crenshaw, K., 119
creole, xx, 58, 61, 64–65
critical incidents, 113–14; career progression, 120–23; cultural dissonance, 124–27; data collection, 115–16; theorising, 116–19
critical race theory (CRT), 14, 116–17, 121
cultural capital, 85, 87
cultural dissonance, 124–27
cultural identity, 35–37
cultural racism, 11

Davis, S. M., 71
degree classifications, 81
DeGruy, J., 52
DEI. *See* Diversity, Equity and Inclusion offices
Delgado, R., 102
Delgado Bernal, D., 119
disassociation, 141–42
discrimination, and wellbeing, 100
disruptor behaviour, 20–24
diversity, 46
Diversity, Equity and Inclusion (DEI) offices, 44
documenting racism, 136
Dodgson, E., 92
Donnor, J., 40
double consciousness, 41, 68, 100, 118–19
double minorities, 102
Douglas, Jenny, 97
dress style, 73
Du Bois, W. E.B., 41, 68, 100, 118
Duncan, S., 89
Dweck, Carol, 145
Dyer, R., 117

education: non-verbal and paralinguistic communication in, 69–70; and occupational status/progression, 93; presentation of self in, 65–69; racism in, xviii, xix, 13, 47–48, 137–40; wellbeing in, 100–101, 108. *See also*

academia; higher education; school context
educational achievement/ underachievement, 82–87, 93
educational qualifications, 81, 83, 93
ego identity, 120
Emecheta, Buchi, 79
emotional burden of racism, 123, 133–34, 141–42; biographical narratives, 136–41. *See also* psychological trauma
employment: Black women's labour market participation, 89–91; occupational status and progression, 91–95, 114–15, 120–23; relationship with parenting, 89; in UK academia, 114–15; wellbeing and search for, 106–8, 111. *See also* workplace
empowered behaviour, 135
equity, 46
Esposito, J., 68
ethical issues in research, 104–5
ethnic absolutism, 130
ethnicity/ies, and terminology, 31–32, 144, 145
ethnic pluralism, 30–31
ethnography of speaking, 63
Evans, G., 65–66, 68
Evans-Winters, V. E., 68
everyday racism: in contemporary workplace, 24; emotional burden of, 133, 137–38; examples of, 51, 53, 55; micro-aggressions, 52–53

family structures, 82
family support, 80
feminism, 3, 15, 29–30
Floyd, George, xv
focus groups, 103–4
Fordham, S., 66, 68
foster care, 80

gangs, 87–88
Garner, S., 117–18
gender, intersection with race and class, 11, 13

gendered stereotypes, 27, 102–3
gender passing, 68
Georgiou, S. N., 85
Gilroy, P., 38, 130
Goffman, E., 120
Golombisky, K., 68
Griffin, R. A., 66

Hall, S., 37–38
health. *See* mental health and wellbeing of Black women
healthcare contexts, racism in, 140–41
health inequities, 12–13
Hersi, F., 36
higher education: challenges to participation in, 78–82; employment in. *See* academia; retention/dropout rates, 78–79; UK context, 114–15; wellbeing of students, 108–9
Hill Collins, P., 3
hooks, b., 40, 67
Horowitz, Donald L., 19
Hottentot Venus, xix
Hung, D., 35
Hunter, M., 117
Husband, C., 9
Hymes, D., 63

identity/ies: authors' backgrounds and experiences, xvi–xxii, 119, 123–27; British and Black, xx–xxii, 37, 110; class dimension, 38–39; concept of, 35; concept of Black identity, 35–38, 130; construction of, 130; and cultural dissonance, 123–27; multiple, 41, 68, 100, 101, 118–19; shifting, 40–41, 101–2
Ignatiev, N., 10
institutional racism, 11–12, 143
International Day for the Elimination of Racial Discrimination, 144
interracial relationships, 19–20, 25–26
intersectionality, 11, 13, 101, 119
Irish people, 10
Ivy, J., 77

Index

Jamaican Creole (JC), xx, 58, 61
Jean-Marie, G., 122
Jensen, R., 118
Jews, 10
Jezebel stereotype, 27, 102
Jones, C., 101
Jones, L., 94
Juneteenth, 144

Keohane, Nigel, 78
King, Martin Luther, 55, 144
kissing teeth, 69–70
Koonce, J. B., 66, 69

labour market participation, 89–91. *See also* employment; workplace
Ladson-Billings, G., 40
language(s): and African world view, 62; Black British talk (BBT), 63–64, 72; of Black women in Britain, 61; code-switching, 64, 72–74; creole, xx, 58, 61, 64–65; and educational underachievement, 83; non-verbal and paralinguistic, 69–70; and presentation of self, 64–69
Lareau, A., 86
Larsen, Nella, 45
Latin America, 33, 34
Lawrence, Baroness Doreen, 131n3
Leonardo, Z., 14, 117
Levine, N., 62
liberalism, 44
loudness, 65–68
Lynch, M., 80

MacPherson Report (1999), 11–12
Malcolm X, 43, 55
Mammy stereotype, 102
Manchester University and Joseph Rowntree Foundation ESRC Report (2014), 77
mature students, 78–79
Maylor, Uvanney, 51. *See also* Black female reflections on academia
McGregor-Smith Review (2017), 93
McIntosh, P., 117

media portrayals, 111
mental health and wellbeing of Black women, 97, 103, 111; appearance, 105–6; Britishness and identity, 110; in education, 100–101, 108; emotional burden of racism, 123, 133–34, 136–42; identity and shifting, 101–2; impact of stereotypes, 102–3; and policymaking, 99, 111; research background, 98–99; research findings, 105–10; research methodology, 103–5; research on, 98–100; seeking work, 106–8, 111; struggle and resilience, 27–28, 109, 141–42; suffering in silence, 108–9. *See also* psychological trauma
mental illness: media portrayals of, 111; suffering in silence, 108–9
mental schemata, 44
micro-aggressions, 52–53, 123, 131n1
migration, 2, 38, 73, 85, 93; Windrush generation, 35–36, 58–59, 92
Miller, K. J., 106
MIND, 98
mindsets, 145
minority cultures, sophisticated racism between, 45
minority ethnic groups, terminology, 31–32
Mirza, H. S., 76–77
Mitton, L., 91, 93
mixed heritage, 2, 33, 37. *See also* Mulattoes
Mocombe, P. C., 39
Morgan, M., 63
motherhood: challenges of, 88, 89, 93; and higher education participation, 79, 80; involvement in children's education, 82, 84–87, 139–40
Mulattoes, 19–20, 25, 33, 102
multiculturalism, 30–31
Multicultural London English, 63
Musoke, W. N., 86–87

Nesbit, A., 80
noise, 65
non-verbal communication, 69–70, 73
Nzgewu, N., 122

occupational status and progression, 91–95, 114–15, 120–23
'othering', xix, 35, 44

Pachter, L. M., 100
paralinguistic communication, 69–70
parenthood: challenges of, 87–89, 93; involvement in children's education, 82, 84–87, 139–40
Parfitt, T., 10
Parker, P. S., 71
Parker Review (2017 and 2020), 94–95
passing, 45, 68
passive behaviour, 20–24
Patois, 61
patriarchy, and silence, 67
pay gap, 93–94
Pentecostal Church, xx, xxi, 79
personal identity, 120
Petrie, Katherine, 78
plantocracy: and colourism, 19–20, 33–34; interracial relationships in, 19, 25–26; myth of seductive temptress in, 26–27; and origins of 'Big House' metaphor, 18–19; and strategic behaviours, 20–21; White women in, 24–25, 27, 28
police, 53
policymaking, 99, 111
postgraduate students, 77–78
post-traumatic slave syndrome, 19, 52
presentation of self, 64–69
privacy, xx, 73
profiling, 53
projecting, 56
promotion, 94, 120–23
psychological aggression, 21
psychological trauma, 19, 52–54. *See also* emotional burden of racism

psychological wellbeing. *See* mental health and wellbeing of Black women
Pulido, L., 14

questioning, 134–35

race: intersection with class and gender, 11, 13; as social construct, 9–11; use of term, 144, 145
Race Disparity Audit (2017), 12
racial categorisation, 19–20, 33–34
Racial Disparities in Mental Health Review (2019), 97, 99–100
racial identity construction, 119–20
racial micro-aggressions, 52–53, 123, 131n1
racial profiling, 53
racial stereotypes, 10, 27, 55–57, 102–3
racial trauma, 19, 52–54, 141–42. *See also* emotional burden of racism
racism(s): author experiences of, xvii–xviii; biographical narratives, 136–41; casual racism, 51; as cause of racial trauma, 19, 52–54, 141–42; challenging. *See* strategic response to racism; concepts and understandings of, 10–15; emotional burden of, 123, 133–34, 136–42; initiatives to tackle, 143–44; institutional racism, 11–12, 143; reverse racism, 54–55; in rural communities, 47; 'ways of knowing', 3–5. *See also* everyday racism; sophisticated racism
racist bullying, xvii–xviii
Rafiq, Aseem, 53–54
raw racism, 47
Reece, R. L., 21
reflexivity, 116
Reisman, K., 64–65
religion, xx, xxi, 67, 79
research design, 103–4
researcher reflexivity, 116
research ethics, 104–5
research samples, 105

resilience, 27–28, 109, 141–42
resistance capital, 87, 123
resistance strategies. *See* strategic response to racism
reverse racism, 54–55
Reynolds, T., 4, 75, 82, 91
Rickford, A., 69
Rickford, J., 69
Rigby, K., xvii
role flex, 73–74
Rollock, Nicola, 41, 86
rural communities, 47

Sapphire stereotype, 102–3
school context: authors' experiences of, xvii–xviii, xx; identities in, 101; presentation of self in, 65–69; racism in, xviii, xix, 47–48, 137–40. *See also* educational achievement/ underachievement
school exclusions, 83–84, 87
science, and constructions of race, 9
Scott, K. D., 72
Sefa Dei, G. J., 101
self, presentation of, 64–69
self-care, 135
self-definition, 145
semi-structured interviews, 104
Sewell Report (2021), 11–13, 53–54, 143
sexual exploitation of slaves, 25–27
shadism, 45. *See also* colourism
Shealey, M., 4
shifting, 41, 101–2, 111
Shorter-Gooden, K., 71–73, 101
Showunmi, Victoria: background, xv, xvi–xix, 123; works by, 56–57, 91, 94. *See also* Black female reflections on academia
silence, 67–68
slavery: and 'Big House' metaphor, 18–19; and language, 61, 62
slaves: distinctions between, 19; myth of seductive temptress, 26–27; sexual exploitation of, 25–27; strategic behaviours of, 20–21; trauma suffered by, 19; White women's relationship with, 25, 27, 28
Smith, W., 116, 131n1
social capital, 87
Social Darwinism, 9
social identity, 120
socialisation, xvi, 56–57, 123–27
socio-economic status, 145. *See also* class
sophisticated racism: in academia, 48–52, 54; compared with raw racism, 47; in contemporary workplace, 23–24; definition and framework, 43–46; emotional burden of, 133; equity, diversity and, 46; in school context, xix, 47–48; strategies to resist. *See* strategic response to racism
Sow, Papa, 88, 89
Spears Brown, C., 100
speech: Black British talk, 63–64, 72; creole, xx, 58, 61, 64–65; ethnography of speaking, 63; loudness, 65–67; paralinguistic communication, 69–70
speech style, 62–63; code-switching, 72–74
splitting, 21
Standard English (SE), 64–65
Steele, Shelby, 123–24
Stefancic, J., 102
stereotypes/stereotyping, 10, 27, 55–57, 102–3
stereotype threat, 57
strategic response to racism, 5, 133–34; in academia, 122–23; advocating as, 135–36; in the 'Big House', 20–21; biographical narratives, 136–41; caring as, 135; communication strategies, 70–74; in contemporary workplace, 21–24, 70–74; documenting as, 136; in education, 70; empowered behaviour as, 135; questioning as, 134–35
structural racism, 12

success: Black women as threat to White women's, 50; challenges in higher education, 76–82; challenges in labour market, 89–91; challenges in occupational status/progression, 91–95; defining, 75–76; parental challenges, 87–89
sucking teeth, 69–70
Sue, Derald Wing, 52–53
Sullivan, K., xviii
swimming club narrative, 138
Syed, J., 9
systemic racism, 12

talking with attitude (TWA), 69
Taylor, Breonna, xv
teaching careers, 81
terminologies, 2–3, 31–32, 144–45
Theodossiou, I., 107
Tomlin, Carol: background, xv, xix–xxii; works by, 39, 61, 64
trauma: suffered by slaves, 19. *See also* psychological trauma
Tripp, D., 113
Tsolidis, G., 102
TWA. *See* talking with attitude

UK context, 1–2
unemployment, 91, 107–8, 111
university. *See* academia; higher education
US academia, xxi–xxii

Van Dijk, T. A., 11

'ways of knowing', 3–5
wellbeing. *See* mental health and wellbeing of Black women
West Indies, racial categorisation in, 33–34
White guilt, 126
White higher education students, 77–78
Whiteness: 'acting White', 56–57, 126; authors' experiences of, xvi–xvii, xviii, xxi, 124–27; and colour hierarchies, 33; understandings of, 13–15, 32, 49, 57–58
Whiteness theory, 117–18
White privilege, 14, 32, 44, 48, 117–19, 125
White rage, 34–35
White supremacy, 14, 32, 54
White women: Black women as threat to, 27–28, 49–50; and feminism, 15, 29–30; in plantocracy, 24–25, 27, 28
White women syndrome (WWS), 25, 28, 50
Wilkinson, J., 122–23
Williams, P., 87–88
Windrush generation, 35–36, 58–59, 92
'woke' ideology, 44–45
workplace: Black women as threat in, 27–29, 49–50; communication style in, 70–74; strategic behaviours in, 21–24. *See also* employment
WWS. *See* White women syndrome

youth offender statistics, 87

About the Authors

Dr. Victoria Showunmi is associate professor at University College London in the Faculty of Institute of Education. Her research interests are gender, identity, race and class in relation to leadership and the development of Black girls and Black women. Her scholarly work is acclaimed nationally and internationally. She is on the Special Interest Groups (SIG) Executive Committee as a Member-at-Large for the American Educational Research Association (AERA); conference chair for The British Educational Leadership, Management & Administration Society (BELMAS); and equality lead and an executive member of the Gender and Education Association (GEA). She is on the editorial board of *Bloomsbury Educational Leadership: Innovative Critical and Interdisciplinary Perspectives and Transforming Education* through 'Critical Educational Leadership, Policy and Practice' (Emerald) as well as assistant editor for the *International Journal of Leadership in Education*.

Dr. Carol Tomlin is a multi-award winning academic and educational consultant who is a visiting fellow at the University of Leeds. She has a long and distinguished academic career teaching in universities both nationally and internationally. She is the principal of Kingdom School of Theology with several years of pastoral ministry. Dr. Tomlin is the author of several academic publications, including co-authored works with Dr. Paul Mocombe, such as *Race & Class Distinction in Black Communities* (2014) and her most recent book *Preach It: Understanding African Caribbean Preaching* (2019).

www.ingramcontent.com/pod-product-compliance
Lightning Source LLC
Chambersburg PA
CBHW020744020526
44115CB00030B/919